Tourism, Tourists

& Society

Tourism, Tourists & Society

Tutor's Manual

Exercises, case studies, OHPs and materials
to support and extend the textbook.
The Tutor's Manual and the book together offer
tested class material for a full year's course.

ISBN 1 85450 233 6
A4 loose leaf with copying rights in a display binder.

Tourism, Tourists & Society

Richard Sharpley

This first edition of **Tourism, Tourists & Society** is published in August 1994 by ELM Publications, Seaton House, Kings Ripton, Huntingdon, Cambridgeshire, PE17 2NJ. Telephone 04873 254, Fax 04873 359.

Printed by St Edmundsbury Press, Bury St Edmunds, Suffolk, England.

Bound by Woolnough Bookbinding, Express Works, Church Street, Irthingborough, Northamptonshire, England.

ISBN 1 85450 159 3

British Library Cataloguing-in-Publication Data

A catalogue record for this publication is available from the British Library.

Contents

To Mum and Dad

Acknowledgements

My interest in adopting a sociological approach to the study of tourism first developed as I became involved in research linked with tourist motivation and sustainable tourism development, and I am grateful to John Urry and Caroline Schwaller at Lancaster University for their advice and help. Thanks are also due in no small measure to my colleagues at the University of Luton, in particular Peter Grabowski, whose personal collection of books and articles proved to be an invaluable source of material, and to those third-year Travel and Tourism students with whom many of the ideas in this book were 'tested'. I am also grateful to my publisher, Sheila Ritchie, for supporting this project and to Pauline Hornsby, Senior Editor at ELM Publications, for her help, comments and rapid proof-reading. In particular, my most sincere thanks go to Julia for her support and patience, and for her advice and inspiration during the writing of this book.

About the Author

Richard Sharpley is a senior lecturer in Travel and Tourism at the University of Luton, specialising in tourism and leisure in the countryside and the sociology of tourism. His other interests include the impacts of tourism and tourism motivation and he is presently engaged in research with the Sociology Department at Lancaster University for his PhD in sustainable tourism development.

Introduction

It is impossible to ignore tourism. During the twentieth century it has grown into the world's largest industry and, for many destinations, it represents a vital source of income, foreign exchange and employment. More importantly, however, tourism is about people. The number of international tourist arrivals is rapidly approaching 500 million and an estimated six times that number participate in domestic tourism each year, figures which represent an enormous, yet temporary, migration of people both across international borders and within their own countries. Thus, tourism, above all, is a social phenomenon, and an understanding of the social processes involved is of fundamental importance to the study of tourism.

This book approaches tourism from a sociological perspective, considering both tourists themselves and the societies which generate, sustain and receive tourism. Easy to read and to understand, it introduces basic sociological theories and their relevance to tourism before examining the major themes and issues concerning the social nature of tourism. It is based upon an existing course at the University of Luton and is aimed at HND and first degree students majoring in Travel and Tourism. It may be used either as a general course text or, as at Luton, as an integral part of more specialised modules within the travel and tourism field. Extensive and up-to-date references are used throughout, and each chapter develops arguments which are of relevance to the practical planning and management of tourism.

Permission has been asked of the relevant publishers to use the quotations in this book. Full details of the sources of the quotations are given in References.

Chapter One

Tourism: A Sociological Approach

INTRODUCTION

Tourism is all things to all people. To a holiday-maker, tourism may be the chance to relax and escape from the stress of everyday life, whilst to any one of the hundreds of thousands of tourism businesses, from large, multinational organisations to small, independent operators, tourism is a source of income and employment. Governments may promote and encourage tourism as a vital contribution to a nation's balance of payments but local residents in a popular destination may see the annual influx of hordes of tourists as something to be suffered or endured.

Equally, the *study* of tourism may be approached from a variety of academic backgrounds or disciplines, each providing a valid basis for explanation and argument. For example, economists treat tourism as a discrete form of economic activity, relating the demand, motivation, growth, scale and form of tourism to economic factors; even the impacts of tourism, or externalities, may be explained or justified in economic terms. More generally, whilst much of the early research and academic study of tourism originated as a branch of geography, a multi-disciplinary approach has been increasingly adopted since the 1970s. There now exists a broad range of tourism literature based on academic specialisms, such as anthropology, psychology, law, marketing

1

and geography, on particular types of tourism itself, such as heritage tourism, rural tourism and special interest tourism, or on geographical or political classifications such as, for example, the UK, Europe, or developing countries.

Despite the enormous variety of standpoints or academic approaches to tourism, there is one aspect or feature of tourism that cannot, or should not, be ignored. Unquestionably tourism is, or soon will be, the largest single industry in the world. In 1991 the total number of international tourist arrivals amounted to some 450 million with worldwide foreign exchange receipts from tourism reaching £185 billion. If the value of domestic tourism in all countries and the earnings of tourism related businesses, such as transport operators, are added to this then, globally, tourism is worth an estimated £2 trillion (WTTC, 1991). No other industry can match the growth rate of international tourism; from 1980 to 1990 international arrivals and receipts achieved annual growth rates of 4.2 per cent and 9.3 per cent respectively.

Underlying these staggering figures is the simple fact that tourism is about *people*; it is about millions of individuals who comprise local, regional and national societies, travelling domestically or crossing international borders and experiencing and impacting upon different societies. It is about people who are influenced and motivated by the norms and changes in their own society, who carry with them perceptions, expectations and standards based on their own personal experience and background. Above all, tourism is about people, tourists, interacting with other places and other peoples, undergoing experiences that may influence their own or the host community's attitudes, expectations, opinions and, ultimately, lifestyles.

In short, then, the very basis of tourism is people and society.

Thus, the study of tourism in general cannot, or should not, be divorced from an examination in particular of what may be termed the 'sociology of tourism'. A fundamental problem, however, is the extent to which tourism, as an essentially social but nevertheless diverse activity, lends itself sociological study. Specifically, the question to be asked is, is it possible to develop a sociological theory of tourism or is it only possible to apply sociological theory to different aspects of tourism? Moreover, other academic disciplines, such as psychology and anthropology, have equal claim as a basis for research into social aspects of tourism; one of the first major texts concerned with the tourist-host relationship and social impacts of tourism is sub-titled *The Anthropology of Tourism* (Smith, 1989a). The purpose of this introductory chapter is to define the context for a sociological approach to the study of tourism. The first step is to examine what is meant by a sociological approach or, more precisely, the meaning, purpose and extent of sociology as an academic activity. This may then be related to, and used as a basis for the consideration of, the human and social aspects of tourism throughout the rest of this book.

WHAT IS SOCIOLOGY?
It is probably true to assert that, although most people have some notion of what sociology is about, relatively few are able to define the term accurately. Unlike many other academic disciplines, such as history, geography and chemistry, the scope and the purpose of sociology are either vague or incomprehensible to the lay person. As a result, sociology is often regarded with disinterest or, in the extreme, with distrust by those who have little knowledge or understanding of the subject. Indeed, as Bilton *et al* (1987:1) point out, sociologists themselves may often feel tempted to say that they are historians or economists rather than sociologists in order to avoid the difficulty of having to explain what they really do!

3

This difficulty in defining sociology arises, in part, from the nature of the subject itself. A simple explanation or description of sociology might be the study of the structure of human society and behaviour. Although essentially accurate, this is somewhat simplistic. Sociology is certainly concerned with specific aspects of society, such as the family, class and gender divisions, work, or deviance (behaviour which does not conform to what is considered to be 'normal', crime being the most obvious example), but this is only half of the story. Of equal, if not greater, importance is the approach or perspective which determines how these particular aspects of society and the behaviour of individuals within society are studied. Sociology is, in effect, a *way* of looking at society.

In other words, the basis of sociology is society. Society is made up of individuals who, with the exception of those who make a conscious decision to avoid contact with other people, perform or participate in a huge variety of actions every day. The great majority of these actions are socially acceptable (i.e. 'normal' behaviour); they are also, however, socially determined. That is, an individual's behaviour is generally constrained, or determined, by society's rules, rules which may be set down by custom, by religion, or by laws. As a result all the individual actions within a given society tend to occur in a co-ordinated fashion so that social life remains reasonably ordered and predictable. For example, it is considered 'normal' for a young person to take a year off in between school and university to go travelling (see Chapter Three for a discussion of back-packing) whereas an individual who does so in, say, his or her forties, might be considered unusual, eccentric or even, perhaps, irresponsible.

The important point, therefore, is that sociology is concerned not only with the structure of society and the behaviour of individuals within society but also with the rules, or wider social

4

forces, that determine social structure and patterns of behaviour. It is this latter characteristic that differentiates sociology from other disciplines, such as anthropology, and that causes most confusion amongst non-sociologists. Whereas many people attempt to explain or describe different forms of human behaviour as natural, instinctive or just plain common sense, all of which place the emphasis firmly on the ability of the individual to make his or her own decisions, sociology rejects notions of individuality and places human behaviour within the context of wider social forces which are beyond the control of the individual. Furthermore, socially normal or acceptable behaviour is relative to different societies and reflects a society's rules or constraints that must be learned by the individual. Thus, *one person's 'common sense' is somebody else's nonsense* (Bilton *et al*, 1987:6). For example, in the Western world it is generally accepted as common sense or normal that it should be men, rather than women, who undertake heavy labouring work; in India it is more often that such work is done by women, a role determined by the social forces of religion, male dominance and the caste system.

The basic tenet of sociology, then, is that human society and behaviour is structured, moulded and constrained by wider social forces and influences, and it is this approach that underlies sociological research and analysis. Yet, although sociologists share this common approach, there are a variety of theories about what society actually is, how it may be explained and, hence, how it determines individual behaviour. The following section briefly traces the development of sociology as an academic discipline and the evolution of the different theories of sociology (see Swingewood, 1991, for the history of sociological thought). The relevance of these theories to the study of tourism is then discussed.

THE DEVELOPMENT OF SOCIOLOGY

Modern sociology, as a distinct discipline, has its roots in Europe in the mid-nineteenth century. The 'father' of sociology is generally held to be the Frenchman Auguste Comte (1798-1857). Not only did he coin the term 'sociology' but also he was the first to adopt a rigorous, scientific approach to the study and explanation of society. Prior to this time, many people had concerned themselves with the development and structure of society; early Greek philosophers, such as Plato and Aristotle, had developed theories about the nature of society, but even by the mid-eighteenth century the work of social theorists, such as Jean-Jacques Rousseau (1712-1778), was largely based on a philosophical, rather than a formal, scientific, approach to the study of society. As Bilton *et al* (1987:2) point out, *philosophers and thinkers frequently constructed grand models and schemes about humans and their societies without looking at how societies actually worked.*

One exception was Robert Owen. Born in Newtown, Wales, in 1771, by the age of 28 he was a successful businessman and co-owner of a cotton mill at New Lanark in Scotland. As a social reformer, his business success allowed him to test his theory that individuals are formed by their environment and that the basis of a happy, harmonious society is education. In other words, Owen believed that people are not born with inherently good or bad traits but that they acquire them from their environment. Thus people, particularly children, can be taught *any language, sentiments, belief, or any bodily habits and manners, not contrary to human nature* (Owen, 1991:12). He therefore developed a model village around the cotton mill at New Lanark, the purpose of which was to provide a stable, healthy and happy environment for his employees and their families. He provided medical care funded by what was, in effect, an early and local form of National Insurance, the village shop was run as a co-operative, various forms of unacceptable behaviour, such as excessive drinking, were discouraged, and all the children in the village received schooling at his Institute for the Formation of Character. In short, Owen adopted and put into practice a sociological approach to providing for his workforce. His motives were treated with suspicion in many circles yet he made what was, arguably, the first practical attempt to test a sociological theory. Interestingly, New Lanark is, today, a major tourist destination in the Clyde Valley near Glasgow.

In contrast to Owen's practical work, Comte was the first academic to develop a sociological theory, or a basis for the study and explanation of society. His work evolved against a background of profound change in Europe; the Industrial Revolution and rapid scientific and technological developments were transforming traditional rural society whilst dramatic advances were being made in the scientific understanding of the world. As a result Comte attempted to apply scientific method to the study of society, believing it to be the path to a full understanding of society and, thereby, the means for improving it. In other words, Comte asserted that true knowledge is scientific knowledge and that social phenomena could be explained, understood and controlled in much the same way as natural phenomena. He called this a *positive* approach and, thus, he established Positivism as a distinct school of sociological thought.

Positivism falls under the broader heading of Structuralism, a wider sociological perspective that dominated much sociological research and thought up to the late 1950s and which is one of the two major competing theories about the way in which society is structured and develops. Structuralism refers to any form of sociological analysis that is concerned with society as a whole and how it is structured. Structuralists adopt a macro-sociological approach, taking as their starting point the assumption that there exists a *central value system which, either by constraint or consensus, normatively prescribes and sanctions role attitudes and behaviour* (Dann and Cohen, 1991). An individual's values, beliefs and behaviour are, according to structural theory, predominantly shaped, developed and constrained by the social world in which that individual lives. Conversely, structural theory tends to ignore or to play down the role of the individual, the 'human actor', in the formation and development of society; human individuality is, in effect, subordinated to the constraining influence of society. It is this latter characteristic of Structuralism that has attracted most criticism, as it *reifies* society. That is, Structuralism views society as being real or as a 'thing' rather than as an abstract concept. (Reification is a term used by sociologists to describe the interpretation of a general concept, such as society, as something solid or real.)

Despite this and other criticisms, the structural perspective dominated much sociological analysis from the birth of modern sociology until the mid-twentieth century. Within Structuralism, there are two distinct and opposing camps. Both adopt the holistic approach to the study of society but whilst one group concentrates on what is known as *consensus theory* the other advocates *conflict theory* as the basis for sociological analysis.

(i) Consensus Theory

A basic assumption of structural sociology in general is that the values, beliefs and behaviour of all the individuals who comprise a particular society are formulated and, most importantly, constrained by what may be described as the rules of that society. Some of these rules may be prescribed by a society's laws which constrain an individual's behaviour by the threat of punishment or sanctions. Not all of society's rules and constraints are backed up by laws; indeed, most social behaviour is constrained by an individual's own beliefs and values. As a simple example, the British are well known for forming queues while waiting to be served in, say, a post office. Jumping the queue is normally considered to be bad manners, yet in many other countries queuing is unheard of and seen, perhaps, as a quaint British custom.

The important point is that, continuing with this example, queuing is not instinctive; people learn that, at least in Britain, it is normal social behaviour to form queues. More generally, individuals are not born with a concept of right and wrong, of what constitutes good or bad manners. These beliefs and values, which effectively constrain an individual's behaviour, are determined by society. To put it another way, at birth an individual is rather like a new computer; the hardware, with particular capabilities, exists but the software has to be installed to make the computer function effectively. A child inherits certain characteristics from its parents but, like a computer, 'software' (i.e. beliefs, rules, values) needs to be installed through a process called *socialisation*.

Socialisation continues throughout an individual's life and in all spheres of life. Society's rules and constraints are learned, or *internalised*, from a variety of sources. Initially it will be an individual's immediate family which has the most influence but school friends, peer groups, institutions such as schools, colleges and universities, the work environment, religion and even the media will constrain and shape an individual's beliefs and behaviour during his or her lifetime. Moreover, the rules that an individual learns are those rules which are generally accepted by a particular society to be appropriate or acceptable. There is a *consensus* about how members of a society should behave, about what the central values and norms of that society are. It is this, according to consensus theory, that determines people's roles and behaviour and ensures the continuation of an integrated, regulated and stable society.

One of the first sociologists to develop a theory of society based on a structural-consensus approach was Emile Durkheim (1858-1917). Following on from and developing the ideas of Comte, Durkheim viewed modern, as compared with primitive, pre-industrial, society as being held together by what he termed *organic solidarity*. While society as a whole determines an individual's role and behaviour, organic solidarity develops from a new moral consensus which, Durkheim believed, could be disseminated through education. Indeed, one of his objectives was the creation of social harmony through the state's use of sociological knowledge.

A central assumption of organic solidarity as suggested by Durkheim is that society is differentiated into separate areas and institutions, such as education, religion or the family, each of which deals with a particular aspect of social life. Each part plays a necessary role or *function* in the harmonious continuation of society, the analogy being that society is like a living organism; each part, or organ, is essential to the well-being of the organism. Yet the character of the organism can only be viewed as a whole, rather than being reduced to its constituent parts. Thus, society should, likewise, be viewed as a whole, with societal institutions examined and explained on the basis of their function in society. This approach to sociology became dominant during the first half of the twentieth century and developed into what was seen at the time as *the* sociological theory, namely, *Functionalism*. The American sociologist Talcott Parsons (1902-1979) was, in particular, at the forefront of the functionalist approach to sociology.

Although functionalism has become less popular since the 1960s it is nevertheless of direct relevance to a sociological approach to tourism. As discussed in Chapter Four, an analysis of tourist motivation cannot be divorced from the function of tourism as, say, an escape from the 'real' world. At a more socio-psychological level, functionalism provides a framework for examining the satisfaction of needs, such as adventure or curiosity, provided by tourism, whilst the functionalist perspective may also be applied to the classification and analysis of tourism as a social system (see Nash, 1981).

(ii) Conflict Theory

Whereas Durkheimian sociology views human action and behaviour as resulting from wider social forces and influences developed by consensus, conflict theorists, although still adopting the macro, holistic approach, believe that sociological study should be concerned primarily with the influence of societal conflicts, such as domination and subordination. In other words, consensus theory favours the harmonious evolution of society and its rules, values and norms; conflict theory is based on the assumption that these rules, values and norms, which are then internalised through the socialisation process, are founded on the ability of dominant group in society to impose their values and behaviour onto subordinate groups. Through the imposition of their values dominant groups are able to sustain a social structure that favours their own position in society; social change must result not from evolution but revolution.

Charles Darwin (1809-1882) attempted to show that evolution was based on conflict and a clash of interests but it was Karl Marx (1818-1883) who, although a philosopher and an economist rather than a sociologist, was to have a profound influence on this branch of sociology. In brief, Marx believed that the basis of society and social structure is the economy; in order to survive people need to produce economic necessities, such as clothing and food. The production of such economic necessities entails an individual's involvement in the system of production; people enter into *relations of production*. It is these relations which influence and determine social structure and, hence, roles, values and behaviour, because relations of production become class relations. In particular, the working class, the *proletariat*, become subordinate to the capitalist class, the *bourgeoisie*.

Under the burgeoning European capitalist system of the nineteenth century, Marx saw the human condition becoming one of *alienation*. With the new methods of mass production and the division of labour, individuals became involved in relatively meaningless tasks which were only part of the wider production system. As a result, workers became alienated from their work, from the product of their labour, from their fellow human beings, from nature and, ultimately, from themselves. In effect, their labour became a commodity, bought by capitalists for the cheapest price. Thus, labour has a value; Marx labelled the difference between the value of labour (i.e. wages paid to a worker) and the value of the commodities produced as *surplus value*. This surplus is extracted from the subordinate class through the process of *exploitation*.

It is surplus value that is the very foundation of the capitalist system, for the surplus created, the profit, enables capitalists to own and control the system of production, including labour, thereby becoming the dominant class. The economically dominant class is also able to dominate other spheres of life, from politics to religion, in the extreme creating an ideology that hides the true nature of social relationships from the subordinate class. Therefore social progress can only be achieved, Marx argued, by removing exploitation, alienation, and economic domination, which in turn can only be achieved by abolishing, through revolution, the economic system (capitalism) which creates those conditions. The responsibility for such revolution lies with the, subordinate, working class.

Conflict theory, especially the work of Marx, has attracted both widespread support and criticism. Within the context of this book it provides a valid basis for a neo-Marxist perspective on tourism. It may be argued, for example, that mass tourism, as a subset of leisure in general, is no more than a capitalistic domination or exploitation of the working class' leisure time. Since the beginning of the nineteenth century the development of leisure, both as the social condition of time free from work and specific activities that leisure encompasses, may be seen as having been shaped and controlled by the needs of the dominant, capitalist classes (see, for example, Clarke and Critcher, 1985). Tourism, and mass tourism in particular (in the narrow sense of the mass tourism product - the package holiday), is designed, produced, marketed and sold by the capitalists, the tour operators. The consumers (mass tourists) are deceived by the lure of a holiday that promises escape from the capitalist system yet which is, in effect, an extension of it. Thus, the 'revolution' in tourism could be manifested in a widespread rejection of the mass, package tour in favour of more individually orientated forms of tourism. Conflict theory is, therefore, of relevance to the study of the social determinants of tourism, tourist motivation and the structuralist theory of tourism as a reflection of societal change.

The major criticism of both consensus and conflict theory is that they both, in different ways, over-emphasise the socialisation process and thereby ignore the ability of individuals to influence and change society. In addition to the reification of society, an interpretation which attributes society with abilities and powers only possessed by humans (for example, thought and reason), consensus theory tends to view individuals as robots conforming to predictable patterns of behaviour. Conflict theory is based on the premise that the majority of people within society are subordinate to the rules and values of the dominant class; conformity results, therefore, not from harmony and consensus but from power and dependence. Both theories adopt an ahistorical approach, ignoring the historical development of society, and minimise human involvement in society's structural development. In contrast, the second major school of sociological theory, the micro approach, highlights the role of individuals and groups of individuals in the determination, explanation and understanding of social reality. This micro approach to sociology is known as Social Action Theory.

(iii) Social Action Theory
Social Action Theory, which essentially adopts a humanist perspective to sociology, is a broad heading under which a number of sociological approaches are found. These include the formal sociology of Georg Simmel (1858-1918), a German sociologist who was one of the first to reject the positivist, structural approach to sociology; the work of Max Weber (1864-1920), who introduced the concept of *Verstehen* (meaningful understanding) to sociological analysis and explanation; *symbolic interactionism*, which developed primarily as an American branch of sociology; and the more recent and radical *ethnomethodology* and *phenomenology* (see Jary and Jary, 1991, for definitions and explanations of sociological terminology).

The basic perspective of social action theory is that society is not distinct from but is formed by the individuals who comprise it and that social reality results from the social action between individuals. Such action, or behaviour, in turn results from the way in which one individual understands or interprets the behaviour of another individual, with one of the simplest forms of interpretation between individuals being the spoken word. Through this ability to interpret and understand, the individual thereby takes on a more active and creative role in the development of society. Thus, for action theorists the development and continuation of society and culture is still dependent on socialisation, but the rules and values that are internalised are neither static, nor are they determined by society. Rather, individual members of society have the ability to adapt and change their behaviour within a process of negotiation, or meaningful encounters, with other members of that society. In short, the rules and values that influence an individual's behaviour are not determined and fixed by a reified society, as proposed by structural theorists, but are being continually being changed and adapted by the actions and decisions of individuals within society.

Simmel argued that the fundamental subject of study should be the individual or, more precisely, the ways in which individuals act socially. Society, therefore, results from an intricate amalgamation of the multitude of interactions and relations between individuals; that is, society is made up of individuals who are connected by social interaction. The type of interaction determines different social institutions or groupings, such as the family, marriage or religion, and it was with the *form* rather than the content of these social groupings, or sociations, with which Simmel was concerned (hence, 'formal' sociology). Thus Simmel defined the form of a social relationship between two individuals as a *dyad*; the content may vary (e.g. husband and wife, manager and subordinate, teacher and pupil) but the form of the relationship depends on the continued interaction and participation of the two individuals concerned. Should a third person join the group (a triad), then the form of the relationship changes from two-way interdependence into interaction based on mediation. Formalism, then, presents a way of looking at tourist groups, such as comparing the difference between individual and mass tourism or the role of a tourist guide as the mediator between tourist and local people.

Similarly, Weber defined society in terms of sociation but he also sought to link the meaning attached to social action with a more positivist cause-and-effect approach. In other words, he introduced the concept of motivation into sociology, combining an understanding of the meaning of social action with the result of such action. The Weberian perspective is of direct relevance to the study of tourism in general and tourist motivation in particular, providing an alternative basis of analysis to, for example, the functionalist explanation of tourism (see Chapter Four). Of the more recent social action perspectives symbolic interactionism is, arguably, of most relevance to tourism analysis and research.

(iv) Symbolic Interactionism
Symbolic interactionism concentrates on the way in which social rules and identities are established through social interaction emphasising, in particular, the importance of the response of other people to an individual's behaviour. Rather than simply internalising society's rules, individuals are able to analyse and adapt their own behaviour; social identity results from the interpretation of the responses of others to an individual's behaviour. To put it another way, social identity, knowing oneself, can only be achieved by interpreting how others respond to our actions, the response being communicated through symbols, such as language, in a social situation. Behaviour and values are developed, therefore, through social interaction.

The most immediate and general relevance of symbolic interactionism to tourism is its potential contribution to an understanding of the tourist-host relationship. Tourist-host encounters are, more often than not, characterised by inequality and a variety of differences between the participants and their expectations. Symbolic interactionism provides the foundation for the analysis of, and potential solutions to, the socio-cultural impacts of tourism. These issues are discussed in Chapters Six and Seven. Dann and Cohen (1991) point to a number of other ways in which symbolic interactionism may be applied to tourism. For example, it provides a basis for researching issues of authenticity/inauthenticity in tourist experiences and, in terms of motivation, it may lead towards an explanation of the desire to escape from the rules and morals of the home society whilst on holiday. That is, the *ludic* (play) qualities of tourist behaviour such as excessive drinking and eating or casual sexual encounters, may be associated with an avoidance of normal social interaction (see, for example, Lett, 1983).

These and other social action theories, including phenomenology and ethnomethodology, have been criticised for over-emphasising the role and influence of the individual in the development of society. It is true that people possess the ability to act individually and creatively, to reason and to make individual decisions, and to make sense of their physical and social world, yet the great majority of people live according to the rules, values, morals and constraints of their societies and, as a result, most societies maintain a sense of order and harmony. Thus, neither of the two primary sociological perspectives, the macro, structuralist, theories or the micro, social action, theories, can alone fully or adequately explain all social phenomena. Indeed, a kind of halfway house has been proposed by the British sociologist Anthony Giddens (1938-). His *structuration theory* develops the notion that social structure is both the medium and the outcome of social action. That is, both structuralism and social action play a role in the development of society, yet neither is afforded primacy.

Inevitably, perhaps, these conflicting perspectives on sociology continue to be a subject of debate amongst sociologists themselves. It is important to point out that they are just that; different approaches, but united by the objective of studying and explaining the development, structure and functioning of human societies. Indeed, most general texts on sociology utilise some, if not all, of the sociological theories in the analysis of different aspects of society. There is, therefore, no single, all-encompassing theory of sociology and, by implication, no single sociology of tourism. This brief review of the development of sociology and sociological thought has served simply to highlight the scope and breadth of sociology as a perspective on society, and it is now important to consider how such a perspective may be applied to the study of tourism as a distinct area of social activity.

TOURISM AND SOCIOLOGY
Tourism is about people and societies. It is a social activity generated by some societies and impacting physically, economically, socially and culturally on others. Some, adopting a structuralist, neo-Durkheimian perspective, would argue that tourism is a reflection of the condition of modern society as a whole (see MacCannell, 1989, and Chapter Eight). In other circles, tourism is viewed as a vehicle for the development of international peace and understanding, a social force for overcoming international barriers and conflict. For example, the World Tourism Organisation (WTO) states that *tourism stands out as a positive and ever-present factor in promoting mutual knowledge and understanding and as a basis for reaching a greater level of respect and confidence among all the peoples of the world* (WTO, 1980:3). On the other hand tourism, and mass

tourism in particular, is often accused of being a destructive influence on host societies and cultures. During the early 1970s, in particular, a number of books questioned the true value of tourism by highlighting the non-economic costs of tourism development (for example, Young, 1973; Turner and Ash, 1975; de Kadt, 1979).

Whichever standpoint is taken tourism is a widespread social activity and is a valid and important subject for sociological analysis; furthermore, as a perspective on tourism, sociology offers the potential for explanation and understanding of many factors and issues within tourism. It is possible to study tourism within the encompassing discipline of sociology (that is, treating tourism as another social institution, along with the family, work, education and so on), permitting a broader approach to the subject than is often taken. As much, if not more is to be gained by taking tourism itself as the starting point. In other words, a sociological approach to the study of tourism is adopted, utilising different and relevant sociological theory as necessary. It is the latter perspective that provides a platform for much of the discussion throughout this book.

A number of issues immediately become apparent but two questions in particular arise. Firstly, which aspects of tourism can be usefully examined from a sociological viewpoint and, secondly, which sociological theories are most applicable to those aspects? In answering these questions another problem becomes evident, namely, which is the most appropriate 'ology' to use? This refers specifically to the study of the socio-cultural impacts of tourism which is not only one of the four main areas of research identified by Cohen (1984) in his review of the *sociology* of tourism but also the prime concern of what has been called the *anthropology* of tourism. *Hosts and Guests: The Anthropology of Tourism* (Smith, 1989a) includes a number of case studies that could be legitimately claimed as sociological research. Conversely, issues of authenticity and the commoditisation of culture, topics frequently examined in the literature by sociologists (see, for example, Cohen, 1988a) are no less a valid subject for anthropologists.

A simple response to the first two questions might be that tourism is concerned primarily with the movement of people and, therefore, all areas of tourism should justifiably be included under the umbrella of sociological analysis. A clearer picture is obtained from a brief review of sociological approaches to tourism in the literature and a summary of the sociological theories outlined above and their relevance to the study of tourism.

(i) Tourism and sociology in the literature

In addition to the socio-cultural impacts of tourism, a field of study to which socio-*economic* impacts may quite legitimately be attached, Cohen (1984) lists three other principle areas of analysis that have emerged in sociological treatments of tourism in the literature. These are: firstly, tourists themselves and their motivations, attitudes, perceptions and so on; secondly, the tourist-host relationship; and thirdly, the structure of the tourism system. In fact, since the publication of his seminal paper *Toward a Sociology of International Tourism* (Cohen, 1972) Cohen himself has been a leading figure in the development of the link between sociology and tourism. A list of his work appears in the References.

The earliest contributions to sociological research in tourism originated in Germany. Research was undertaken as early as 1930 but the first major work appeared in 1960 (Knebel, 1960, referred to in Cohen, 1984), around the time that mass tourism as we know it today was emerging as a major social force.

Nuñez (1963) adopted a strictly empirical, as opposed to theoretical, approach in his study of the development of a tourism destination, as did Forster (1964) who documented changes in the structure of the work force in Pacific island societies resulting from tourism development. In contrast, Boorstin (1964) lamented what he called the *Lost Art of Travel* in his criticism of mass tourism in general and mass tourists, who he perceived as cultural dopes easily satisfied by inauthentic, pseudo experiences, in particular.

Boorstin's elitist sentiments were echoed to an extent by Mishan (1969), an economist who argued that the growth of mass tourism resulted from the cost of travel being too cheap. That is, the tourism industry, *in a competitive scramble to uncover all places of once quiet repose, of wonder, beauty and historic interest to the money-flushed multitudes* (1969:141), ignored the environmental and social costs of tourism development in calculating their prices. The danger was that the longer term survival of host destinations and communities was threatened by short term profit motives. The solution: to ban all international air travel!

Despite their elitism, the approach of both Boorstin and Mishan is of relevance to the present concern for the impacts of mass tourism (see Chapter Seven). Their critical stance with respect to mass tourism was also continued, albeit with a less generalised and more balanced and considered approach, by a number of authors, especially Young (1973) and Turner and Ash (1975). It was also during the 1970s that a more rigorous and theoretical sociological approach was applied to the study of tourism. Cohen (1972) was the first to challenge the generalised notion of the 'tourist' with his model of tourist typologies (discussed in Chapter Three); he went on to develop a phenomenology of tourism (1979), arguing that not only is there a variety of tourist types, or roles, but also a variety of experiences by which tourists may be categorised. Perhaps the most influential work to emerge at this time was that of MacCannell (1973 and 1976). In firmly rejecting Boorstin's arguments, MacCannell proposed a new sociological theory of tourism based upon the notion that tourists actively seek the authentic in times and places away from their normal lives. What they actually experience, though, is a reality which is constructed for their benefit, a *staged authenticity* (MacCannell, 1973). Similarly, Cohen and Taylor (1976) presented the case that tourism is an escape from the alienated condition of modern Western society and a search for self identity. The concept of authenticity and tourist experience/ expectations has been developed by other authors (see, for example, Pearce and Moscardo, 1986) and is directly related to broader issues, such as the development of eco tourism, the commoditisation of culture, heritage and the commercialisation of history, the marketing of 'authentic experiences', and so on.

The theoretical approaches of the 1970s were balanced by empirical studies which were also undertaken during the same period. These were primarily concerned with the different relationships and perceptions embodied within tourist-host encounters and the socio-cultural impacts of tourism development (see Smith, 1989a, and de Kadt, 1979), and signified the advancement of anthropology as a separate area of tourism research.

Since the early 1980s there has been nothing less than an explosion in the range and depth of research and literature concerned with tourism. Most general tourism texts include sections concerned with the social and cultural impacts of tourism, tourist demand and motivation, types or categories of tourists, definitions of tourism, resort life-cycles and other topics that can be linked to sociological treatment, yet most tend to adopt an empirical, 'face-value' approach. At a more specialised level, a number of books and many papers and articles have considered particular aspects of tourism which could be categorised under the heading of the sociology of tourism. Many, for example, are concerned with tourism as a form of escape (see Rojek, 1993), as a reaction to modern society (Krippendorf, 1986 and 1987), as a search for meaning, self-identity and authenticity (drawing parallels with religious experience), or even as a return to a childlike stage of existence (Dann, 1989). One notable exception is the work of Urry who has developed a sociological examination and explanation of tourism based upon the central theme of the tourist 'gaze' (Urry, 1990a).

(ii) Tourism and sociological theory - a summary
Although the brief review of the literature demonstrates the evolution of the sociological and anthropological treatment of tourism, it does not indicate the extent to which sociological theory can be usefully applied to tourism. It is important, therefore, to consider not only the ways in which tourism and sociology have already been linked, but also to identify areas of potential research. This is best done by relating the major sociological perspectives outlined earlier in this chapter to relevant issues within tourism.

(a) Structural-Consensus Theory
The structural, macro sociological perspective firmly places tourism within the study of society as a whole whilst, at the same time, directing attention towards the wider tourism system than towards the individuals who participate in tourism. As a basis for studying tourism the structural approach may be criticised for reifying what is, in effect, the combined actions and behaviour of tourists and those who are employed in, benefit from, or whose lifestyles are affected by, tourism. Nevertheless, a general macro

perspective and the more specific functionalist approach provide a foundation for tourism research in a number of areas.

Firstly, it is important to explain and describe the development of tourism within the context of the development of society as a whole and, in particular, how tourism has become institutionalised. The growth and democratisation of tourism from what was once an activity enjoyed by the privileged few to the mass social phenomenon that it is today is frequently explained by the three facilitators: increases in free time, more disposable income and advances in technology. Whilst undoubtedly true this is a rather simplistic explanation. Tourism is directly related to the development of leisure which, in turn, is linked to societal change and forces. Thus, for example, factors such as industrialisation, urbanisation, mass production and consumption, environmentalism and even the 'yuppie' culture have directly influenced the development of tourism and may help to explain the transformation of tourism from luxury to perceived necessity.

Secondly, as Dann and Cohen (1991) point out, a macro perspective can be adopted when considering the evolution of the tourism system itself, either as a linear development from local, small-scale beginnings through to international business, or as a cyclical process such as that proposed by Butler (1980). A functionalist approach either places tourism in the context of its role in the functioning of society as a whole, such as its function in promoting international understanding, or views tourism itself as a social system. In the latter case, different parts of the tourism system may be categorised by function and linked to, for example, product development and marketing.

The greatest potential for tourism research within the holistic, macro approach is in adopting the basic assumption that tourism is a reflection of society. In particular, the positioning of tourism as a search for the authentic (MacCannell, 1976) as a reaction to the contrived, inauthentic condition of modern life in tourism generating societies, or even as a sacred experience (Graburn, 1989) compared with the ordinary, demands the consideration of factors such as the authenticity of the tourist experience, the commoditisation of culture and tourist motivation, and thematic issues such as the link between postmodernism and contemporary tourism.

(b) Structural-Conflict Theory

Conflict theory is a valid basis for research into a variety of tourism issues. Brief mention has already been made of the conflict-based relationship between the tourism industry and its customers, manifested in the domination and control of the mass tourism, package holiday market by the tour operators. This relationship is, arguably, founded on paradox and deceit. The product is sold as an escape from the mundane, the ordinary, the routine; it promises change, excitement and temporary freedom from day-to-day institutionalised life. Yet, despite the apparently huge choice available to the customer, the product is standardised and mass produced. Rooms may have more or less facilities, accommodation may be self-catering, bed and breakfast or half board, a hotel is near the beach or a bus ride away, but the basic product is still the same: transport, accommodation, food and entertainment. Furthermore, in cases where a tour operator also owns the travel agent, the airline and possibly the accommodation, the entire process is controlled by one organisation. Customer choice is, generally, constrained by price and, far from escaping from the capitalist system, the tourist is actually contributing to it.

Within the broader, international tourism system conflict theory brings issues of dependency and neo-colonialism into clearer focus. The international tourism industry is becoming increasingly dominated by large multinational corporations (MNCs) based in Western tourism generating countries (see, for example, Dunning and McQueen, 1982). These organisations frequently support, finance, manage or own the tourism facilities in destination countries or regions, particularly in the developing world, which lack the necessary financial and human resources to develop tourism. The MNCs gain increasing control over tourism to and in the destination (Bull, 1991:181-197) which, in turn, becomes increasingly dependent on Western finance, products and tourists. Britton (1982) found that many previously colonised nations, such as Kenya, are particularly susceptible to overseas domination of their nascent tourism industries, a situation he describes as neo-colonialism whilst, more generally, Nash (1989:39) comments that it is the *power over touristic and related developments abroad that makes a metropolitan center imperialistic and tourism a form of imperialism.*

The third area in which conflict theory is of relevance to tourism is the study of the tourist-host relationship and the concept of *commercialised hospitality* (Dann and Cohen, 1991). What is, possibly, a unique experience for a tourist may be business as usual for the host whose 'hospitality', in reality, is motivated by profit. Conflict theory also highlights the unequal, transitory basis of tourist-host encounters and the growing incidence of what may be termed 'inverse-exploitation'. Increasingly, tourists may be invited to take a photograph or to visit a local home, only to be asked afterwards for a 'gift', usually money. Such behaviour may be seen as exploitation of both the tourist and a country's tradition of hospitality whilst, overall, conflict theory directly challenges the notion that the development of tourism can lead to greater knowledge and understanding between different peoples and nations.

(c) Social Action Theory

The micro-sociological approach directs research and analysis towards the tourist as an individual as opposed to the tourism process and system.   Focusing as it does on the interaction between individuals, the most logical application of social action theory is to the explanation of the different expectations, perceptions, relationships and outcomes of tourist-host encounters. The success of such encounters is often undermined by misunderstandings based on differences in race, gender, class. For example, potentially meaningful encounters between southern European males and northern European female tourists or between European vistors and Gambian beachboys (known locally as 'hustlers') may be limited by opposing expectations and cultural differences. The analysis of tourist-host encounters may then be related to the broader field of socio-cultural impacts of tourism and an exploration of the practical ways in which such impacts may be reduced.

Social Action Theory may also be applied to the study of tourist motivation, one of the primary themes in the sociological treatment of tourism.   Examining and explaining tourist motivation or, in simple terms, determining the reason why people travel, is a complex process. Motivation is related to both *push* and *pull* factors (Dann, 1981); push factors are those which directly influence motivation and may be socially, psychologically, economically or physically determined, whereas pull factors are the attractions of the destination.   Thus, the various social action approaches are of direct relevance to an examination of both push and pull factors. These are discussed in greater detail in Chapter Four.

(iii) The sociology or anthropology of tourism?

Within the tourism literature there appears to be a degree of confusion as to what constitutes a sociological or an

27

anthropological approach to the study of tourism. For example, Selwyn (1992:354) describes Cohen as *one of the most prolific anthropological writers on tourism* and Dean MacCannell's *The Tourist* (1989) as *one of the most influential books in the anthropology of tourism*, whereas both Cohen and MacCannell are more generally considered to be sociologists. This blurring of the boundaries between the two disciplines arises, perhaps, because of the overlap in their subject matter. Anthropology is the study of humankind; *anthropologists are interested in everything human, whenever and wherever it occurs* (Nash and Smith, 1991). Thus, sociology is, arguably, a discipline that falls within the broader concerns of anthropology. Furthermore, anthropology's claim on tourism cannot be disputed: *modern tourism accounts for the single largest peaceful movement of people across cultural boundaries in the history of the world. Given that, tourism is unavoidably an anthropological topic* (Lett, 1989:276). Little is to be gained here from a semantic discussion of the two disciplines but a brief consideration of anthropological concern with tourism will clarify the approach adopted in this book.

The application of anthropology to tourism was relatively late in comparison to other disciplines. This, according to Nuñez (1989:265), was because tourism was considered by anthropologists not to be a proper or serious subject worthy of their attention. Indeed, it was Nuñez himself who was responsible for one of the first anthropological works on tourism (Nuñez, 1963), but it was the publication of *Hosts and Guests* (Smith, 1989a) that firmly established tourism as a valid target for anthropologists. Since that time, a sizeable body of literature has been produced concerned with tourism, literature which, according to Lett (1989:276) can be divided into two broad categories:

(a) work which empirically assesses the impact of tourism on host societies and

(b) cultures and the meanings of tourism to the tourist.

The latter category includes such topics as motivation, tourist roles and the semiology of tourism, whilst the dichotomy between the two is embodied in the work of Graburn (1989), who views tourism as form of sacred journey, and that of Nash (1989) who describes tourism as a form of imperialism. Crick (1989) adds the political economy of tourism to the list of identifiable categories of the anthropological treatment of tourism.

It is immediately apparent that there is a large area of overlap between sociology and anthropology within the context of tourism research. Indeed, the only major difference is that anthropology is traditionally constrained by its holistic, comparative, cross-cultural approach, a fundamental basis of the discipline being that anthropological theories must be applicable to all peoples in all places. However, returning to the main points made throughout this chapter that tourism is, essentially, about people and societies and that tourism itself, rather than associated disciplines, should be the starting point for any analysis or research, then inter-disciplinary conflict becomes irrelevant. It is the perspective adopted that is important so that what we are concerned with, in effect, is the 'humanology' of tourism.

WHAT IS TOURISM?
Ryan (1991:6) shows that tourism may be defined from a variety of viewpoints. For example, an economist might define tourism in terms of the supply of and demand for tourism products, a tourist board might adopt a technical, statistical definition based

on purpose and length of stay, or an environmentalist might describe tourism in terms of the legitimised exploitation of natural resources.

One of the first attempts was made by the League of Nations in 1937 which defined a tourist as someone who travels for twenty-four hours or more outside their normal country of residence. A similar definition, which included journeys for the purpose of either leisure (including recreation, holiday, health, study, religion and sport) or business was proposed by the International Union of Official Travel Organisations (IUOTO), the precursor of the WTO, in 1963. However, a more widely accepted definition of tourism is that of the Tourism Society:

> *Tourism is the temporary short-term movement of people to destinations outside the places where they normally live and work, and their activities during the stay at these destinations; it includes movement for all purposes as well as day visits or excursions*

The major drawback with this definition is that it implies that anyone who travels, for virtually any purpose, is a tourist. It is probably of most use as a guideline for the collection of statistical data at, say, an international airport. It is, however, very generalised and describes the action involved in tourism rather than placing it in any particular concept. Furthermore, by including business travel it ignores the generally held perception that tourism is a leisure activity whereas, interestingly, the word travel comes from the French *travail*, or work.

Others have adopted definitions more related to their disciplinary background. Nash defines tourism as the activity of *a person at leisure who also travels* (Nash, 1981:462), firmly placing tourism as the antithesis to work activities. Smith continues the theme, recognising the position of tourism as a leisure activity but introducing the notion of motivation: *a tourist is a temporarily leisured person who voluntarily visits a place away from home for the purpose of experiencing a change* (Smith, 1989a:1). Both of these definitions concentrate on the tourist; to do so, as Crick (1989) argues, is to miss out, even in the sociological context, much about the tourism system. By creating the work/leisure dichotomy, certain categories of travel activity which are strictly neither leisure nor work, such as religious pilgrimages or long-term budget travel (see Chapter Three), are omitted, thereby creating a narrow set of parameters within which to place the activity of tourism.

The essential point is that, given the vast array of activities, motivations, organisations and so on that comprise tourism, to attempt a single, all-encompassing definition is a difficult, if not impossible task. It is, perhaps, better to describe tourism in both broad and more specific terms. Thus tourism, generally, is a modern social phenomenon which involves the movement of people to various destinations and their stay there. As a widespread activity that is embedded in modern society, tourism also embraces the following characteristics:

1. It is normally viewed as a leisure activity and generally associated with the short-term escape or change from the routine or ordinary. An implicit assumption is that tourism involves freedom from work, although some forms of non-leisure travel (e.g. pilgrimage, exploration/adventure travel) or work-related travel (e.g. conferences, incentive travel) are also accepted as forms of tourism.

2. It is socially determined. Often described as the democratisation of travel, tourism is, nevertheless, shaped and divided by wealth, gender, age, class, education and other

social factors, all of which have an influence on the frequency, duration, destination and style of tourists' trips.

3. The international tourism industry is diverse, fragmented and multi-sectoral. Extensive vertical and horizontal diversification has resulted, however, in the domination of the industry by a relatively small number of multinational corporations, mostly based in the industrialised, tourism generating countries.

4. It is dependent on the physical, social and cultural attributes of the destination. These attributes are marketed to potential tourists as the promise of excitement, of authenticity, of the exotic and of the extraordinary.

5. It is a commercial activity based on encounters between tourists and local people or communities. Tourism acts, therefore, as a catalyst in the development of commercialised hospitality, the potential commoditisation of culture, and as an agent of social change.

6. It is a sector of the broader leisure market and reflects trends and changes in tourism generating societies.

Many of these characteristics and issues are addressed throughout this book. Indeed, they constitute a form of agenda for the following chapters. This chapter has shown that there is a variety of ways in which sociological theory may be applied to these issues as a valid basis for explanation and understanding. Before considering these specific issues it is important to remember that tourism is inextricably linked to the societies that both generate and receive tourism and that it is, in effect, a product of society. The next chapter briefly traces the historical development of tourism as socially determined activity.

Chapter Two

A Social History of Tourism

INTRODUCTION

The roots of modern tourism lie in the industrial, economic and social transformations that occurred during the nineteenth and early twentieth centuries. Technological innovation and increasing levels of income and free time provided the means for more widespread participation in travel and tourism, whilst changes in the social condition, resulting, in particular, from rapid urbanisation and the new, industrial work practices, provided the motivation. Thus, it would be logical to assume that tourism is a phenomenon of modern society, emerging as a kind of inevitable by-product of the modernisation of society.

However, *like many other modern industries, tourism can trace its ancestry back to the Old Testament* (Young, 1973:9), with the means of travel having been available, albeit to a privileged minority, for thousands of years. For example, sea-going ships were first designed and built around 3000 BC (Casson, 1974:21) and chariots were first introduced around 1600 BC. Similarly, people have been able to be tourists, in the sense of travelling for pleasure, education, spiritual fulfilment and interest rather than trade or warfare, for as long as they have been physically able to travel from one place to another. Indeed, some of the earliest indications of tourism are to be seen in Egypt, where ancient graffiti dating back to 1300 BC have been found scratched onto the great pyramids at Giza (Casson, 1974:32). Therefore, although modern, mass tourism is, undoubtedly, a feature of the late twentieth century, tourism has existed in one form or another for almost as long as societies have existed. This chapter briefly traces the historical development of tourism, considering how the nature and meaning of tourism, as a socially determined activity, has evolved into the mass phenomenon that it is today.

TOURISM IN ANCIENT TIMES

For the earliest civilisations, the major factors which inhibited the development of tourism were the difficulty and danger of travelling any distance and, for most people, a lack of money. With the exception of the Minoan (2000-1500 BC) and the Mycenaean civilisations (1600-1200 BC), road building was virtually unknown and, even by the end of the fourth century BC in Greece, roads were poor and highwaymen frequently preyed on unsuspecting travellers. The most convenient and safest mode of transport was by ship, although even sea travel was not immune to danger from either the elements or piracy, and, as most travel was motivated by either trade or warfare, the opportunity to travel for pleasure was very limited.

Nevertheless, tourism of a sort existed within ancient Greece, although normally associated with attending religious or sporting festivals or consulting oracles. For example, the oracle at Delphi drew people from far and wide to seek advice on various matters whilst the Pythian Games, also at Delphi, were a popular event. Many sick people travelled to Epidaurus in the hope of being healed by the gods, similar to modern day pilgrimages to Lourdes in France, but Olympia, home of the Olympic Games, was probably one of the most popular tourist destinations in ancient Greece. The first Games were held in 776 BC and thereafter attracted thousands of visitors from both Greece and abroad to witness the sporting contests and other events which gave the Games their deep religious significance. Thus, tourism in ancient Greece *was not so much a voyage of adventure as a trip in accordance with tradition and ritual. The man who travelled tightened his links rather than liberated himself from his social background* (Sigaux, 1966:10). Visits to oracles or festivals were part of Greek life and travel for pleasure was uncommon; tourism as a form of escape or relaxation, a common motivation for much present day tourism, did not become widespread until Roman times although holiday resorts were developed near major cities. The most famous of these was Canopus near Alexandria.

One notable exception was Herodotus, a Greek historian who lived during the fifth century BC and died around 425 BC. An educated man from a wealthy background, he spent much of his life travelling and recording what he experienced and is, therefore, often considered to be the first travel writer. Usually travelling by ship, a fact which accounts for his frequent descriptions of harbours and river towns, Herodotus travelled widely around Egypt, Syria, Persia, and Asia Minor, reaching as far as Sicily and Italy in the west and Babylon in the east. In his writings he describes what he encountered on his travels, sometimes relating his own experience and observations, sometimes relying on information from guides and other people he met. He wrote to both inform and to entertain and his work is a unique record of early tourism.

One of the major hurdles which limited the development of tourism in ancient times was overcome by the Romans. In order to administer their expanding empire and to maintain the *Pax Romana*, it was necessary for the Roman authorities to build a network of roads which not only allowed for the rapid movement of troops and administrative personnel but also increased the opportunity for ordinary citizens to travel. One of the first major highways to be built was the Via Appia, the Appian Way, the construction of which commenced in 312 BC. It eventually stretched across Italy from Rome to the port of Brindisi on the east coast and was one of literally thousands of major and minor roads which, by the first century AD, crossed the length and breadth of the Roman Empire. It was possible to travel along first-class, paved roads all the way from Hadrian's Wall in the north to the southern corners of the Empire in Ethiopia (Young, 1973:10), with travellers being able to break their journeys at staging-posts, or hotels, along the route. Indeed, travel and tourism during the Roman period was both relatively safe and convenient, yet long distance travel for purposes other than trade or military service was still uncommon. Even though general holidays and other festivities occupied about half the Roman year, most festivals and other events took place locally and there was no widespread touristic movement between provinces (Sigaux, 1966:11). Only the wealthier members of Roman society were able to indulge in foreign tourism; Athens and the Greek cities of what is now Turkey, such as Ephesus, were popular destinations and, as a forerunner of the Grand Tours of the sixteenth to eighteenth centuries, young Romans were sent to Athens or Rhodes to be educated. Many Romans also visited Egypt and were as anxious as previous visitors to scratch their names onto famous structures.

More generally, the Romans introduced the concept of tourism as a form of escape. Those in positions of authority, or who could afford to do so, built themselves villas or country houses beyond the confines of the cities, often in the hills to escape the summer heat. The Alban and Sabine hills around Rome offered cool relief from the heat of the city and by the first century BC were dotted with summer homes and villas. Nor was this practice restricted to Rome; villas and second homes were found around most cities throughout the Empire. The development of the road network also allowed easy access to coastal areas during the summer months and a string of resorts developed along the northern shore of the Bay of Naples, over one hundred miles from Rome. The wealthier members of Roman society owned villas both in the hills and in coastal resorts; of the latter, the most famous was Baiae, the first of Rome's summer resorts. Originally favoured as a winter resort because of its hot springs (taking the waters being an important ritual in Roman life), Baiae gradually expanded from a peaceful place to relax and to go fishing and boating into a major resort. As it developed the town gained a reputation for moral laxity; loud parties, excessive drinking and nude bathing were commonplace and it soon attracted criticism from more straight laced members of Roman society. For example, Seneca described the resort as *the home of vice...*[where]*...licence is triumphant*, a complaint which fell largely on deaf ears. Indeed, Baiae survived as long as the Roman Empire itself.

Despite the popularity of the coastal resorts around Naples, the establishment of a number of spa towns in various provinces, such as the French towns of Vichy and Aix-les-Bains, which became popular entertainment centres, and the relative ease of travel with the extensive road network, tourism during Roman times was still limited and sporadic. The distances to be travelled were often great and travel during the winter months was often impossible. Nevertheless, the Romans added an important dimension to travel and tourism. Previously, tourism was motivated by trade, health and attendance at festivals or other religious events; the Romans introduced the summer holiday, a form of tourism that disappeared with decline of the Roman Empire during the fifth century AD and not reappear until the twentieth century. Indeed, the fall of Rome signalled the virtual end of tourism as a leisure activity for almost a thousand years, although specific forms of travel and tourism emerged during the intervening period.

TOURISM IN THE MIDDLE AGES

With the end of Roman rule many roads fell into disrepair and, as a result, most people's mobility was severely impaired. However, this was not the only reason for a decline in tourism; in addition to being extremely uncomfortable, travelling also became a much more dangerous activity whilst the decline and widespread poverty of Europe during the Dark Ages meant that few people had the means, purpose or inclination to undertake journeys of any distance. Such tourism as existed at this time was limited to local fairs, festivals and religious holidays (literally, *holy days*); travelling was usually only undertaken for the purpose of trade or government business.

However, one form of voluntary tourism which was popular during this period was pilgrimage. *In its purest form pilgrimage was a voluntary journey to worship at some holy shrine, and the journey itself was expected to be hard and fraught with difficulties, a form of penance* (Jebb, 1986:3). Pilgrimages had been undertaken for some time; indeed, Bethlehem was frequented by Christian visitors as early as the third century (Sigaux, 1966:18) but about the tenth century, when overland travel became more practicable and as more facilities for travellers became available, greater numbers of people set out on such journeys. Most travelled on foot (although, by the time of Chaucer's Canterbury Pilgrims, horseback had become the favoured means of transport) and the three main destinations were Jerusalem, Rome, and Santiago de Compostella in north west Spain. All three attracted large numbers of pilgrims. For example, some three hundred thousand people visited Rome in 1300, but shorter journeys within one country, such as English pilgrimages to Canterbury or Winchester, were also popular.

Thus, during the Middle Ages, tourism, as opposed to obligatory forms of travel, was largely associated with religion. However, the more adventurous also embarked on long distance journeys seeking fame and fortune, perhaps the most well-known being Marco Polo who travelled to China in the thirteenth century. The accounts of his journeys are one of the very few examples of travel writing remaining from this era and it was not until the sixteenth century that individuals not only began to travel for travel's sake, but also began to record and publish details of their travels and adventures for a public that was becoming increasingly interested in stories of faraway, exotic places. One of the better known of these early adventurers was Thomas Coryate who, in 1608, undertook a trip to Venice and whose account of his travels, *Coryate's Crudities*, was to inspire others to follow in his footsteps. His writing was both vivid and humorous. For example, during a rough crossing of the English Channel he describes *varnishing the exterior parts of the ship with the excremental ebullitions of my tumultuous stomach*, an experience that has undoubtedly been frequently repeated over the centuries!

Coryate was typical of many tourists of that time in as much as his destination was Italy. Though a nation in decline it was still the intellectual centre of Europe (Turner and Ash, 1975:31) and academics, writers, artists and the aristocracy visited and were inspired by Italian art and culture. The artist Dürer, the philosopher Erasmus and the poet John Milton were amongst the many people who travelled there, whilst the Palladian style of architecture was introduced in Britain by Inigo Jones following his own visit to Italy in the early 1600s. However, it was not only to Italy that tourists, in particular the English, travelled. It was one of a variety of destinations that made up what became known as the Grand Tour, a form of travel which was indicative of the re-emergence of tourism as a leisure activity for the first time since the decline of the Roman Empire.

TOURISM FROM 1600 TO 1800

The seventeenth and eighteenth centuries are of particular importance in the historical development of tourism because, although they preceded the modernisation and industrialisation of society, it was then that the pattern of tourism development through to the present time was set. In other words, it was this period which marked both the start of the social democratisation of tourism, a process which has culminated with the emergence of mass tourism, and the beginning of the transformation of the fundamental meaning and purpose of tourism.

(i)   The Grand Tour

Like all tourist movements, the Grand Tour was the product of a particular social and cultural environment (Towner, 1985). At the start of the seventeenth century it was customary for the English aristocracy to send their sons, once they had graduated from university, on a tour of Europe. Usually accompanied by a tutor, the young aristocrats spent a period of anything up to three or four years abroad, the purpose of this extended trip being to complete a young man's education. In a sense, the cultural centres of Europe became a large finishing school for young Englishmen. They enrolled on courses at the universities in major cities and learn not only academic subjects and languages but also social refinements, preparing themselves for careers as diplomats or in government. For example, amongst those who travelled in Europe in the early days of the Grand Tour (and by the mid-1700s, it is estimated that some 20,000 English were abroad at any one time) was Henry Wooton who, having gone on an extensive tour starting in 1589, was eventually to become the English Ambassador in Venice. The travels of these early Grand Tourists inevitably took them to Italy as part of what Towner

(1985) describes as the *Classical Grand Tour*. The northern Italian cities of Turin, Verona and Venice were on the usual itinerary and the classical tastes of the tourists were also reflected in their routes along the Rhone valley in France. Switzerland, Austria, Germany and Holland were also included on longer tours.

The important point about the Grand Tour, in terms of the historical development of tourism, is that the characteristics of both the Tour and those who participated in it changed over time. In other words, during the two centuries or so that preceded the Napoleonic Wars, the Grand Tour underwent a fundamental transformation and by the beginning of the 1800s the purpose, destinations and length of trip of the tourists bore little relation to earlier tours. A greater number of tourists started to tour Europe, but their trips were shorter both in distance and duration, they came from increasingly older age groups, they tended to belong to the professional middle classes rather than the aristocracy, and their purpose was more for pleasure and sightseeing rather than education (for more detail, see Towner, 1985). In short, the Grand Tour became popularised and the tourists themselves began to gain a reputation for showing little or no interest in the people, language or culture of the countries through which they passed, an accusation that may be directed towards certain forms of modern, mass tourism.

As the Grand Tour became *invaded by the bourgeoisie* (Turner and Ash, 1975:41), the aristocracy abandoned the traditional European tour in favour of more socially exclusive resorts or areas elsewhere in a pattern of behaviour that has been repeated throughout the development of tourism since the late eighteenth century. However, the character of the Grand Tour was also transformed; whereas the early Grand Tourist travelled abroad for *discourse* (Adler, 1989), to learn languages, to read and to meet and converse with eminent persons, later travellers relied more on visual observation or, in other words, on sightseeing. Initially, such sightseeing was impartial and objective, *the 'eye'... was deliberately disciplined to emotionally detached, objectively accurate vision* (Adler, 1989), but soon an element of subjectivity was injected. Nature, landscape and scenic beauty became the object of the tourists' gaze as the romantic movement emerged, influenced greatly by the writing of Rousseau. Mountain scenery, once feared or simply considered to be monstrous and ugly in comparison with more gentle, ordered landscapes, became the object of the tourists' attentions and their routes through Europe were adapted accordingly. Switzerland became popular and towards the end of the eighteenth century a number of visitors, including William Wordsworth, undertook walking tours there.

In England, too, the romantic movement came to dominate the ways in which people viewed the landscape, epitomised by the transformation of the Lake District from what Defoe described as *a country eminent only for being the wildest, most barren and frightful of any that I have passed over in England, or even Wales itself* into an area revered by writers, poets and artists alike. Importantly, what had changed was not the landscape itself, nor even the modes of transport, for travel was still slow and relatively uncomfortable, but people's attitudes towards landscape and scenery. In other words, tourism during the eighteenth century responded to cultural changes which have continued to guide and influence the way in which mountainous and rural areas are viewed as tourist destinations.

(ii) Tourism and the spa resorts

At the same time as the Grand Tour was becoming popular amongst the English aristocracy the spa towns of England and

Europe were once again becoming popular for the first time since the decline of the Roman Empire. Often described as the first step towards the development of resort-based tourism, renewed interest in the spas resulted from the belief amongst the medical profession at the time that mineral water could be beneficial to the health. Bath, in particular, became nationally and internationally famous, largely because of a book published by Dr William Turner in 1562, drawing attention to the alleged medicinal properties of its waters. Other spas were soon established in England, including Scarborough, Epsom and Tunbridge Wells, and the fashion soon spread across the English Channel as spas in France, Germany and Italy were re-developed to cater for the needs of an increasing clientele.

It was not long before the spa towns became social centres as well as health resorts; indeed, health considerations rapidly took second place as visiting spas became an annual event on the social calendars of the upper classes. By the beginning of the eighteenth century Bath was at the height of its popularity with Richard 'Beau' Nash, the Master of Ceremonies, organising the social life of the town and welcoming each visitor personally. Gradually, more and more facilities were provided to entertain visitors at the spas and they soon became, in effect, holiday resorts disguised as health centres, with only a minority of visitors being in anything but the best of health. A similar process was also occurring in Europe and some German spas, such as Baden-Baden, became little more than gambling resorts. Inevitably, perhaps, the spas began to attract increasing numbers of visitors from the expanding middle and professional classes and their social exclusivity began to suffer. Improvements in transport further increased their accessibility and, as shopkeepers, innkeepers and a variety of other trades moved in to take advantage of the increasing numbers of visitors, the resorts began to move down market. By the end of the 1700s, the spa towns were rapidly being transformed into residential and commercial centres as tourists turned their attention to the seaside resorts and new developments that were to emerge during the following century.

TOURISM IN THE NINETEENTH CENTURY

The nineteenth century is, without a doubt, the most important period in the history of tourism. Even by 1800, after two hundred years of the Grand Tour and the rise and decline of the spas, tourism was still an activity enjoyed by a relatively small, privileged proportion of the population. For example, it is estimated that about 40,000 English citizens were either living or travelling in Europe at that time (Sigaux, 1966:66) yet, by 1840, some 100,000 people were crossing the English Channel each year, a figure which rose to one million by the start of the twentieth century (Young, 1973:18). The main factor which brought about this rapid growth in tourism was, of course, technological advance, especially the introduction of the railways, but society itself underwent a fundamental transformation that was to influence how and where people spent their leisure time in general, and the development of tourism in particular. In other words, the improvements in transport and communications during the nineteenth century enabled a far greater proportion of the population to participate in travel and tourism but changes in the structure of society also determined where, when and how different social groupings participated in tourism. Indeed, the development of tourism reflected broader social transformations. Thus, although the greatest growth in tourism has been experienced during the latter half of the twentieth century, the foundations for such growth were laid during the nineteenth.

(i)   The development of the seaside resort

As the spas declined in popularity during the late 1700s, the attention of tourists turned towards coastal resorts. Once again, the initial impetus was provided by the medical profession which extolled the supposed recuperative powers of sea water. In 1753, Dr Richard Russell published a famous paper in which he described the benefits of bathing in, and even drinking, sea water and, to practice what he preached, he moved to Brighthelmstone (now Brighton) on the south coast. By the turn of the century Brighton had become a fashionable destination, its popularity having been given an important boost following a visit by the Prince of Wales in 1783, and the town expanded rapidly. Similarly, a number of northern coastal resorts, such as Blackpool, Southport and Scarborough, also grew in popularity. For example, in 1795, Blackpool was described in the *Blackburn Mail* as being *the first watering place in the Kingdom, whether we consider the salubrity of the air, the beauty of the scenery, the excellence of the accommodation or the agreeable company of which it is the general resort.*

The initial exclusivity of the seaside resorts was dependent on two factors. Firstly, sea bathing was considered to be a medicinal rather than a pleasurable activity and was, therefore, a structured ritual (see Urry, 1990a) which, frequently, took place during winter. Secondly, travelling at the end of the eighteenth century was still slow and relatively expensive; for example, the trip from London to Brighton could take up to two days and the cost of such a journey was beyond the means of most people, even if they had the time. Thus, up until the 1830s, the seaside resorts were still the preserve of the wealthier, leisured classes, although some resorts had become accessible to other social groups, largely as a result of new transport services. In particular, the resorts near the Thames estuary became increasingly popular following the introduction of steamboat services. The first service between London and Gravesend started in 1815 and to Margate in 1820 (Holloway, 1994:19).

By 1830, paddle steamers were carrying Londoners in their thousands down the Thames to the Kent coastal resorts, where the famous piers were originally built for landing passengers rather than entertainment.

In 1829, Stephenson's *Rocket* travelled from Liverpool to Manchester at an average speed of about thirty miles (48 kilometres) per hour, signalling the advent of rail transport and the technological revolution which brought about the birth of mass tourism. The expansion of the railways was remarkable. In 1836, there were 700 miles (1126 km) of track in England, in 1843 there were some 2000 miles (3218 km) and, by 1848, the total length of the railways exceeded 5000 miles (8045 km). This expansion was matched by the rapid increase in the number of passengers travelling by rail and by 1847 the annual number of train passengers had risen to 51 million (Holloway, 1994:20). For the first time, cheap, safe and relatively fast transport was available to the majority of the population, although the railway companies were slow to recognise the potential opportunities of mass leisure travel, and the seaside resorts expanded rapidly. The growth and success of some individual resorts was almost entirely dependent on the railways. For example, Rhyl in north Wales developed entirely as a result of the construction of the Chester to Holyhead railway line and, furthermore, the social status of resorts also depended to some extent on the rail links, although other factors were also important (Urry, 1990a:22). Some destinations, such as Torquay and Bournemouth, remained relatively exclusive owing to their distance from major industrial cities and the later arrival of the railways, whereas Blackpool had moved down market by the 1850s (for a detailed history of the English seaside resorts see Walvin, 1978, Walton, 1983, or, more generally, Pimlott, 1947).

It was not only the development of the railways that led to the growth and democratisation of tourism at the seaside resorts; of equal importance were the social changes that were occurring during the nineteenth century which created the time, the money and, perhaps most importantly, the desire to participate in tourism. At the beginning of the century, Britain was still a pre-industrial, rural society. About 80 per cent of the population lived in rural areas rather than in towns and cities and social life, including leisure, was determined by traditional customs and the agricultural calendar. However, the Industrial Revolution, which led to the developments in transport technology, also brought about a variety of transformations created the social and cultural conditions under which tourism could thrive. From a positive point of view, there was a general increase in wealth amongst the industrial population as the average income per head quadrupled over the course of the nineteenth century (Urry, 1990a:18). For the first time, some working people were able to accumulate savings to pay for holidays, holidays with pay not being made available until well into the twentieth century, although poverty was widespread in the rapidly expanding industrial cities. However, free time for leisure and tourism was initially limited. Most people worked a six day week, with Sundays reserved for rest and worship, until half-day holidays were introduced during the second half of the century and bank holidays in 1871. It was during this period that working class leisure activities, often structured and organised by the dominant class, began to emerge and it is no coincidence that both the Football League and Rugby League were formed in the northern industrial areas towards the end of the 1800s (see Clarke and Critcher, 1985:62).

As life became industrialised and urbanised, work time and leisure time became differentiated and the different social classes emerged, often with their separate, class-defined residential areas within towns and cities. The working classes, in particular, found their lives becoming increasingly structured, organised and dominated by the capitalist system. Long working hours, the Protestant work ethic, social reform campaigns and cramped urban areas which lacked space for leisure and recreation all combined to create the conditions under which people longed to escape from the towns and cities. Employers began to realise the benefits of offering regular, official holidays to workers, and wakes weeks, when factories, mills or even entire towns closed for a week's holiday, became commonplace in the industrial north. Importantly, this meant that communities took holidays together and, for many towns, this was manifested in trips to the seaside, with particular resorts becoming associated with different industrial cities or regions. For example, Morecambe catered for tourists from Yorkshire whilst Blackpool was favoured by Lancashire workers; south coast resorts near London were mainly visited by day-trippers and others, such as Southport, managed to retain a more exclusive atmosphere.

Thus, mass tourism to the seaside resorts was a direct result of the Industrial Revolution and tourism, generally, came to be seen as a formalised and regular form of escape from the stress and strain of modern, industrial life. The development cycle that had become evident through the popularisation of the Grand Tour and the spas once again meant that, as the nineteenth century progressed, the higher social classes had to look further afield to retain their exclusivity. International train travel was introduced with services such as the Orient Express offering luxurious travel across Europe. It is also interesting to note that proposals to build a Channel Tunnel were first mooted during the nineteenth century and, at a Select Committee meeting in 1883, the potential cost of building the tunnel was put at £3 million! The Mediterranean resorts along the French Côte d'Azur became popular amongst the European aristocracy and became the favourite haunt of Royal tourists. For example, Queen Victoria visited Cannes in the 1890s, as did the Russian Czar, and at the end of the century the Riviera was about five times more expensive in real terms than it was during the 1950s and 1960s (Turner and Ash, 1975:69). However, another vital characteristic of the development of tourism during the nineteenth century was the institutionalisation of tourism and the beginnings of an identifiable tourism industry.

(ii) Thomas Cook

Although travel opportunities became available to increasing numbers of people with the rapid development of the rail network, greater wealth and a more formal approach to the provision of free time for those, other than the leisured classes, to whom work was a necessity, *there was no tradition of travel amongst the new Victorian middle classes* (Young, 1973:20). In other words, most people had little idea about how to overcome the potential problems of overseas travel, such as language barriers, exchanging money, knowing where to go and where to stay, and so on. What was needed to bring overseas travel within the reach of these potential tourists was an organisation that would provide all the services and help necessary, and that organisation was set up by Thomas Cook. Cook was not the first person to organise tours for the public; Sir Roland Hill is accredited with 'inventing' excursion trains and by 1840 such trips were not unusual. However, it was Thomas Cook who did more than anyone to revolutionise tourism, transforming it from the preserve of the privileged classes into an international industry and creating the package tour as one of the most popular forms of tourism (see Brendon, 1991, for a complete history of Thomas Cook).

Thomas Cook's main business was printing but he was also a firm believer in temperance. It was as he was walking to a meeting in Leicester in 1841 that he first had the idea of organising a special train to take delegates to a temperance meeting in Loughborough and, on 5th July, 1841, 570 travellers boarded a Midland Counties Railway Company train for the eleven mile journey from Leicester. Each had paid one shilling for the return journey but, more importantly, that short trip was the first step to Thomas Cook becoming a worldwide force in tourism. The success of the first trip soon led to other trips being organised, motivated more by Cook's altruism than a drive to be commercially successful (a characteristic that was to lead to a serious conflict with his son, John, who was more concerned with building a successful business). Soon he was running regular excursion trips; from 1848 tours were made in Scotland, with 5000 tourists each season using Cook's services, and in the same year he took a group to Belvoir Castle. He first contemplated overseas tours in 1850 but the Great Exhibition of 1851, to which he conveyed a total of 165,000 visitors, delayed his ambitions. Indeed, it was not until 1855 that the first overseas Cook's tour occurred and, owing to resistance from the French railway authorities, the tour ended at Calais.

Throughout the 1850s most of Thomas Cook's business was in Britain but from 1862 onwards, following a successful excursion to Paris, his operations abroad began to expand. The first tour to America was undertaken in 1866, John Cook joined his father as a partner in the business and thereafter the organisation's size and prestige expanded rapidly. In some parts of the world, the company began to wield much power and influence. For example, they had control of all passenger steamers on the Nile from 1880 onwards and a virtual monopoly of all tourism from India, including pilgrim traffic to Mecca and the responsibility for the travel arrangements of Indian princes attending Queen Victoria's Jubilee celebrations. In 1872 the first Cook's Circular Notes were issued. These were similar to letters of credit used by travellers during the previous century but were much more flexible in as much as they could be exchanged at any hotel or bank in the Cook's scheme; in effect, they were the ancestors of the modern traveller's cheque which was first developed in the 1890s by American Express. 1872 was also the year when Thomas Cook's first round-the-world tour was organised.

One hundred and fifty years on, Thomas Cook is still a major force in international tourism and the company continues the tradition of innovation started by its founder in the 1840s. For example, early in 1994 a revolutionary new information and booking system using a mobile travel kiosk was launched, reducing the need for customers to visit a travel agency and making information and booking services more widely available, thereby making it even easier to book a holiday. Indeed, the greatest contribution that Thomas Cook made to the development of tourism was just that; through his organisational skills, his eye for detail and his contacts he took the worry out of travelling and brought the opportunity of travel to millions. In other words, Thomas Cook was a major influence in the democratisation of travel and tourism, removing much of the mystique of overseas travel and undoubtedly influencing people's attitudes towards tourism. Not that he was without his critics; on the one hand, he set standards of comfort and convenience that brought tourism to the masses but, on the other hand, he could also be accused of diminishing the authentic travel experience (see Chapter Five) and of creating, in the broader sense, the institutionalised mass tourist. However, whichever viewpoint is adopted, there is no doubting his contribution to the what was, in effect, the socialisation of tourism.

TOURISM IN THE TWENTIETH CENTURY
In the early years of the twentieth century, the development of tourism continued along the course that had been set during the previous century. The English seaside resorts became increasingly popular and greater numbers of tourists travelled

abroad. The upper classes spent their summers on the French Riviera but, for the majority, tourism was still very much based around the mass exodus to the seaside. Already there were signs of the internationalisation of tourism as large numbers of Americans crossed the Atlantic and it was estimated that in the years preceding the First World War up to 150,000 American tourists came to Europe each year. Travelling was becoming increasingly comfortable and easy. No passports were required in Europe and many countries were becoming increasingly reliant on tourism as a source of income. New types of tourism were also becoming popular; skiing holidays in Switzerland had been introduced by Sir Henry Lunn in the 1880s (Holloway, 1994:22) and, domestically, the countryside was becoming a popular destination for walkers and cyclists. The first holiday camp, Cunningham's, on the Isle of Man, had already been established at the turn of the century (see Ward and Hardy, 1986) and, generally, tourism expanded rapidly. Furthermore, the pattern of development also continued. Those with time and money went abroad, those with less of both went to the seaside resorts and, as more and more people were able to travel, once exclusive resorts became popularised.

(i) The inter-war years
Following the First World War the growth in tourism continued, although there were a number of important developments which had both a direct and indirect influence on the evolution of tourism. Passports were introduced but, in the Europe of the prosperous 1920s, this had little effect on the numbers of people participating in tourism. Trans-Atlantic travel, in particular, grew spectacularly as Americans visited Europe in their thousands, bringing with them styles and fashions that were to dominate the European social scene for a number of years. Tourism offered wealthier Americans the opportunity to escape from the restrictions of their own society, in particular the

Prohibition, and many spent their summers travelling in Europe or staying on the French Riviera.

Indeed, it was on the Riviera during this period that sunbathing first became popular. Until the 1920s, most middle and upper class Europeans and Americans avoided exposing their skin to direct sunlight; pale complexions were considered to be a symbol of higher social status, whereas darker, sun-tanned features were identified with lower, rural classes or coloured people. Thus, British women in colonial countries, such as India, maintained their strict dress code in order to avoid darkening their skin and, hence, being identified with local people. However, during the years immediately following the First World War, sunbathing became an increasingly popular leisure activity and the sun tan became highly fashionable. By the early 1920s, social life on the French Riviera centred on the beach and the sun tan became a symbol of wealth and of the leisure classes. A hot summer in 1928 finally made sunbathing more popular in England (see Turner and Ash, 1975:80) and with it emerged an entire new industry, supplying bathing costumes, sun tan lotion and so on. Achieving a sun tan soon became a major motivation for tourism. It was a visible sign of wealth and prestige in the major northern European urban centres, differentiating between those who could or could not afford a summer holiday by the Mediterranean, and, even with the onset of mass tourism in the 1950s and 1960s, the symbolic importance of the sun tan did not decline. Indeed, despite scares about skin cancer caused by excessive sunbathing, escaping for two weeks in the sun remains a primary motivation for many tourists.

During the 1920s and 1930s, travelling became much easier and more accessible for many people. Initially, the introduction of motorised public transport by road in the form of the charabanc, an early type of coach, improved accessibility and the ride on the charabanc became part of the attraction of a trip to the seaside. However, it was the motor car that did more than anything to improve personal mobility. International travel was still beyond the means of most people and the car provided a new found freedom for the middle classes who were no longer dependent on public transport services. Motoring became a popular leisure activity, new destinations, such as the countryside, became popular, and by the outbreak of the Second World War there were some two million cars on the road in Britain. Inevitably, increasing car ownership and less reliance on public transport resulted in the beginning of the decline of the railways, a process that has continued throughout the twentieth century. Nowadays there are over 20 million cars on the roads in Britain and car travel is, without a doubt, the most popular mode of tourism transport, both domestically and abroad. Indeed, the great majority of tourism within Europe is based upon the car and the opening of the Channel Tunnel in 1994 will open up more opportunities for motoring on the Continent. Cycling also became more widespread in the early part of the twentieth century; the Cyclists' Touring Club was founded in 1878 and, coinciding with a trend towards healthy activities, the founding of organisations such as the Youth Hostels Association in 1930 and a growing interest in the outdoors, cycling became a popular form of tourism during the 1930s.

With regard to air travel, the First World War had stimulated research into aircraft design and, following improvements in safety, the first scheduled fare-paying passenger flight took place between London and Paris in August, 1919 (Young, 1973:24). However, the service was not a success; flights were relatively slow, noisy and usually very uncomfortable and the service was soon cancelled. Longer journeys required frequent stopovers for refuelling and aircraft tended to be unreliable. It was also, initially, a very expensive way of travelling compared with rail and sea transport and so it was not until after the Second World War (international conflict, once again, having provided the impetus for rapid advances in aircraft technology) that air travel became a viable and realistic mode of transport for large numbers of tourists. Nevertheless, by 1939 there were regular air services between all the major European cities and Pan Am was operating a regular trans-Atlantic service.

Another factor that stimulated the growth of tourism in during the inter-war years was the increasing amount of free time that people were able to enjoy, in particular socially-sanctioned free time. Throughout the latter half of the nineteenth century, various pieces of legislation had improved working conditions and reduced the length of the working week. By the 1920s, most people worked a 48 hour week. A number of enlightened employers also gave their workers paid time off, but there was no legal requirement to do so. However, throughout the early twentieth century there was increasing pressure for holidays with pay. By the mid-1920s up to 17 per cent of the work force were receiving paid holidays, but it was not until 1938 that the Holidays With Pay Act was passed, giving all employees a legal right to enjoy paid holidays. With the onset of the Second World War it was to be some years before the legislation fully took effect and since then peoples' holiday entitlement has gradually increased. For example, in 1969, 97 per cent of all full-time manual workers in Britain received two weeks paid holiday; by 1988, 99 per cent received four weeks. The introduction of holidays with pay firmly established the popularity of the British seaside resorts, confirming their virtual monopoly on British holidays; even by the late 1960s, three-quarters of all domestic holidays were spent at the seaside. Many resorts, such as Scarborough and Brighton, were at the height of their popularity and Blackpool at the end of the 1930s attracted some seven million visitors between June and September each year.

Importantly, it was during this time that the family holiday became socially institutionalised.

(ii) The holiday camp

One of the major features of tourism in Britain during the inter-war years was the development of the holiday camp (for a history of the holiday camp, see Ward and Hardy, 1986). Indeed, as a result of publicity and nostalgia embodied in television programmes such as *Hi-de-Hi!*, the holiday camp is probably the most widely recognised symbol of British tourism up until the late 1950s. The person normally accredited with the concept and development of holiday camps is Billy Butlin and, certainly, his vision, flair and entrepreneurial skill were significant factors in the growth and popularity of the camps. However, the idea of holiday camps dates back to the turn of the century; Cunningham's Young Men's Holiday Camp was established on the Isle of Man in 1897 and, by the time Butlin's first camp opened in 1936, about 60,000 visitors a year stayed at Cunningham's. The Caister Camp on the Norfolk coast was founded by John Fletcher Dodd in 1906 as a summer camp for socialists and throughout the 1920s and early 1930s a number of organisations set up camps around the coasts of Britain. Some, such as those run by the Holiday Fellowship, were run as non-profit schemes to provide the opportunity for healthy holidays and fresh air for young people and others, such as camps organised by the Co-operative Holidays Association and the Workers Travel Association (by 1939, the second largest holiday organisation in Britain), provided holidays for workers and their families. A number of these early camps had rudimentary chalets for accommodation but in many others people slept in tents; indeed, *by 1939 it was estimated that a million and a half people spent their holidays under canvas and in camps of all kinds* (Ward and Hardy, 1986:42).

Butlin's first camp opened at Skegness on Easter Sunday, 1936 and, compared with earlier holiday camps, it was relatively luxurious. It comprised 600 chalets, dining and recreation facilities, a swimming pool, a theatre, tennis courts, services such as child-minding and organised entertainment and, perhaps most important of all, modern sanitary arrangements which had been noticeable by their absence at many other camps. Holidays, with full board and free entertainment, were offered at an all in price, ranging from 35 shillings (£1.75) to £3 per week, depending on the season, and the camp was an immediate success. His second camp opened in Clacton in 1938 and more followed after the Second World War, with other entrepreneurs such as Fred Pontin and Harry Warner building up their own holiday camps. By 1948, it was estimated that one in twenty holiday makers stayed at a Butlin's camp each year (Ward and Hardy, 1986:75) and throughout the 1950s and 1960s the camps remained popular. The Clacton camp was closed in 1983, along with those at Filey and Barry Island, and in recent years the remaining camps have been extensively modernised in order to compete with newer inland resorts, such as Center Parcs.

Holiday camps were successful for a number of reasons. They provided all-in holidays aimed at the middle, rather than working classes, they retained the atmosphere of a seaside holiday but with much better facilities than in the traditional hotel or boarding house, there was plenty to do, especially in poor weather, and they were bright, fantasy lands where 'campers' could forget about life outside and immerse themselves in a dream world. Their success also depended on peoples' willingness to be organised; holiday camps were developed when the great majority of the population first enjoyed paid holidays and, for many people, having free time was a novel experience. They were used to the routine of work and the culture of mass production and consumption and, thus, the regimented life of holiday camps reflected the broader social condition of the time. However, from the 1960s onwards, the popularity of holiday camps diminished. Their image as 'camps' became unfashionable and developments in tourism, in particular the growth in overseas holidays, provided competition with which the camps, in their original form, were unable to compete.

(iii) The development of mass tourism

The Second World War effectively put an end to the development of tourism for a number of years but the fifty years since the end of the war have been the most spectacular and, from a sociological point of view, the most significant in the history of tourism. Within the modern, Western world, international tourism has been transformed from a luxury enjoyed by a privileged minority into a leisure activity enjoyed by a large majority of the population and, as a social activity, tourism has become internalised. That is, it has become an accepted, or even expected, part of life, a necessity rather than a luxury, and a mass activity. For example, in 1950 there were approximately 25 million international arrivals, a figure which is expected to rise to 500 million in 1994. If the number of people taking holidays in their own country is added to this (it is estimated that there are six times as many domestic tourists worldwide as international tourists), then the size and scale of tourism becomes apparent.

This remarkable and rapid growth in tourism since 1950 has resulted from the same three factors that have enabled the development of tourism from earliest times, namely, time, money and technology. Reference has already been made to the increasing amount of socially-sanctioned free time that most people in Britain enjoy, including holidays with pay and bank holidays. It is likely that the amount of time available for tourism will continue to increase as people retire earlier and live longer and as new forms of employment, such as job-sharing, become more widespread. It has also been forecast that, in the future, peoples' careers may be based on '35's'; thirty-five hours a week, thirty-five weeks a year and a thirty-five year working life. Whether this is likely to occur is open to debate but there is no doubt that people will generally have greater amounts of free time in the future. Increasing wealth has also played a significant role in the growth of tourism; for example, real disposable income in Britain increased by 25 per cent between 1981 and 1988 and *it can be demonstrated that, historically, a growth of one per cent in incomes tends to be accompanied by a growth of rather over one per cent in travel* (Cleverdon and Edwards, 1982:7). Taken together, greater amounts of income and free time are most likely to result in an increase in the number of holidays that individuals take, rather than an increase in the number of people having holidays. Thus, although there has been an increase in the number of British tourists travelling abroad over the last decade, the volume of domestic tourism in Britain has remained level as a result of the increase in second and third holidays.

It is technological advance, the emergence of a sophisticated tourism industry and the development of the package tour that has done most to influence the rapid growth of international tourism. Following the end of the Second World War the large number of surplus aircraft and, during the 1950s, the introduction of jet airliners, set the scene for the rapid expansion of the air transport industry in general and charter air travel in particular (see Holloway, 1994:27-28). As the large airlines bought new jets, smaller charter companies were able to buy cheap, second hand aircraft to fly tourists to their holiday destinations and, working on the principle of economies of scale, the cost of international travel became almost as cheap as rail or road travel. The first person to operate a charter holiday flight was Vladimir Raitz who, in 1950, organised a trial trip to

Corsica. He went on to build his business under the name of Horizon Holidays (now owned by Thomsons) and, following his success, a large number of other tour operators were established both in Britain and abroad.

Since that time, the package tourism industry has become increasingly sophisticated and diversified; companies have integrated vertically and horizontally so that some tour operators own their own airline, their own chain of travel agents and, frequently, hotels in resorts. The scale of operations has increased enormously, with some twelve million passengers on package tour flights out of Britain in 1992, and the introduction of wide bodied jets and increasingly efficient aircraft has extended the package *pleasure periphery* (Turner and Ash, 1975). Whilst holidays to Spain, the Balearic Islands, Greece and other traditional package resorts continue to thrive, newer, more distant destinations now appear in the tour operators brochures; Mexico, the Seychelles, the West Indies, Thailand and Bali can all be visited on package tours, and at prices which would have been considered impossible only a few years ago. The package product has also diversified. Cultural or sightseeing tours may be combined with more traditional beach holidays on 'two-centre' holidays, such as a week's sightseeing in Sri Lanka followed by a week on the Maldives, and some of the most remote areas of the world can now be visited on package tours.

A fuller examination of the development of tourism over the latter half of the twentieth century is beyond the scope of this chapter. Different destinations and countries around the world attract different types of tourists, offer different products and suffer different problems related to the growth of tourism. The important point, however, is that the development of tourism over the last fifty years or so has mirrored the pattern of development that has been evident throughout the historical evolution of tourism. In other words, since the earliest times when tourism emerged as an identifiable and distinct sphere of social activity, those destinations or types of travel which were once the exclusive preserve of the well-to-do or the higher social classes have, almost inevitably, become assimilated under the umbrella of mass tourism. The Grand Tour became popularised as the aristocracy were replaced by a middle class more intent on pleasure than learning, whilst both the spas and the seaside resorts soon lost their exclusivity. Similarly, the Mediterranean resorts which were once frequented by the royalty of Europe gradually became less exclusive, firstly with the influx of American tourists in the 1920s and 1930s and more recently as a popular summer destination for car-borne tourists from other European countries. Nowadays the more distant, exclusive destinations also attract the package tourists as international tourism has become geographically more democratic.

This process whereby exclusive destinations become caught in the popular, mass tourism net has been called the *aristocratic model* of tourism development (Thurot and Thurot, 1983) and it is a process which, influenced by the media, technological advance and an increasingly confident travelling public, has accelerated in recent years. Up until the onset of modern, mass tourism, the exclusivity of a resort or a form of tourism was normally 'safe' for at least a generation but, *nowadays, the European upper middle class...has been caught up with by the lower classes within a period of ten years* (Thurot and Thurot). The extent to which this model continues to influence the development of tourism in the future remains to be seen; the mass package holiday of the 1960s and 1970s is gradually being replaced by a more individual approach to tourism, with self-catering holidays, fly-drive packages and special interest holidays becoming more popular. At the same time, a number of factors might influence the future of tourism. For example, if sunbathing became unfashionable owing to health concerns or if technological progress brought electronic imagery, such as virtual reality, within the reach of most people, then the development of tourism may, in fact, go into reverse. However, the present trends indicate that, globally, tourism will become even more widespread and democratised and viewed, increasingly, not as a luxury but as a right.

Chapter Three

Tourists: Roles and Typologies

INTRODUCTION

It is generally accepted that the word 'tourist' first appeared in the English language around the end of the eighteenth century, its first known usage being in a 1780 guide book to the Lake District. William Wordsworth used the word in his 1799 poem *The Brothers* and in 1800 Samuel Pegge wrote in a book on new English usage that *a Traveller is now-a-days called a Tour-ist* (quoted in Buzard, 1993:1) indicating that, originally, 'tourist' and 'traveller' were inter-changeable terms describing, in a neutral sense, a person who was touring. Nowadays traveller and tourist have different connotations. The former, in a touristic sense (as opposed to gypsy, new age traveller, and so on), is usually applied to someone who is travelling/touring for an extended period of time, probably back-packing on a limited budget. It connotes a spirit of freedom, adventure and individuality. The word tourist, on the other hand, is frequently used in a rather derogatory sense to describe those who participate in mass produced, package tourism.

The traveller/tourist dichotomy has, as Buzard (1993:5) argues, *more to do with the society and culture that produce the tourist than it does with the encounter any given tourist or 'traveller' may have with a foreign society and culture.* It is probably true to say that, at some time or another, most people have tried to distance or disassociate themselves from other tourists, convincing themselves that they are somehow better or enjoying a more meaningful experience. This issue is discussed shortly but the important point is that the word tourist is nowadays applied to such a huge number and variety of people undertaking such vastly different types of travel that, as a way of collectively describing the individuals who made 475 million international trips in 1992 and the billions who participated in domestic tourism, it is a virtually meaningless term. Even if, as Witt *et al* (1991:38) point out, about 70 per cent of international tourist arrivals are for holiday purposes, describing all the individuals concerned simply as tourists conceals a whole host of different factors, such as length and type of holiday, a person's demographic, social and psychological characteristics, the purpose of the trip, and so on. For example, strictly speaking a young person embarking on a year's back-packing tour of Asia, a family having a two-week package holiday in Benidorm and an American of Irish descent visiting Ireland to discover his ancestry are all tourists, but there the similarity ends.

If we are to be able to better understand, explain and predict tourist behaviour, it is necessary to look beneath the all-encompassing label of 'tourist'. We have to ask, who is a tourist and what are the different types of tourist? We have to consider how tourists may be categorised by their behaviour (the roles they play) and, adopting a structural approach, the extent to which tourist types and roles are determined by society. This chapter discusses the different attempts which have been made to create typologies of tourists and examines newer, socially determined categories of tourist, such as the 'good' tourist (see Wood and House, 1991) and the 'post-tourist' (see Feifer, 1985, and Urry, 1988 and 1990a). It also suggests that a practical,

64

useful typology of tourists should be based upon a broader approach than has been adopted to date.

TOURIST OR TRAVELLER?

When the word tourist was first used it was synonymous with traveller. That is, it was used in a totally neutral sense to describe a person who was touring for, normally, the purpose of pleasure or leisure. During the first half of the nineteenth century, however, distinctions came to be made between tourist and traveller, or tourism and travel, distinctions which implied as much, if not more, about the character of the individuals concerned as about the actual means of travel. The tourist, as opposed to the traveller, not only became associated with mass forms of travel but also with a particular mentality or approach to the travel experience. In effect, *high culture, the culture of the traveller, saw itself as the polar opposite of low culture, the culture attributed to the tourist* (Rojek, 1993:174), a distinction immortalised, perhaps, by Henry James' description of tourists as *vulgar, vulgar, vulgar*.

Writing in 1869, James was referring specifically to American tourists in Europe but his sentiments reflect the continuing dichotomy in the way that people view tourists and travellers. This dichotomy is most evident in the literature on travel; again, it was in nineteenth century writing that the distinction emerged (see Buzard, 1993) but the trend continues in the late twentieth century. Nowadays much travel literature tends to emphasise and, perhaps, glorify in the unusual, the different or the unique way of travelling from one place to another. Authors' accounts of cycling, walking, running, or sailing particular journeys predominate; if it has been achieved against a background of political turmoil or civil war, under harsh weather conditions or without the approval of the authorities, then so much the better! More recent series of guide books, in particular the Lonely

Planet *Travel Survival Kits*, also emphasise the individualistic, adventurous approach in contrast to the easy, comfortable, package tour. Thus, as the number of places around the world yet to become tourist destinations continues to diminish, for travellers it is not *where* but *how* that has become important.

In a physical sense, therefore, the traveller/tourist dichotomy emerged as a result of, and is sustained by, technological advance. During the latter half of the eighteenth century the train was seen as the prime culprit of the demise of 'real' travel; for example, John Ruskin wrote that the train *transmutes a man from a traveller into a living parcel* (quoted in Buzard, 1993:33). A century later it is ironic that, in an age of supersonic air travel, international train journeys (preferably hauled by a steam engine) are now promoted as a return to the days of real, authentic travel. In short, it is not the actual form of transport but its degree or stage of technological advance that determines its acceptability to travellers. No doubt a trip on Concorde will one day be sold as an authentic experience of real travel!

Of more importance are the social distinctions inherent in the traveller/tourist argument. All tourists, in general, are looked down upon by other tourists who, arguably, consider themselves to be undeserving of the tourist label. Furthermore, it is a process or reaction that is found across the entire spectrum of touristic activity and one which does not always respect traditional social groupings or distinctions. For example, back-packers, particularly those on longer-term trips, are at pains to call themselves travellers rather than tourists (see Riley, 1988); travel is associated with adventure, authentic experience, taste, individuality and self-discovery, whereas tourism is pre-packaged, pre-paid, comfortable and predictable. Travellers make their own choices; tourists have their decisions made for them. Travel is seen to be somehow 'better' than tourism, travellers 'better' than tourists, irrespective of class, wealth, education, age, nationality and other social distinctions.

Similarly, distinctions are made within forms of tourism, such as package beach holidays. Some people believe that certain destinations are not suitable or are too 'touristy' and so a fortnight's holiday in, say, the Seychelles may be perceived to be better than two weeks on Majorca; the two products are, in effect, the same, the primary difference being the cost. Comparisons may also be made between different nationalities of tourists. For many years the American 'if it's Tuesday it must be Belgium' style of touring Europe bore the brunt of the anti-tourists' criticism; attention nowadays has shifted towards coachloads of camera-toting Japanese. Tourist differentiation is even apparent within the context of a single mode of transport. As the opportunity for travel became more widespread during the 1800s, *status distinctions came to be drawn less between those who could and those who could not travel but between different classes of traveller* (Urry, 1990b). For example, charter flights are more 'touristy' than scheduled flights and even in China rail travel is segregated into two classes of travel - 'soft seat' (i.e. first class) and 'hard seat' (i.e. second class).

Simply put, all tourists (and travellers), as Culler (1981) argues, *can always find someone more touristy than themselves to sneer at*. Disliking and trying to avoid other tourists at the same time as trying to convince oneself that one is not a tourist is, in fact, all part of being a tourist. The basis of the conflict is a kind of social arrogance which can be linked directly to the aristocratic model of tourism development described in Chapter Two. Throughout the nineteenth century criticism was directed at ordinary people who, taking advantage of the new forms of transport, were able to travel both at home and abroad in ever increasing numbers, thereby threatening once exclusive destinations. The implication was that not only would the new mass tourists impinge on the enjoyment of the previously privileged minority who had the time and money to travel but also that they were, somehow, unable to appreciate the travel experience. For example, Wordsworth fought vigorously against the extension of the railway line to Windermere in the Lake District, fearing it would bring large numbers of people more intent on simple pleasures than admiring the sublime beauty of the region. Thus, as travel became increasingly democratised, the moral and cultural benefits of travel were seen to be becoming correspondingly diluted. As the growth of mass tourism has continued throughout the twentieth century, this perceived gulf between the traveller and the tourist has intensified; as more and more people become tourists, the less and less do they wish to be labelled as such.

One of the fiercest critics of mass tourists, highlighting the traveller/tourist dichotomy, is Daniel Boorstin. In lamenting what he terms *The Lost Art of Travel* (Boorstin, 1964), he describes the onset of mass tourism as *the decline of the traveller and the rise of the tourist*. The difference, he continues, is that:

> *The traveller, then, was working at something; the tourist was a pleasure seeker. The traveller was active; he went strenuously in search of people, of adventure, of experience. The tourist is passive; he expects interesting things to happen to him...he expects everything to be done to him and for him.*
>
> (Boorstin, 1964:85)

The modern tourist, according to Boorstin, has become a passive onlooker who travels in organised groups, enjoys contrived, pseudo-events, rarely experiences, or seeks, the real or authentic and, as Cohen (1988a) puts it, *seeks to enjoy the extravagantly strange from the security of the familiar*. Boorstin is, in fact, concerned with the overall state of modern society and simply uses mass tourism as an illustration for his arguments. Nevertheless, his opinions reflect the continuing and widely held belief that travellers are different and in some way superior to tourists, a belief that is based upon a number of misconceptions and generalisations.

1. The art of travel imagined and, perhaps, romanticised by the protagonists of the traveller/tourist dichotomy has not been lost; it has been overtaken by modern technology. In particular, advances in information technology have rendered the recreation of 'traditional' travel impossible. It matters little what mode of transport is used for what distinguishes early from modern travel is not the speed, comfort or type of transport but the expectations and knowledge of what will be encountered either *en route* or at the destination. Television, radio, magazines, education, guide books and even the experiences of family and friends have irrevocably altered the fundamental experience of travel to the extent that the traveller/tourist knows what to expect and what will be found.

2. Rather than leading to greater harmony and understanding, tourism serves to highlight social distinction and conflict. Different modes and standards of travel, different classes of accommodation, different destinations and even the difference between those who are able or unable to participate in travel and tourism are no more than a reflection of wider social differentiation and stratification.

3. Travel cannot be separated from tourism. Not all travellers

are necessarily tourists but all tourists are, by definition, travellers and there is little point in attempting to distinguish between the two in a collective sense except, perhaps, as a marketing exercise. That is, the perceived difference between travel and tourism may be used as means of distinguishing between different types of holiday and for appealing to different market segments. For example, a month-long overland trip in a truck through South America may be sold as authentic travel but, from the tour operator's point of view, it is no less a package holiday than a two week beach holiday.

4. By attempting to differentiate between the traveller and the tourist, generalised characterisations of each emerge. The word tourist, in particular, has come to be associated in a derogatory sense with mass tourism (which is also an overused and misunderstood term) and those who continue to denounce mass tourism disregard the enormous variation in the motivation, experience and behaviour of different tourists. Similarly, there is no single type of traveller. In short, there is no such thing as *the* tourist or *the* traveller and, within the context of the modern tourism system, it may be concluded that a traveller is simply one type of tourist.

TOURISTS: TYPES, CATEGORIES AND ROLES

An understanding of tourist categories and roles is essential, along with other factors, to the explanation and prediction of consumer behaviour within tourism. One of the earliest attempts to distinguish between different types of tourism was made by Gray (1970) who coined the terms *sunlust* and *wanderlust* tourism. Sunlust tourism is essentially tourism that is resort based and motivated by the desire for rest, relaxation and the three S's - Sun, Sea and Sand, whereas wanderlust tourism is based on a desire to travel and to experience different peoples and cultures. Implicit in each term are the characteristics of each form of travel; for example, climate and comfortable and familiar accommodation and cuisine will be more important to the sunlust tourist whereas the wanderlust tourist will be more interested in different cultures and the potential for experience and learning. However, as the two terms imply, sunlust and wanderlust are basically categorisations based upon the purpose of the trip.

Since then a number of typologies, concentrating on the tourists themselves, have been developed. Some of these concentrate on tourists' behaviour whilst others adopt a more psychological approach.

(i) Cohen's Typology of Tourists

Cohen was the first sociologist to propose a theory of different types of tourists and his work is still widely used and quoted in the study of tourism. Rather than looking at tourists in isolation his typology of tourists rests *on the basis of their relationship to both the tourist business establishment and the host country* (Cohen, 1972). His work is also based on the fundamental assumption that all tourists, even those with a thirst for adventure and excitement, are unable to escape totally from the influence of their home environment, carrying with them as they travel their values and behaviour patterns. Thus, all tourists, according to Cohen, need something to remind them of home, such as a newspaper, familiar food or a friend, whilst the way in which they view, and react to, new places and cultures is also determined, to a greater or lesser extent, by their home environment and culture. In short, tourists travel in an *environmental bubble*.

Cohen's starting point is, therefore, similar to Boorstin's view of the mass tourist but, unlike Boorstin's single generalisation, he suggests that different tourists are more or less able experience and adapt to the unfamiliar and fall into four different categories:

(a) The organised mass tourist
The organised mass tourist is probably the type that conforms most closely to the stereotypical image of the tourist. On a package tour, the organised mass tourist travels around in air-conditioned coaches on a pre-arranged, inflexible itinerary, stays in hotels which recreate the home environment, makes virtually no decisions and at all stages of the trip is shielded from any possible contact with the host country's culture. If on a beach holiday, the organised mass tourist remains within the hotel complex with the exception of an occasional organised tour and at no time does he or she venture outside the environmental bubble. Domestic tourists on package trips (e.g. a week in Blackpool) also fall into this category.

(b) The individual mass tourist
Individual mass tourists are similar to the organised mass tourists in as much as their holiday or trip is arranged and booked through an operator but they are able to exercise a degree of personal choice and control. For example, a fly/drive holiday, where tourists choose their itinerary but still stay on the beaten track combines familiarity with a certain amount of novelty and is likely to appeal to individual mass tourists. They rely on the established tourism system but are able occasionally to escape from their environmental bubble.

(c) The explorer
The characteristics of the explorer approximate to the behaviour of the independent traveller. The explorer makes his/her own travel arrangements, tries to avoid the tourist trail as far as possible by getting off the beaten track and attempts to associate with local people and culture by learning the language, eating in

local restaurants and so on. Nevertheless, a reasonable level of comfort and security is sought and although the explorer, for the most part, is able to escape the environmental bubble, some of the values and routines of home life are retained. For example, accommodation used by fellow travellers may be preferred and many explorers travel secure in the knowledge that they have their return ticket home.

(d) The drifter
At the opposite extreme from the organised mass tourist, the drifter attempts to merge into local communities, living and working with local people. The drifter has no fixed itinerary and becomes immersed in local culture and customs. Tourism and tourists are considered to be phoney and so all contact with the tourism system is avoided. Escape from the environmental bubble is almost complete, contact with the familiar is minimal and the sense of novelty is at its highest.

Cohen categorises the first two types of tourist, the organised and the individual mass tourist, as *institutionalised* tourists. That is, their tourism experience is planned, controlled and provided by the mass tourism industry. In order to serve their large number of customers as rapidly and efficiently as possible each part of the tour or holiday is planned, packaged and predictable; novelty for the customer is, in many instances, a mass produced and inauthentic version of local culture (see Chapter Five). Drifters and explorers are *noninstitutionalised* tourists, requiring little contact with the tourism establishment. As Cohen argues, drifters and explorers often act as pathfinders for the mass tourism industry; destinations 'discovered' by or popular amongst explorers and drifters often become commercialised and open up to the mass tourism market. For example, Goa was once a famous haunt of travellers in India; it is now directly served by charter flights from Europe.

One problem with Cohen's typology is that the institutionalised/ noninstitutionalised forms of tourism are not entirely distinct. For example, independent travellers, explorers, tend to rely on specialist guide books referring them to destinations, accommodation, restaurants, transport routes, budget flight agencies and so on that are frequented by other travellers. They often follow popular trails and in many countries a local tourism industry has emerged to serve the particular needs of independent travellers. In short, independent travel has become as institutionalised as mass tourism. It is also debatable whether or not the drifter is a feasible categorisation at all. As the world gets smaller and more homogeneous it becomes less likely that any individual can fully escape the home environment; as the 'global village' emerges so too does a global environmental bubble.

Another criticism is that this categorisation is based on observable tourist behaviour but gives no indication of the reason for that behaviour. Thus, an individual might prefer to be an explorer but, constrained perhaps by financial, work or family commitments, a form of organised mass tourism may be chosen in order to optimise the benefits at a given time. Nor does this typology allow for variable tourist behaviour over time; the implication is 'once a mass tourist, always a mass tourist' whereas tourists frequently take different types of holiday from one year to the next or even within a year.

(ii) Tourist Types, Tourist Numbers
A similar typology to Cohen's is suggested by Smith (1989a). It is again based upon the behaviour of tourists, but Smith also links types of tourists to their numbers with implications about their impacts on the host environment.

(a) Explorers

There is a very limited number of explorers, constrained by the ever diminishing supply of areas to be explored. They are more akin to anthropologists than tourists and fully accept local lifestyles and culture.

(b) Elite Tourists

Elite tourists, rarely seen, *usually include individuals who have been 'almost everywhere'* (Smith, 1989a:12). They participate in unusual activities and adapt fully to local ways but are, nevertheless, on a pre-arranged and, most likely, expensive tour.

(c) Off-beat Tourists

Equivalent to Cohen's explorer, off-beat tourists are uncommon but seen. They try to avoid tourists and adapt well to local norms, staying in local accommodation and using local services.

(d) Unusual Tourists

Tourists who occasionally break away from an organised tour in order to experience some local culture are relatively few in number. They will adapt to local norms for a time but are happier within their own environmental bubble.

(e) Incipient Mass Tourists

Incipient mass tourists represent a steady flow of visitors to a destination that has a reasonably established, but not dominant, tourism industry. The incipient mass tourist will tend to seek out Western style amenities.

(f) Mass Tourists

There is a continuous influx of large numbers of mass tourists to a destination or resort and they expect Western amenities.

(g) Charter Tourists

Charter tourists arrive by the planeload in massive numbers. They demand Western style food and accommodation and, in the extreme, the actual destination may be of little importance to them as long as they enjoy their holiday.

Based as it is on tourist behaviour, similar problems emerge with this typology of tourists as with Cohen's. There is also little distinction sometimes between the different categories of tourists; the difference between a mass tourist and a charter tourist is not always clear. Other proposed typologies of tourists also suffer from the same limitations. Cohen (1974) suggests that different types of tourist are distinguishable by what he terms the *dimensions of the tourist role*. Factors such as permanency, voluntariness, distance and purpose of trip, and frequency of recurrence determine whether or not an individual is a tourist and, if so, what type of tourist. Pearce (1982) reviews a number of attempts to formulate tourist typologies and proposes fifteen different types of tourist based upon five role-related behaviour patterns. For example, a jet-setter is identifiable by a luxury life style, a concern with social status, a search for sensual pleasures, interaction with similar people, and frequenting famous places.

Typologies of tourists which rely upon observations of the behaviour and roles of tourists indicate the enormous diversity of activities that are included under the broad heading of tourism but frequently reveal more about the researcher and the research methods used than about the tourists themselves (Lowyck *et al*, 1992:13). They also tend to be static, not allowing for variations in an individual tourist's behaviour, and view tourists in isolation from broader sociological factors which may determine and explain variations in tourist roles. Attempts have also been made to link tourist categories with the tourism experience.

(iii) Tourists' Experiences
Building upon his earlier work in distinguishing between different types of tourist, Cohen (1979b) accepts that it is overly simplistic to assume that tourists can be categorised along a continuum ranging from, at one end, tourists as mass consumers accepting the superficial, inauthentic product of tour operators (as proposed by Boorstin, 1964) to, at the other end, tourists as modern pilgrims on a voyage of exploration and self-discovery (e.g. MacCannell, 1989). This continuum adopts a structural approach in as much as each category reflects, or results from, the influence of the tourism generating society. Recognising that tourism is a multi-dimensional phenomenon, Cohen proposes that a micro approach is equally valid in developing an understanding of different tourist types and roles, concentrating not on observed behaviour but on different tourist experiences.

The starting point is to ascertain where the 'spiritual centre' of the individual tourist is located. That is, different individuals identify with and accept to a greater or lesser extent their home culture and society. At one extreme, the 'centre' is located entirely within the home society and the individual finds no meaning in any other societies and cultures; as a tourist, the individual is not concerned with experiencing and learning about other peoples and cultures. At the other extreme lies the modern (in the sociological sense) individual who, alienated from the meaning and values of home society, locates his or her 'centre' elsewhere and, as a tourist, seeks authentic experiences. Between these two points it is possible to identify five categories of tourist experience:

(a) Recreational
The tourist whose centre is located in the home society seeks recreational experiences and has little or no interest in learning

about or experiencing the society and culture in which the recreational experience is taking place.

(b) Diversionary

The diversionary tourist is an intermediate category. Although alienated to an extent from his or her own society, the individual does not seek authentic experiences elsewhere. In a sense, the purpose of a holiday or trip is to temporarily forget about home.

(c) Experiential

The experiential tourist is the modern, alienated individual who seeks authentic experiences elsewhere. Although seeking to experience alternative cultures and societies, the experiential tourist neither identifies with them nor rejects his own society. The trip thus compensates for the inauthenticity of home life to which the tourist inevitably returns.

(d) Experimental

The experimental tourist is seeking to relocate his or her 'centre', but lies midway between the 'centre' at home and an identified 'centre' elsewhere. Authenticity of experience is essential, but the experimental tourist does not become totally immersed in any one culture.

(e) Existential

The existential tourist is the opposite extreme to the recreational tourist. Alienated from the home society, the 'centre' is firmly located elsewhere. The tourist becomes fully immersed in the local, foreign culture and society, finding meaning and belonging in the new chosen 'centre'.

Actual types of tourist may be identified with any one of these five categories. For example, the mass tourist on a two week beach holiday or a skiing trip closely resembles the recreational tourist whilst a cultural tourist on a tour of, say, the Far East, may be categorised as an experiential tourist. Whilst adding an extra dimension to the behavioural typologies this typology still does not allow for the different needs or requirements of an individual tourist. Nor is it based on any empirical research; it is a theoretical categorisation within which different tourists may be located but, as with other typologies, it considers tourists *per se* rather than in their broader social context.

(iv) Psychocentrics and Allocentrics

One of the better known attempts to link personality traits to tourist types and roles is Plog's tourist typology (Plog, 1977). Researching the reasons why people who, even though they could well afford it, did not fly, Plog identified two opposing character types at each end of a continuum. Psychocentrics are those who are inward looking, who concentrate on small problems and tend to be less adventurous. The corollary in tourism is the mass tourist looking for the familiar. The psychocentric tourist frequents popular, mass tourist resorts either at home or abroad and feels more comfortable surrounded by other tourists. Allocentrics, on the other hand, are adventurous and are prepared to take risks, as with Cohen's explorer and drifter. The allocentric tourist, therefore, prefers unusual, exotic destinations and enjoys the freedom of relatively autonomous travel. In between the two extremes lie the categories of near-psychocentric, mid-centric and near allocentric.

Unlike other tourist typologies, Plog goes on to link different types of tourist with different destinations which they are most likely to visit. He suggests that (American) psychocentrics go to resorts such as Coney Island, near New York, whereas allocentrics are to be found travelling in Africa. Mid-centrics, the most numerous category, take their holidays in places such as Europe or Hawaii, destinations which offer the experience of a new, yet sufficiently similar, culture. One problem with attempting to link tourist type with destination in this way is that it is a static model. Destinations change and develop over time; as a resort is discovered and attracts growing numbers of visitors it will evolve from an allocentric to a psychocentric destination. Equally, the parameters of each category of tourist may change or become vague. For example, as long haul charter flights become more available and more exotic destinations are publicised and packaged, psychocentrics might be found travelling to destinations which, according to Plog's model, normally attract allocentrics.

A number of other attempts have been made to create typologies of tourists (see Lowyck *et al*, 1992:13-32). Little is to be gained from a consideration of them all but, generally, they may be sub-divided into two distinct groups. Firstly, there are those typologies which concentrate on the tourists themselves, their behaviour and their experience (e.g. mass tourists, independent travellers, vacationers, cultural tourists, and so on). The great majority of typologies fall within this category. Secondly, there are typologies which are based upon the life style of tourists, such as Dalen's (1989, quoted in Lowyck *et al*, 1992). He applies a four segment categorisation of life style to tourism and suggests that, for example, the *traditional materialist* looks for low prices and safe products and, therefore, purchases the mass, package tourism product.

Neither approach is entirely satisfactory in explaining and predicting tourist behaviour. Typologies that concentrate on the tourist *per se* are, generally, descriptive, static and theoretical whilst life style categorisations are often developed in isolation from the tourism system. Some combination might be desirable but, as Lowyck *et al* (1992:26) point out, *studies in which tourism consumer behaviour is linked to general life style variables are generally lacking.* From a sociological point of view, a typology of tourists should be based upon both a micro analysis of tourists themselves and a macro, structural approach which locates actual tourist behaviour and experience within a broader social context. This issue is discussed shortly but, firstly, it necessary to consider what may be described as socially determined tourist typologies.

SOCIALLY DETERMINED TYPOLOGIES

When a structural perspective is applied to the analysis of tourist typologies it becomes evident that types, or categories, of tourist have emerged which have more to do with the values of society as a whole than with the behaviour or life style of individual tourists. In other words, certain types of tourist have been given labels that reflect broader, societal attitudes towards tourism and tourists rather than being based on any empirical research of individual tourists. In particular, the term 'mass tourist' is a general and over-used categorisation of tourists that bears as much relation to the widespread and growing concern for the impacts of mass tourism on host societies and environments as it does to the traditional, Boorstin-type attitude towards the tourists themselves. Mass tourism, however, is not simply *one monolithic, static sort of phenomenon* (Graburn, 1983) but an activity that encompasses a huge variety of products, demands, destinations and so on. Therefore, clarification is required of what is meant or understood by mass tourism and, hence, the mass tourist label.

(i)   What is Mass Tourism?

Since the 1960s the criticism surrounding mass tourism has increasingly shifted away from the tourists themselves onto the perceived negative impacts of mass tourism around the world. A number of well-known books published during the 1970s

(Young, 1973, Turner and Ash, 1975, de Kadt, 1979, Rosenow and Pulsipher, 1979) all point to mass tourism's potentially destructive impact on societies, cultures and environments whilst during the 1980s the adverse publicity surrounding some Mediterranean destinations added to the negative opinions of mass tourism (and mass tourists). Thus, mass tourism has evolved from what Crick (1989) describes as the *degenerate offspring* of early travel into what some see as an internationally destructive force: *The tourism industry is in crisis...a crisis of mass tourism; for it is mass tourism that has brought social, cultural, economic and environmental havoc in its wake, and it is mass tourism practices that must be radically changed to bring in the new* (Poon, 1993:3).

This criticism is indicative of a widespread condemnation of mass tourism which is founded upon a subjective, socially constructed view of mass tourism. Just as mass tourists have come to be seen collectively as what may be described as the lowest common denominator of tourism, so too has the phenomenon of mass tourism itself achieved a notoriety based on generalisations and misconceptions rather than a balanced consideration of the situation. There are, in fact, a number of different ways of defining mass tourism which provide a more objective basis for analysis.

(a) Mass tourism: the product

Mass tourism is a social, economic, political and geographic phenomenon, commonly used as a means of describing the movement of large numbers of people, usually on standardised, inclusive tours, for the purpose of holiday taking. This movement of people is the manifestation of the fundamental nature of mass tourism, namely, the mass purchasing of a product. In turn, the product has evolved through technological advance, economies of scale and the combination of a variety of services into a single package. It is both a tangible and intangible product; the purchase of transport, accommodation and so on is combined with the anticipated benefits of the holiday but, nevertheless, mass tourism is a product that is 'manufactured', marketed and sold.

Following this argument, the mass tourist is simply an individual who purchases the mass tourism product, a product supplied by the mass tourism industry. To categorise tourists as mass tourists, or even to sub-categorise them as organised, individual, incipient or charter mass tourists, simply identifies them as individuals who, to a greater or lesser extent, purchase a mass tourism product. Assumptions about the character, limitations or needs of the mass tourist thus become irrelevant unless the decision making process leading up to the purchase of the product is also taken into consideration.

(b) Mass tourism: tourism for the masses?

A second way of defining or interpreting mass tourism is that it is tourism that is enjoyed by the masses as opposed to the privileged few, at least in the developed, industrialised nations of the West. As described in Chapter Two, technological advance and increased levels of leisure time and disposable income have gradually brought travel, and international travel in particular, within reach of the great majority of the population. If the increasingly rapid process whereby once exclusive destinations are becoming assimilated under the umbrella of mass tourism is also taken into consideration, then it becomes evident that tourism is becoming increasingly democratised. Simply put, all tourists are part of the mass democratisation of tourism and, hence, are mass tourists. The distinction must then be made not between mass tourists and other tourists, but between tourists and non-tourists, demanding a sociological explanation of why individuals choose, or are able or unable, to be tourists.

(c) Mass tourism or mass tourists?

A third and final way of interpreting mass tourism returns to theme of mass tourists as individuals who are satisfied with inauthentic, 'pseudo' events experienced from the safety of their environmental bubbles. This derogatory connotation has been compounded in recent years by the publicised inappropriate behaviour of a minority of tourists, such as 'lager louts', to the extent that the problem of mass tourism is seen by some to be not the number of tourists, nor the type of tourism, but the tourists themselves. The socially defined mass tourist has become, in effect, an individual who is neither able to appreciate the tourism experience nor knows how to behave in an appropriate manner whilst on holiday.

This is, of course, an extreme and inaccurate view. Being a mass tourist is easy, it is safe and, perhaps most importantly, relatively cheap, a combination that continues to ensure the popularity of mass, package tourism. More importantly, *people seem to enjoy being mass tourists* (Butler, 1992) and they choose to be so. Categorisations that link mass tourists with recreational experiences, with an inability to escape the environmental bubble and with an implied lack of cultural awareness deny the mass tourist any individuality and any ability to choose and to make informed decisions. Thus, typologies which include the mass tourist as a separate category say more about the researcher than the researched. Lumping together all mass tourists as a single, socially defined category is adopting what Emery (1981) calls the *lemming hypothesis. We do not know why [mass tourists] move, but we know that, at certain times of the year, they all start moving - and we have a fair idea of the destination.* The inevitable conclusion is, again, that a practical and realistic tourist typology should be based in the broader, social context.

(ii) The Good Tourist

A second, socially determined type of tourist that has emerged from the present concern for the negative impacts of mass tourism is the 'good tourist' (Wood and House, 1991), the implication being that to be a traditional, mass tourist is being a 'bad' tourist. The way forward to more appropriate, less damaging forms of tourism, collectively known as alternative tourism (see Smith and Eadington, 1992), is seen to be the responsibility of not only the tourism industry as a whole but also of the individual tourist. In a sociological sense, the emphasis must shift from the structural, mass tourism perspective towards the individual, social action approach. The individual tourist responds to the reactions of others (in this case environmentalists, pressure groups and the impacts of other tourists on host environments and cultures) and demands new forms of tourism. The new, responsible tourist seeks quality rather than value, is more adventurous, more flexible, more sensitive to the environment and searches for greater authenticity than the traditional, mass tourist.

In particular, the good tourist is exhorted to adopt a new code of travel although, interestingly, not being asked to question whether any form tourism is appropriate (some would argue that the only good tourist is a non-tourist!). For example, the good tourist prepares for the trip by learning in advance about the destination, ensures that he or she uses a tour operator which is aware of and supports environmental programmes in the host country, behaves in an appropriate manner and recognises local customs whilst abroad and, wherever possible, tries to benefit the local economy rather than international tourism businesses. Thus, the good tourist is a category of tourist that could, potentially, embrace all other types of tourist although it does overlook some fundamental features of tourism and tourist motivation (see Chapter Four and McKercher, 1993). Generally, tourism is associated with holidays which, in turn, conjure up visions of rest, relaxation, fun, escape from the regular and the mundane, freedom from work and so on. The good tourist, conversely, is being asked to work at tourism, to adopt a fundamentally different approach and interpretation of the tourism experience. Additionally, the concept of the good tourist frequently attracts criticism that it is no more than an attempt to attach an explorer/drifter image to certain tourism products and to develop a niche market for 'aware' tourists. This has led to accusations that the overall idea of alternative tourism is no more than a marketing ploy, a *green mantle* (Wheeller, 1991, 1992a and 1992b) behind which the tourism industry is hiding. The link between the good tourist and modern tourism generating societies is explored in Chapter Eight.

(iii) The Post-Tourist

One feature that unites all the typologies of tourists is that they propose separate and identifiable tourist roles but without an allowance for either a combination of roles at any one time or a variety of roles over time. For example, an individual may be categorised as a mass tourist, an explorer or a special-interest tourist. Equally, a tourist may be concerned with a safe, recreational experience within the constraints of the environmental bubble or, at the opposite extreme, seeking an 'existential' experience, but there is no room in the typologies for an individual to adopt different tourist characteristics or experiences whereas, in reality, the distinctions between different categories are likely to be much more blurred. A tourist might be on a pre-paid, packaged tour but as Rojek (1993:177) explains, *there is always room for tourist bypassings and deviations from the tourist script.*

In short, most tourist typologies are static in both time and breadth. Furthermore, most typologies are also limited by the proposed links between tourist behaviour and the assumed character of tourists. The explorer-wanderlust-allocentric tourist is typecast as being bold, adventurous, independent and empathetic to new cultures and societies, whereas the mass, institutionalised tourist is unadventurous, indecisive, easily pleased by staged, inauthentic events and has little or no interest in expanding his or her cultural horizons beyond the limits of the environmental bubble. Such categorisations, as has already been pointed out, have been developed without taking the broader social context into account but, especially in the case of the mass tourist, they also deny tourists the ability to make choices.

In direct contrast, it may be argued that tourism and tourists have come of age. In other words, the distinction between the traveller and the tourist is, in fact, no more than a manifestation of the first two stages in the evolution of travel and we have now reached the third stage, the era of the *post tourist* (Feifer, 1985, and Urry, 1988 and 1990a:100). The post tourist lives in an age of mass communication and rapid advances in information technology; most tourist sights and destinations can be seen, if not actually experienced, on video and television in the comfort of the tourist's own living room. The post tourist is able, therefore, to make informed decisions and delights in the choice available.

More importantly, the post tourist recognises and understands the fundamental change that has occurred in the nature of tourism. Armed with a mass of information and images, the post tourist knows that it is no longer possible to experience authenticity because nothing is new. The pseudo-event or the cheap souvenir is accepted for what it is. Tourism has become a kind of game, *or rather a whole series of games with multiple texts and no single, authentic tourist experience* (Urry, 1990a:100) and the post tourist understands the role he or she plays in that game. The post tourist chooses sometimes to be a mass tourist, sometimes an independent traveller and sometimes not to be a tourist at all and accepts the conditions and constraints of each role. For example, the organised, packaged tour is purchased for what it offers; not an authentic cultural experience but the opportunity to collect a set of pre-determined images and sights, saved for all time, perhaps, as photographs. Above all, the post tourist is aware of being a tourist, of being an outsider, *not a time traveller when he goes somewhere historic; not an instant noble savage when he stays on a tropical beach; not an invisible observer when he visits a native compound* (Feifer, 1985:271).

For the post tourist, then, the traveller/tourist dichotomy is irrelevant. The traveller has matured and evolved into an individual who experiences and enjoys all kinds of tourism, who takes each at face value and who is in control at all times. In effect, the post tourist renders tourist typologies meaningless!

TOURIST TYPOLOGIES: A BROADER APPROACH

Throughout this chapter it has been emphasised that a realistic typology of tourists is essential to the explanation, understanding and prediction of tourist behaviour. If this is combined with other factors, such as a consideration of tourists' motivation (Chapter Four), a broader foundation for understanding and predicting the demand for tourism is then provided. A number of issues have emerged that point to limitations both in existing tourist typologies and the more general, all-embracing categorisations, such as the 'mass tourist' and the 'good tourist'.

1. Most typologies are static and do not take into account variations in tourist behaviour or experience over time. It is perfectly feasible for an individual to knowingly choose different types of holiday or trip at different times subject to

broader constraints or needs. Furthermore, people may mature as tourists as they become more experienced, giving credence to the concept of the post tourist. As Lowyck *et al* (1992:28) argue, it must be questioned *whether it makes sense at all to divide people into different types without taking into account their full life spans.*

2. Most typologies are isolated from the wider social context of the tourist. As a simple example, the most convenient and affordable holiday for a young family might well be of the package variety, yet the parents may have well have travelled extensively as explorers or independent travellers before being constrained by financial, job or family restraints. Thus, being a mass tourist does not necessarily imply an inability to escape the environmental bubble or, in terms of Cohen's experiential typology, having one's 'spiritual centre' firmly embedded in one's home culture and society.

3. Each typology, in particular those concerned with tourist roles or behaviour, employs a variety of names to describe a lesser or greater number of categories, from Gray's two-category to Pearce's fifteen-category typology. The important point is that, in the absence of universally accepted parameters and names for tourist categories, researchers create descriptions of different types of tourists according to their own sphere of interest. Thus, some typologies, though looking different, say the same thing.

4. Typologies of tourists tend to be *etic*, a word used by sociologists to describe a study that is undertaken from the researcher's point of view rather than centring on the object of the research. In other words, the typologies depend more on what the researcher puts into it rather than on unbiased, empirical findings. For example, longer-term independent

travellers may be described as adventurous, individual and culturally aware on the one hand, or as lazy, irresponsible 'drop-outs' on the other hand, depending on the experience and opinion of the researcher.

Overall, typologies of tourists tend to be descriptive and, although of interest in terms of highlighting the variety of tourist types and experience, fail to be of direct relevance to a better understanding of the demand for tourism. By concentrating on the tourists *per se* rather than locating tourist categories within the broader social context of the tourists' home environment, many important, if not dominant, factors which determine different types of tourists are excluded from the equation. Therefore, a tourist typology should not be based upon a one dimensional, linear progression of observed (or imagined) behaviour or experience, such as the mass tourist to individual drifter continuum, but upon a multi-dimensional matrix which incorporates tourist roles with other factors which influence tourist types. These other factors fall under two broad headings:

(i) Demographic and socio-economic factors
Tourism is not a single product. It encompasses a whole host of different products which are designed, packaged and marketed by the tourism industry to appeal to different potential tourists or, in marketing terms, different market segments (see Middleton, 1988:65-76). Simply put, the tourism industry recognises that different types of tourism suit different people according to a variety of demographic and socio-economic factors. Logically, therefore, each of these factors should be taken into account in the formulation of a tourist typology. There are four principal variables to be considered:

(a) Age
An individual's age will determine, to a great extent, the type of

tourism that he or she participates in. A younger person is more likely to be attracted to independent travel or, perhaps, to the '18-30' style of beach package holiday, whereas older tourists may be less inclined to subject themselves to the relative uncertainty or possible discomfort of independent travel. Equally, an older person may, in a touristic sense, be more experienced and demand more specialised forms of tourism.

(b) Life cycle

Life cycle characteristics play a dominant role in the determination of tourist types. For example, a young, single person has greater freedom to choose different types of holidays (within the constraints of availability of free time, financial resources and psychographic considerations) than, say, a family with young children. At the other end of the scale, 'empty nesters' or people who have retired early have fewer family responsibilities and are able to be more flexible in the timing and duration of trips. They are also likely to more disposable income.

(c) Gender

The gender of tourists may well influence their holiday decisions, irrespective of other factors. For example, some women may decide to not travel independently or to avoid certain countries for safety reasons. Gender is also of importance within the context of the family because although *the rigid roles which normally provide the base of family life become blurred* (Clarke and Critcher, 1985:172), under certain conditions those roles may become amplified. With the growing trend towards self catering holidays, women may simply find that their domestic work has been transferred to a new location and decide, therefore, that other forms of tourism are more suitable.

(d) Income/employment

Income and occupation or, more generally, socio-economic grouping, are, perhaps, the most influential factors in determining tourist types. Generally, research has shown tourism to be highly price elastic (for example, see Gerakis, 1965, or Edwards, 1987); that is, small increases in the cost of a holiday are very likely to result in tourists choosing cheaper destinations. More specifically, those employed in professional or managerial positions (social groups A and B) benefit from higher levels of income and longer holidays than, say, skilled manual workers (C2) and therefore have a much wider choice of what type of holiday to take. The latter group may also be more restricted with respect to the timing of holidays. Thus, it is not surprising that, of the 41 per cent of the British population who did not take a holiday in 1992, 45 per cent belong to the D and E (unskilled manual workers, unemployed and pensioners) social group (ETB, 1993). At the same time, the D and E groups (32 per cent of the British adult population) account for just 13 per cent of all holidays taken overseas whilst social groups A and B (17 per cent of the population) account for 30 per cent.

Some of these factors are inter-related and also point to other determinants of tourist behaviour. For example, there is an obvious link between age and life cycle characteristics whilst socio-economic grouping may be related to other variables, such as the level and type of education, which in turn can influence the type of tourism that an individual participates in. Essentially, a clearer and more practical tourist typology may be created by combining the more traditional, role based approach with the techniques of market segmentation. For example, in the case of independent travellers, the characteristics of a spirit of adventure, an interest in new cultures and so on certainly apply, but they are also more likely to be younger, single, and of student status (i.e. with more time but less disposable income).

(ii) Structural social factors

Most tourist typologies adopt a micro perspective. They concentrate on the tourist as an individual and, even when demographic and socio-economic factors are taken into account, the emphasis is placed firmly on the ability of individuals to decide what type of tourist they wish to be. In other words, different types of tourist are taken, in most cases, to be self-determined. The one exception is the 'mass tourist', the implication of most typologies being that people become mass tourists more by default than by design.

It is true that most people are able to choose, within the constraints of time, money, family commitments and so on, what type of tourists they wish to be. An equally valid approach is to consider the extent to which tourist types are structurally determined. The manner in which certain tourist labels, such as the 'mass tourist' and the 'good tourist', are socially constructed has already been considered but a holistic approach reveals that, in some situations, society plays the dominant role in the determination of tourist types.

(a) Non-tourists

Non-tourists, or people who, for whatever reason, do not participate in tourism, are a valid and identifiable category of tourist but not one that is normally included in tourist typologies. In Britain, the proportion of people who do not take a holiday (a holiday being defined as a stay of four or more nights away from home) has remained at around 40 per cent of the population for a number of years, despite increasing levels of disposable income and paid holidays. Some of these will be people who have made conscious decisions not to be tourists, whilst others may be restricted by factors such as illness or family constraints. For many people, their status as non-tourists has been determined by society in as much as their labour has been deemed as excess to requirements. In other words, for the unemployed the decision to be or not to be a tourist is beyond the control of the individual. The loss of paid employment and an income other than state benefits, effectively removes an individual's access to most forms of tourism, especially overseas tourism. The unemployed, non-tourist is, therefore, a manifestation of the conflict theory of society.

(b) Capitalist tourism

As discussed in Chapter One, a structural-conflict perspective on tourism reveals that the tourism industry is, in effect, a microcosm of capitalist society. The tourism industry, though diverse, fragmented and comprising a large number of private operators, is dominated by a few powerful, multinational corporations (MNCs). These organisations have concentrated the ownership of different sectors of the tourism system (i.e. transport, accommodation, entertainment, travel agencies) to the extent that it is possible for one company to own and control all the components of a package holiday. Therefore, the extent to which tourists as consumers of tourism products are able to influence the kinds of products that are on offer and, hence, the types of tourist they can choose to be, is in the hands of the larger tourism organisations.

In other words, the pluralist approach (power being shared by a multiplicity of groups or organisations), which implies that tourism suppliers follow market trends and consumer demand, *greatly underestimates the power of business to persuade consumers, through advertising in particular, to make the right choices* (Clarke and Critcher, 1985:103, and generally for a neo-Marxist perspective on leisure). Tourists can choose to purchase or not to purchase different tourism products, but they have little control over what is on offer. On the other hand, the tourism industry and, in particular, MNCs produce a range of products to appeal to a variety of tourists, products which recognise and, perhaps, reinforce social characteristics and divisions such as age, gender and class. New products are introduced not to satisfy customer demand but to increase diversity, market share and, ultimately, profit. For example, a number of tour operators now offer trips or holidays that are designed to attract the 'good' tourist, more likely to be a younger, relatively affluent, better educated and well travelled person looking for authentic yet environmentally friendly holidays. Arguably, such trips play on the environmental conscience of the individual and, whilst developing an image of 'good' tourism, are little more than a niche within the mass tourism market; ironically, the 'good' tourist becomes a mass tourist.

To develop a tourist typology that incorporates a multi-dimensional approach is, perhaps, an impossible task. Nevertheless, given the limitations of existing typologies, a broader foundation that locates tourists in a social context provides a clearer picture and explanation of tourist categories and roles, thereby contributing towards a better understanding of the demand for tourism. Chapter Four continues on this theme with an examination of tourist motivation.

Chapter Four

Tourism and Tourist Motivation

INTRODUCTION

The study of tourist motivation is concerned with the question, *why do people travel?* Many attempts have been made to answer this question, ranging from theories based in psychological research to more speculative or apocryphal explanations. For example, the desire to travel is still widely seen as resulting from the 'the travel bug' or 'having itchy feet', a supposed medical condition which John Steinbeck described in *Travels with Charley* as a *disease [that] is incurable* (quoted in Pearce, 1982:48). The actual meaning of the motivation to travel is also open to wide interpretation; for some, tourist motivation results from deep, psychological needs often unrecognised by tourists themselves, whereas others equate motivation with the purpose of a trip or the choice of holiday.

Whichever viewpoint is adopted, motivation represents the how, why, when and where of tourism. In other words, *the importance of motivation in tourism is quite obvious. It acts as a trigger that sets off all the events in travel* (Parrinello, 1993). It is not surprising, therefore, that many authors and researchers in tourism have concerned themselves with motivation, recognising it as *one of the most basic and indispensable subjects in tourism studies* (Wahab, 1975:44). It is also one of the most complex areas of tourism research. In contrast to early travellers who were motivated by basic needs for survival, present day tourists are motivated by an enormous variety of factors, many of which are rooted in modern society. Equally, there have been a number of different approaches, some based on a variety of disciplines, to the analysis of tourist motivation. This chapter examines tourism motivation from a sociological perspective considering, in particular, the link between the motivation for tourism and modern society.

MOTIVATION AND THE DEMAND FOR TOURISM

Before looking at the different approaches to tourist motivation it is important to understand the role of motivation within the overall consumer decision making process. At a basic level, tourism is a product that is purchased and consumed. Hence, tourists go through a process of *acquiring and organising information in the direction of a purchase decision and of using and evaluating products and services* (Moutinho, 1987:5). In other words, unless a trip or a holiday is an impulse purchase, tourists make a choice on the basis of their personal needs and desires and the extent to which they perceive those needs will be satisfied by a particular trip, holiday or destination (see Goodall, 1991:59). That choice will normally be influenced by factors such as the image or known attributes of the destination, the impact of advertising, the distance and mode of travel to the destination, previous experience, the advice of family and friends and so on. Additionally, holiday choice is constrained by factors such as family and work commitments, financial considerations and, of course, the range of products supplied by the tourism industry.

If all the knowledge, information, images and perceptions of a particular holiday or destination are combined they add up to the overall attraction, or *pull*, of that holiday choice. Pull factors may be described as *destination-specific attributes* (Goodall, 1991:59) within the decision making process. For example, the destination-specific attributes of a skiing holiday might include accommodation, entertainment facilities, the probability of good snow, the availability of skiing instruction and so on. At the same time, there usually exists a variety of factors that influence, or *push*, an individual into making a purchase decision. These *person-specific motivations* are what push an individual into wanting a particular type of holiday or, indeed, a holiday as opposed to another product, such as a new washing machine. Thus, the skiing holiday might be chosen in preference to, say, a summer beach holiday because an individual has a need or preference for a healthy lifestyle.

The distinction between push and pull factors is of fundamental importance to understanding the role of motivation within the demand for tourism. Generally, it is the push factors, the needs and wants of an individual, that lead to the decision to purchase a holiday in the first place, the nature of those needs determining the type of holiday the individual wants. For example, a person might want to visit friends and relatives but may be motivated by a need for love and affection. Once the decision to take a particular type of holiday has been made, the pull factors of different destinations determine which one is chosen. Thus, *the key to understanding tourist motivation is to see vacation travel as a satisfier of needs and wants* (Mill and Morrison, 1985:4).

In short, motivation is the very basis of the demand for tourism. The distinction between push and pull factors may not, in practice, be always clear cut and a whole host of other factors, including the socio-economic and psychographic characteristics of the individual, may influence the final choice of tourism product. Nevertheless, it is motivation that translates an individual's personal needs into goal-orientated behaviour,

behaviour from which the tourism decision making process evolves and progresses. The motivation to satisfy needs, combined with personal preferences, pushes the tourist into considering alternative products; the final choice depends on the pull of alternative holidays or destinations. Gilbert (1991:79) highlights the role of motivation in his four stage description of the tourist decision making process:

(a) Energisers of Demand
These are the forces, including motivation, which lead the tourist into deciding to take a holiday in the first place.

(b) Filterers of Demand
Demand is constrained by a variety of demographic and socio-economic factors.

(c) Affectors of Demand
The information about a destination and the tourist's image of it will affect the course of action taken.

(c) Roles
The role of the tourist as a consumer (e.g. as a family member) may determine the final choice of holiday.

An understanding of tourist motivation is, therefore, of fundamental importance to the study of tourism demand; *an analysis of the motivational stage...can reveal the way in which people set goals for their destination-choice and how these goals are reflected in both their choice and travel behaviour* (Mansfeld, 1992). There is also great practical value in the explanation and analysis of tourist motivation. Those organisations which are best able to cater for and predict tourist motivation and demand, and hence satisfy the needs of tourists, are likely to be most successful in an increasingly diverse and competitive tourism market.

PERSPECTIVES ON TOURIST MOTIVATION

Dann (1981) defines tourist motivation as *a meaningful state of mind which adequately disposes an actor or group of actors to travel, and which is subsequently interpretable by others as a valid explanation for such a decision.* What we are concerned with here are the ways in which this *meaningful state of mind* is determined or, more simply, how it is that people are motivated to be tourists. It must also be stressed that the study of tourist motivation is of most relevance to the category of what may be described as holiday tourism; that is, tourism that is generally non-essential and for pleasure. The demand for other forms of tourism, in particular business tourism, tends to result from the purpose of the trip rather than from the needs of the tourist.

In his review of the study of tourism motivation, Dann (1981) identifies seven different perspectives that have been adopted:

1. *Travel as a Response to What is Lacking Yet Desired*
   The motivation for travel lies in the desire to experience something new or different. People become tourists because their own physical and cultural environment cannot fulfil this need.

2. *Destinational Pull in Response to Motivational Push*
   This approach highlights the importance of push factors in tourist motivation. Such factors may be determined by the tourist's home environment or by an individual's own psychological needs.

3. *Motivation as Fantasy*
   Tourists may be motivated by the perceived opportunity to

indulge in forms of behaviour that would not normally be socially sanctioned or acceptable in their home environment.

4. *Motivation as Classified Purpose*
   In contrast to push factors, this approach views the purpose of a trip or holiday as the primary motivating factor.

5. *Motivational Typologies*
   Typologies of tourists are often used as models of tourist motivation. Within the context of this book typologies and motivation, though connected, are treated as separate issues (see Chapter Three).

6. *Motivation and Tourist Experiences*
   This approach suggests that tourist motivation is largely determined by the expected experience in relation to the home environment, in particular by the promise of authenticity.

7. *Motivation as Auto-Definition and Meaning*
   The principles of social action theory, especially symbolic interactionism, can be usefully applied to tourist motivation. The ways in which tourists define and respond to situations is seen as a better way of explaining tourist motivation rather than simply examining their behaviour.

Within these seven perspectives, there are two distinct approaches which may be used as a basis for an examination of tourist motivation. The first is to consider ways in which motivation results from influences external to the tourist (extrinsic motivation) and the second is to consider the personal needs of tourists themselves (intrinsic motivation).

(i) Extrinsic Motivation

There are a variety of different forces and pressures which emanate from an individual's social and cultural environment and which may, to a lesser or greater extent, influence that individual's needs and motivations. These pressures may flow from sources such as social norms, the influence of family and friends, the work environment and so on. Therefore, although some may argue that *motivation is a purely psychological concept, not a sociological one* (Iso-Ahola, 1982), there is little doubt that, in the case of tourism, motivation often results from societal values, norms and pressures which are internalised and become psychological needs. For example, the motivation for many people to take a holiday is to relax, to rest, to have a change and to get away from the routine, mundane constraints of everyday life. These needs can be grouped together under the general heading of escape, or *avoidance* (Iso-Ahola, 1982) motivations which are, undoubtedly, rooted in society.

It would be logical to propose, therefore, that, sociologically, a structural approach to extrinsic tourist motivation should be adopted in as much as certain categories of motivation, such as escape, result directly from the pressures and condition of life in a tourist's home society. MacCannell's assertion that for modern tourists, *reality and authenticity are thought to be elsewhere: in other historical periods and other cultures, in purer, simpler lifestyles* (1989:3) and that tourism is, therefore, a search for the authentic that results from the inauthentic, alienated condition of modern industrial society is firmly based in structural sociology. More specifically, tourist motivation may be viewed from a functionalist perspective; whether motivated by the desire to rest and relax, to 're-create', or to seek authentic experiences, the function of tourism is to redress the balance and harmony of society: *tourism is social therapy, a safety valve keeping the everyday world in good working order* (Krippendorf, 1986).

Nevertheless, it is important to bear in mind that overall tourism demand results from the needs and motivations of *individual* tourists who, together, comprise the market for tourism; motivation is concerned with the individual tourist and the micro, social action perspective is, therefore, of greater value to the study of motivation. (See Dann, 1981, for a discussion of the disciplinary treatment of motivation).

(a) The Tourism-Work Relationship

Modern tourism and, more generally, leisure, originated as a result of the fundamental changes that occurred in the nature and structure of society from the early nineteenth century onwards. People were motivated to participate in leisure activities or to travel by the need to remove themselves physically or mentally from the conditions of life in the cities of the Industrial Revolution. In particular, leisure and tourism became the antithesis to work, a *status quo* that, for many people, continues to this day. Work is, therefore, a primary extrinsic motivational factor for tourism.

Leisure, tourism and work cannot be separated; work provides both the means and the motivation for leisure and tourism and, up to a point, people need to participate in leisure and tourism to continue in work. Thus, work and leisure are not separate, distinct conditions. A relationship exists between the nature, or experience, of work and the leisure experience (see Parker, 1983). For some people, work is boring, monotonous, repetitive and something to be endured; leisure and tourism represent freedom and escape from work and work, therefore, is a means to an end. For others, work is a way of life. It is exciting, stimulating and, perhaps, the dominant feature in an individual's life; the role of leisure may be subordinated to work. The important point is that different types of work produce different levels of satisfaction; creative, challenging work produces higher levels of satisfaction whereas more mundane, repetitive forms of work result, generally, in lower satisfaction for the individual. Different work environments, therefore, produce different individual needs and, hence, different leisure and tourism motivations. In short, *the experience of work in industrial societies...forms the context for the experience of leisure* (Clarke and Critcher, 1985:17).

It is not only the work environment which determines an individual's leisure and tourism needs; nor does the work-tourism relationship apply to certain groups in society, such as the retired, the unemployed and, arguably, housewives. Nevertheless, Parker (1983) suggests three basic ways in which the work-leisure (tourism) relationship manifests itself, thereby providing a framework for understanding the links between work and leisure experiences and requirements. Similarly, Zuzanek and Mannell (1983) propose four different hypotheses about the nature of the work-leisure relationship.

1. Work and tourism in opposition

Where work and tourism are in opposition, there is a sharp contrast between the experiences of each. The individual is motivated to seek out forms of tourism that offer a distinct change of experience, or even lifestyle, from that found at work. In theory this relationship should operate in both directions; that is, people in monotonous, production-line type employment are motivated to go on holidays which are stimulating and exciting and which allow them to escape, albeit temporarily, from the reality of everyday life. Conversely, it might be expected that those who are employed in challenging, stressful jobs would seek out quieter, restful or even monotonous types of tourism experience. It has been found, however, that this model is most applicable to those in lower status jobs and to whom tourism *compensates* (Zuzanek and Mannell, 1983) for deficiencies at work and, by implication, at home.

Ryan (1991:20) cites the leading role played by the textile workers of Lancashire and Yorkshire in the formation of cycling and rambling clubs at the end of the nineteenth and in the early twentieth centuries as an historical example of the compensatory nature of leisure experiences. He goes on to describe a situation where the tourist escapes to a fantasy life, the life of the 'idle rich', staying in hotels and enjoying standards of service that could normally only be dreamed of. By saving for the holiday, the tourist is able to indulge in a life-style that is in direct contrast to normal life; in compensation for what is missing at work and at home, the holiday represents an inversion of everyday reality. Thus, the tourist is motivated to search out the opposite of the work/home experience. The lower middle-class tourist seeks to be a *king/queen for a day*, whilst the middle-class tourist seeks to be a *peasant for a day* (Gottlieb, 1982).

The opposition/compensation model of tourist motivation is also applicable to the lifestyle or constraints that are imposed by different types of work, rather than the deficiencies of the work itself. People are constrained by time commitments and codes of dress and behaviour; tourism offers the opportunity to indulge in 'ludic' behaviour (i.e. behaviour that can be described as play), to escape from constraining rules and norms. For example, Lett (1983) describes how charter yacht tourists in the Caribbean behave in a manner which is *an inverted expression of many of the pervasive values and attitudes of middle-class US. culture* (1983:54). Constrained only by time, the tourists ignore the social rules and conventions of their home society and indulge in excessive drinking and sexual activities, behaviour which is *licensed and excused only because it is temporary and occurs away from home* (1983:53). Lett emphasises the compensatory character of such behaviour and suggests that it not only refreshes and restores tourists but also prepares them to re-enter their structured, everyday existence.

2. Tourism as an extension of work

Where tourism and leisure are an extension of work there is, again, a direct link between the work experience and the tourism/leisure experience. Unlike the opposition/compensation model, however, where the individual is motivated to seek change and escape, the extension model proposes that there is little distinction between patterns of work and patterns of leisure. In other words, tourism and leisure compliments, rather than contrasts with, work. Thus, people who have challenging, stimulating and satisfying jobs, who are in a position of some responsibility, are more likely to choose an independent and stimulating type of tourism. Conversely, those who work in highly regulated, routine and monotonous jobs, who have a passive work role, will adopt a similarly passive attitude towards their tourism and leisure activities. They will choose the mass produced, package holiday which, in effect, mirrors the production-line environment of the workplace. The extreme case would be the individual whose work is central to his or her life and for whom there is little or no distinction between tourism and work, no boundary between work and leisure. For example, a history teacher's holiday might be spent touring historical sites, an activity which could be described as both leisure and work.

The important implication of the theory of tourism motivated as an extension of work is that as work practices change and adapt, so too will the demand for tourism. Many of the main tourism generating countries are being rapidly transformed from industrial to post-industrial economies; primary, manufacturing industries are being superseded by service industries, traditional production lines are becoming increasingly automated. For example, Glasgow has lost virtually all its traditional manufacturing industries and is basing its economic regeneration on the development of the tertiary, service sector, including tourism. Some would argue that the move towards service industry dominated economies is resulting in more widespread job satisfaction, whilst others would argue that although technology has advanced, the system of production (i.e. capitalism) remains unchanged. Whichever viewpoint is adopted, there is little doubt that changes in work practices and environments will impact upon tourism motivation and demand.

3. Neutrality between tourism and work

Both the opposition/compensation and the extension models of the relationship between leisure and work highlight the role of work itself in determining tourist motivation. That is, there is a causal relationship between work and tourism and leisure. In contrast, the third model occupies the mid-point between opposition and extension, suggesting that work has little or no effect on leisure patterns and *vice versa*. In effect, the experience of work and the experience of leisure remain independent; there is no link between the two. As Clarke and Critcher (1985:19) point out, in this situation it is likely that leisure is seen to be more fulfilling, that work loses its perceived importance and becomes a means to an end. For example, during the 1980s in Britain the work ethic was dominant; by the start of the 1990s, quality of life had become a more widely accepted motivation. The importance of work has diminished and the implication is, therefore, that the influence of work as an extrinsic factor in tourist motivation is also diminishing in terms of the type of tourism chosen. Nevertheless, the position of tourism, in particular the annual summer holiday, as the accepted (or even expected) form of leisure activity is such that the role of work as the prime extrinsic motivator of tourism is virtually unassailable.

(b) Social influences

In addition to work and the work environment as a major factor in influencing tourist motivation, a variety of other extrinsic pressures may affect the individual. These pressures are exerted by other people and together may be termed social influences (Moutinho, 1987:5). There are four main sources of social influence in an individual's tourist motivation:

1. Family influences

The family can play a significant role in the determination of tourist type (see Chapter Three); irrespective of other factors, the family may be a powerful constraint on the choice of tourism product. Equally, the family can have a significant influence on tourist motivation. It is through the family that, initially, most people acquire and internalise their values, beliefs and expectations. Thus, if an individual was brought up in a family which enjoyed regular overseas holidays, it is likely that he or she will be motivated to continue the tradition. Conversely, a negative experience or impression of family holidays may motivate an individual family member into becoming an independent tourist. The VFR (visiting friends and relatives) market is, of course, largely influenced by the family with the desire to visit relatives, both domestically and overseas, being a powerful tourism motivator.

2. Reference groups

A reference group is any group that an individual turns to as a point of reference for beliefs and attitudes; that is, a group against which an individual can judge his or her own beliefs and behaviour. Reference groups may take various forms, such as religious or ethnic groups, work colleagues, or the local neighbourhood, and are either normative (influence general values) or comparative (influence specific attitudes). The level of contact with or adherence to a particular reference group will determine the influence that group has on an individual.

3. Social class

Social class is *a relatively permanent division of categories in a society, a division that brings about some restrictions of behaviour between individuals in different classes* (Moutinho, 1987:7). Members of a particular social class tend to have similar values and lifestyles and it is likely that they will follow standards of behaviour acceptable to that class. Therefore, social class is an important factor in tourist motivation. For example, many destinations are categorised by the social class of the majority of visitors. Different types of tourism may also be class motivated; the working classes tend to be attracted by mass tourism or crowds of other tourists, whereas a more solitary approach to tourism, what Walter (1982) refers to as *romantic tourism*, is of greater appeal to middle class tourists.

4. Culture

The culture of a society is the combination of its values, morals, behavioural norms, dress, cuisine, artefacts and language; in short, a society's way of life which is passed on from generation to generation. The culture of a society may change and adapt over time and it influences the attitudes and behaviour of the individual members of society. In the context of tourist motivation, the culture of a particular society can be a strong influence in the determination of tourism demand. For example, travel and tourism is more deeply rooted in some cultures than others, or more acceptable in some countries than others. Also, different cultures motivate different types of tourism, such as the importance religious tourism and pilgrimage within Islamic culture.

Social influences on tourist motivation are not mutually

exclusive. Indeed, it is likely that a combination, if not all, of these four sources of pressure and influence have a bearing on an individual's decision making process. Some, such as the influence of family, may be more explicit whilst class or cultural characteristics may be so ingrained as to be unrecognised as positive or negative motivational factors. They may also be combined with motivational forces arising from the work-leisure relationship, so that it may be impossible to highlight any one dominant source of motivation.

(c) Modern society and tourism motivation

Leisure in general and tourism in particular have become institutionalised within modern, industrial societies. For the majority of the populations of the main tourism generating countries, the summer holiday is an accepted, or even expected, part of life, celebrated as vigorously as other more traditional festivals in the annual calendar. Rapid advances in technology, economic growth and greater amounts time available for leisure activities have brought to the masses a degree of freedom and mobility once reserved for the privileged minority. Indeed, *mobility, vacations and travel are social victories* (Krippendorf, 1986).

Paradoxically, however, those societies which provide the opportunity for travel and tourism also provide the motivation; modern, industrial society has created not only the means of, but also the need for, tourism. For many tourists, the annual holiday represents the chance to rest, to recover from the stresses and strains of everyday life, to get away from it all: *a hurried mobility has obsessed most of the inhabitants of the industrialised nations. One seizes every opportunity to free oneself from the boredom of everyday life as often as possible* (Krippendorf, 1986). Tourism has become an essential ingredient in a person's life cycle in modern society. In order to survive in modern society, an individual must, periodically, escape from it. Thus, from a structural point of view, tourism is motivated by society and, at the same time, plays an essential function within it. In other words, society itself determines, arguably, the ultimate motivation for tourism.

It is the character of life in modern societies, an amalgamation of the activities, work practices, demands, technological advances, expectations and social values which, together, constitute the modern 'way of life', that has created the need to escape. This need has been satisfied by increasingly fast, economical and widely available forms of transport. Since the beginning of the industrialisation and urbanisation of societies, people have become increasingly alienated. The division of labour, mass production and automation have alienated people from their work and the product of their labour; greater mobility and communication have alienated people from their friends and families; cities have alienated people from nature; people have even become alienated from themselves. Immersed in a world dominated and guided by the economy and economic growth, people have lost their sense of place and belonging; independence and freedom have replaced community, having has replaced giving, materialism has replaced contentment. Manufacturers introduce new products to make every task easier, faster and more painless. Yet every technological advance diminishes human contact and reduces the need for social interaction. As life gets faster, people have less time. The realities of modern life, for many, are a source of stress, constraint, disenchantment and dissatisfaction. People have lost their sense of time and place, they have lost their self-identity. In short, life in modern, industrial society is typified by a sense of 'anomie'.

Anomie is a word used by sociologists to describe *a situation of perceived normlessness and meaninglessness in the origin* [tourist generating] *country* (Dann, 1981). According to Dann (1977), anomie is a major extrinsic tourism motivator. Adrift in modern society's headlong rush to achieve economic and material growth, people find themselves wanting to say 'stop the world, I want to get off'. Whether to simply rest for a couple of weeks on a beach, to participate in physical or cultural activities which the hectic pace of life at home does not allow for, or to search for meaning, fulfilment and authenticity in other places and cultures (MacCannell, 1989), people are motivated to escape, temporarily, from their society. Every year, millions of people join together in a kind of migration, *seemingly of their own free will, but appearing as if they were obeying an order* (Krippendorf, 1986). They willingly subject themselves to traffic jams, delays at airports and all the other problems associated with modern, mass travel in order to refresh themselves, to prepare themselves for work or simply just to convince themselves that, compared to life in other places or countries, things are not too bad after all. Indeed, motivated by the realities of everyday life and spurred on by the efforts of the tourism industry, *people learn to desire vacations...for escape purposes and come to think of such vacations as essential for their psychological well-being* (Mannell and Iso-Ahola, 1987).

In short, tourism has become a fact of modern society. Society has created the need and the motivation for tourism, it has created the means by which the great majority of the population may participate in tourism and, in a sense, society sustains tourism as an essential function in the work-leisure cycle. It is for these reasons that some authors (for example, Krippendorf, 1987) maintain that the root of the 'problem' of tourism, as a mass phenomenon that impacts physically and culturally on destination areas, lies not in tourism itself but in the societies that generate tourists. They argue that, unlike early travel, modern tourism is motivated by the need to escape rather than a desire to discover and, therefore, the only way to minimise the impacts of tourism is to remove the need for tourism in the first place. By fundamentally altering the way of life in modern societies, people will no longer feel the need to escape and, by implication, will not participate in tourism. However, the position of tourism as a socially motivated and maintained activity is such that, unless technological advance in areas like 'virtual reality' can offer a viable and realistic alternative, people will increasingly feel the need to take holidays away from their everyday society.

(ii) Intrinsic motivation
The study of motivation has, traditionally, been concerned with the needs and desires of the individual. It is an individual's personal and deep-rooted needs that lead to motivated, goal-orientated behaviour, the goal being to satisfy those needs. The study of motivation has, therefore, been guided by the assumption that *in order to understand human motivation it is necessary to discover what needs people have and how they can be fulfilled* (Witt and Wright, 1992:34). Every individual has personal and unique needs, needs which may go unrecognised by, but are still intrinsic to, the individual.

(a) Maslow's hierarchy of needs
One of the best known theories of motivation is Maslow's hierarchy of needs (Maslow, 1943). It was originally developed by Maslow in connection with his work in clinical psychology during the 1940s but since that time it has been applied widely as a general theory of motivation. It has also been used in specific fields of research, such as motivation in business, and it also forms the basis for much of the work concerned with tourist motivation.

Underlying Maslow's theory of motivation is the concept that all individuals have a number of needs which fall into five broad classifications:

Physiological Needs:	hunger, thirst, rest, sex, etc.
Safety Needs:	freedom from threat, fear and anxiety, etc.
Love (Social) Needs:	friendship, affection, receiving love, etc.
Esteem Needs:	self-esteem, self-confidence, reputation, prestige, etc.
Self-actualisation Needs:	self-fulfilment, etc.

Furthermore, Maslow proposed that these five classes of needs form a hierarchy, each of which must be satisfied before an individual will be motivated by the next class of need in the hierarchy. If none of the needs in the hierarchy have been satisfied then the basic, physiological needs take precedence and dominate behaviour. However, once this need has been satisfied then it no longer motivates behaviour and the individual will then move up to the next level of the hierarchy. This process continues until the final level is reached, the implication being that self-actualisation is the level to which people should aspire (see Cooper *et al*, 1993:21).

The appeal of Maslow's theory lies, no doubt, in its simplicity. Maslow himself has recognised the limitations of his model, in particular its relevance and adaptability to the work situation. He has also suggested that the linear progression from one set of needs to the next does not necessarily occur in all cases; not only does he identify seven different 'routes' through the hierarchy but he also states that each set of needs may only be partially satisfied before the next set begins to dominate behaviour. Because of these limitations, Witt and Wright (1992:36) suggest that Murray's classification of human needs, developed in 1938, provides a better, although more complicated, basis for understanding and explaining tourist motivation. Nevertheless, Maslow's model has been widely adapted by tourism researchers, perhaps because of the way in which a wide range of differing human needs are presented in a simple and understandable framework (Cooper *et al*, 1993).

For example, Pearce (1988) and Pearce and Caltabiano (1983) have developed a framework for the study of tourist motivation that is initially based on Maslow's hierarchical model. They describe five different levels of motivation, namely, a concern with biological needs, safety and security needs, relationship needs, special interest needs and, finally, self-actualisation needs. They argue that such a framework allows for both biological motives (e.g. rest and recuperation) and social motives to be included and, unlike other theories of tourist motivation, it recognises that motivations may change over time and that tourists may also have more than one motivation. Furthermore, tourist motivation is viewed as a dynamic process; people have a tourism 'career' and move up the tourist ladder at different stages of their life-cycle (see Pearce, 1992). At any stage they may also retire from their tourism career; that is, they may decide not to take holidays.

(b) Psychological motives for tourism
Dann (1977) suggests that tourism is motivated socially by the anomic condition of society and psychologically by the need for ego-enhancement. In other words, people feel the need to travel not only because of the sense of normlessness and meaninglessness imposed upon them by modern society but also by the need to be recognised, to have their ego or confidence boosted. Whilst on holiday, away from their usual surroundings and friends, people are able to act out an alien personality, similar to the *king/queen for a day* situation described by Gottlieb

(1982). However, it is more than an inversion of the normal and more than indulgence in ludic behaviour; the opportunity for ego-enhancement, for status enhancement, links directly to the potential satisfaction of Maslow's concept of self esteem needs. Equally, anomie as a tourist motivator can also be seen as resulting from the need for love and a sense of belonging.

Dann's theory of tourist motivation is based upon research amongst tourists visiting Barbados. He found that anomic tourists were married and tended to belong to higher socio-economic groups, whereas ego-enhancement tourists were from a lower socio-economic group and more likely to be female. The demographic characteristics of the latter group related to lower status roles in the tourists' home countries, thus confirming the ego-enhancement motivation of travel. However, a major criticism of Dann's approach, as argued by Pearce (1982), is that, in addition to ignoring other possible motivations, it is unclear whether the findings are based upon the tourists' own explanations or the researcher's interpretation of the situation. Such criticism is understandable when it is considered that tourists themselves may have difficulty in recognising or articulating the real, underlying motivations for travel. For example, Crompton (1979) found that respondents to his research had difficulty in explaining the true reasons for destination choice. However, he identified seven psychological push motives for travel: escape from a perceived mundane environment, exploration and evaluation of self, relaxation, prestige, regression, enhancement of kinship relationships, and facilitation of social interaction. These psychological motives represented, according to Crompton (1979:415), *a hidden agenda* for tourist motivation.

The same problem in determining the true psychological motivation for tourism has been recognised by Mill and

Morrison: *tourists themselves may be unaware of the true reasons for their travel behaviour. Individuals are often unaware of the real reasons for doing certain things* (1985:2). Additionally, people may not always be willing to reveal the real reason for their holiday, such wanting to impress their neighbours or work colleagues by showing off their suntans. Likewise, Krippendorf (1987:22) suggests that an individual's motivation to travel will normally repeat *all the reasons that feature in advertising and which are repeated over and over again in all tourist brochures and catalogues*, whilst the true motivations lie hidden in the subconscious. Nevertheless, Krippendorf lists eight different travel motivations that can be identified from the literature: recuperation and regeneration; compensation and social integration; escape; communication; broadening the mind; freedom and self-determination; self-realisation; happiness.

(c) Motivation by purpose

Owing, perhaps, to the difficulty in ascertaining an individual's underlying motivations for tourism, some authors relate motivation to the purpose of trip rather than the satisfaction of an identified or hidden psychological need. For example, McIntosh and Goeldner (1990:131) list four categories of what they term basic travel motivators:

1. *Physical motivators*
   These relate to the need for rest, participation in sport, relaxing entertainment and other motivations which are connected with health. Common to all physical motivators is the reduction in tension and the refreshment of body and mind through physical activities.

2. *Cultural motivators*

These are manifested in the desire to see and learn about other countries, their music, food, history, religion, art and so on.

3. *Interpersonal motivators*

These include visiting friends and relatives, the desire to meet new people and to make new friendships, and escape from the everyday social environment

4. *Status and prestige motivators*

These concern ego-enhancement and the desire for recognition, appreciation and attention, and personal improvement. Trips may be related to education or study, the pursuit of hobbies, or business and conference type tourism.

The major problem associated with the motivation by purpose approach is that it describes the outcome or the goal orientated behaviour that results from a specific need, rather than the actual motivation itself. Thus, the desire to learn about other cultures may, in fact, be the outcome of a need to make up for a lack of culture in the home environment, or wanting to make new friends may result from a deeper motivation to avoid loneliness.

(d) Tourism as a sacred journey

Anthropological research into tourism has been divided into two broad areas: assessing the impacts of tourism development on host cultures and societies, and analysing the meaning of tourism to the tourist. Whilst the first area falls under the heading of the social impacts of tourism (see Chapter Seven), the second is, essentially, an anthropological study of tourist motivation and is, therefore, of relevance within the context of this chapter.

According to Graburn (1989:22), *tourism...is functionally and symbolically equivalent to other institutions that humans use to embellish and add meaning to their lives.* If this is so, then it immediately becomes apparent that there is a potential link between the role of tourism as a secular ritual in modern life and more traditional, religious forms of travel, such as pilgrimage. Indeed, as Graburn (1983) asks, *if tourism has the quality of a leisure ritual that takes place outside of everyday life and involves travel, is not it identical to pilgrimage?* Similarly, MacCannell views the tourist's search for meaning and authenticity as a modern form of pilgrimage, with present day tourist sights being the equivalent to *the religious symbolism of primitive people* (1989:2). It is important to note that we are concerned here with holiday tourism as opposed to the specific category of religious tourism; in the latter case, tourism and pilgrimage or sacred journeys become one and the same thing.

Even at a more mundane level, the manner in which thousands of people each year are drawn, as if by some invisible power, to the popular tourist sights around the world is directly analogous to a form of pilgrimage. Many tourist sights or attractions are accorded the status of a religious icon or symbol; they have to be seen by tourists, they are *famous for being famous...* [and] ... *entail a kind of pilgrimage to a sacred centre, which is often a capital or major city* (Urry, 1990a:12). However, it is not the actual sight, nor the original motivation, but the meaning to the individual tourist that is important. In other words, a religious pilgrimage is normally considered to be something serious, legitimate, authentic and of spiritual significance to the participant, whereas tourism, by comparison, is frivolous and superficial (Pfaffenberger, 1983). Yet, if the labels attached to each are stripped away, it becomes apparent that the experience of seeing, for example, the Taj Mahal, may be of equal significance to a tourist as is a visit to, say, Lourdes, for a pilgrim. *The difference between tourism and pilgrimage lies not so much in any radical phenomenological difference between them...but rather in the culturally-supplied language of symbols in which travellers are obliged to express their peregrinations* (Pfaffenberger, 1983).

The argument that tourism is a form of sacred journey is based upon the relationship between work and play (tourism) and, in particular, the location of each. Compulsory activities, such as making a living, take place in the ordinary, home environment, whereas tourism is voluntary and takes place in the non-ordinary environment, away from home. It is, perhaps, for this reason that staying at home during time off from work is not considered to be a true holiday; to stay at home is to do nothing whilst to go away is to do something (Graburn, 1989:23). It also lends credence to the adage that a change (in this case, of location) is as good as a rest. Thus, it is considered proper that people work at home and go away for their holidays.

If work takes place in the ordinary environment then, logically, it represents the ordinary experience. It also represents the passing of ordinary time. Normally, the passage of time is marked by regular festivals or events which, traditionally, have a religious or sacred significance. Thus, festivals such as Christmas or Easter represent a temporary shift from ordinary, secular, profane time into sacred time. During these periods of sacred time, the individual is also transferred from the ordinary, profane existence (usually dominated by compulsory activities) into another, non-ordinary state of existence. In modern, secular societies the annual summer holiday is one such event which has come to be equated with the religious festivals in more traditional societies. The week or fortnight away marks a shift from the profane experience of everyday life to the non-ordinary, sacred experience of the holiday. Thus, by comparing the function of religious festivals in traditional societies to that of holidays in modern society tourism becomes, logically, a sacred journey.

A number of authors have linked the concept of tourism as a kind of sacred journey with Turner's work on pilgrims (see Turner, 1973, and Turner and Turner, 1978). This, in turn, represents an extension to the concept that the passage of time alternated between profane (ordinary) and sacred (non-ordinary) time. It also builds upon the notion introduced in Chapter Three that tourist behaviour is dependent, up to a point, upon the location of an individual's 'spiritual centre'.

Turner develops the idea that, by taking part in religious rituals or undertaking a pilgrimage, people become divorced from everyday social and economic structures and constraints. Typically, this involves a three-stage process. Initially, people go through the *separation* stage, where they become separated from their ordinary home environment and society. In terms of tourism, this is the equivalent of travelling to, and arriving at, the destination. They then move into the second stage, into a condition which Turner describes as *liminality*. That is, people (or tourists) cross the threshold or boundary (from the Latin *limen*) of their normal, ordered and structured society and enter into a state of anti-structure (i.e. a situation where the structure and order of everyday life have disappeared). Normal obligations, such as work, no longer exist and new types of relationships, unaffected by the usual social constraints of status and role, are established between individuals and groups. In other words tourists, while on holiday, are temporarily freed from the demands of their jobs, household chores, social commitments and, generally, the behavioural norms and values of their society. Unrestricted by social barriers, they are able to form groups or relationships with people whom they would not, perhaps, normally mix with and together enjoy the sense of freedom and escape offered by the holiday. Turner describes this sense of togetherness, of sharing, in his context, a religious, spiritual experience, as a state of *communitas*. Passariello (1983) and Lett (1983) use this concept as a basis for explaining the behaviour of, respectively, weekend domestic tourists at a Mexican coastal resort and North American charter yacht tourists in the Caribbean.

The third and final stage is *reintegration*; people return to their ordinary home environment and social structure. In traditional societies, it is likely that the return from a sacred ritual or pilgrimage, such as a Muslim having completed his pilgrimage, or *hadj*, to Mecca, is signified by reintegration into the social group at a higher status. For a tourist, the experience of liminality is more likely to be of a compensatory nature. That is, he or she returns refreshed, renewed and ready to accept the responsibilities and constraints of everyday life. Reintegration is at the same social status or level as separation but the tourist has been spiritually uplifted by the liminal (or *liminoid*, the word used by Turner and Turner (1978) to distinguish between secular and liminal, religious experiences) benefits of the holiday. Therefore, the tourist is motivated in the first place by the psychological need for spiritual regeneration, a need that may be satisfied by a temporary shift away from the ordinary, profane existence into sacred time. The tourist is able to look at life from the outside, from the freedom of the holiday, from the *Centre Out There* (Turner, 1973).

(iii) Tourist motivation and the tourist gaze

Urry (1990a, 1990b, and 1992) describes the activity of tourism as gazing or, more specifically, the tourist 'gaze'. *What is the minimal characteristic of tourist activity is the fact that we look at, or gaze upon, particular objects* (1990b). The actual physical purchases, such as transport, accommodation and food are incidental to this central feature of tourism; the consumption of these goods and services allows the tourist to gaze upon *features of landscape and townscape which separate them off from everyday experience* (1990a:3). Tourist motivation results from the need to gaze on sights, places and peoples that are unusual, that are removed from the experience and routine of normal, everyday life; by implication, tourist activity (gazing) is motivated by the need to collect gazes.

There are two different ways in which tourist gazes may be collected, depending on the needs of the individual tourist (see Urry, 1990a):

(a) The romantic gaze
The romantic gaze (see also Walter, 1982) is motivated by the desire for solitary enjoyment and experience. It is the equivalent to the search for authenticity and the sacred journey to the 'centre out there'. The romantic tourist seeks reality in other cultures and societies and, in a broader sense, tries to recreate the 'lost art of travel'.

(b) The collective gaze
The collective gaze is communal tourism. It is motivated by the need to gaze at the familiar or to share the non-ordinary with other people. Indeed, it is the shared experience that is of fundamental importance to the collective gaze.

TOURIST MOTIVATION: CONCLUSIONS
Throughout this chapter, tourist motivation has been identified with the satisfaction of an individual's needs, needs which push, or motivate, the individual into particular types of behaviour. These needs may result from pressures and forces which are external to the individual, such as the work experience, family obligations or societal norms, from deep-rooted, psychological

needs, such as self-esteem or a need for companionship, or from a combination of both. As such, this approach has provided an indication of the enormous range and variety of forces that have the potential to motivate an individual into goal orientated (specifically, touristic) behaviour. However, as Witt and Wright (1992:44) argue, *the study of needs can at best only provide a partial explanation of motivated behaviour*. Other factors must also be taken into consideration if the explanation of tourist motivation is to be of use in predicting tourist behaviour. In particular, it is necessary to look at tourist motivation over time and the way in which an individual's needs may be translated into motivated behaviour.

In theory, tourist decision making follows a logical process which commences with the translation of needs into motivated behaviour. This behaviour takes the form of a consideration of the different products related to the satisfaction of needs and, based upon the available information and the overall image of the destination, the tourist then makes a decision and purchases a holiday. Thus, each stage can be assigned a separate and identifiable position and function within the overall decision making process. In practice, this process may not be quite so simple and straightforward. The dividing line between different stages is not always distinct and, in particular, the *meaning* of a holiday to the consumer should also be considered. In other words, tourists experience and purchase more than the actual one or two week break. Prior to departure, the process of choosing, of anticipating the holiday (see Parrinello, 1993) is all part of the tourism experience and people may be motivated as much by the prospect of having a holiday as by the potential benefits of the holiday itself. Holidays are often purchased many months in advance and the thought of having a holiday, having something to look forward to and to dream about, can be as equally exciting and beneficial (and in many cases more so) than the holiday itself.

Thus, tourist motivation can *be strictly linked with anticipation* (Parrinello, 1993).

Nor does the process finish when the tourist returns home from a holiday. Although the physical state of being on holiday has come to an end, the memories and images of a holiday may remain with an individual for much longer, particularly if photographs have been taken or souvenirs bought. In a sense, the holiday lasts much longer than the actual period spent away and a tourist might also be motivated by the thought of being able to look back on his or her holiday whilst, at the same time, anticipating and planning the next one. Therefore, the stages of motivation, choice, holiday purchase and the actual trip become merged into a continual process of anticipation, experience and memory, a process which sustains itself in modern, tourism generating societies which are *literally saturated with tourist culture* (Parrinello, 1993).

Again departing from the basic notion of needs resulting in motivated behaviour, tourist motivation is also dependent on the extent to which people *expect* a particular choice of action to lead to certain outcomes. For example, an individual might want to go on a beach holiday to get a suntan, motivated by the self-esteem need, perhaps, of being able to show off his or her tan. The choice of destination will be motivated, therefore, not only by the original need to get a tan but also by the extent to which the individual expects to achieve that goal. Therefore, the individual will be motivated to choose a destination that offers the best opportunity for sunbathing and also, perhaps, at a time of year when a suntan is most noticeable (i.e. a winter sun destination). The same principle can also be applied to the influence of socio-economic restrictions on holiday choice. Thus, a person who has a low expectation of being able to afford a particular holiday will be motivated to choose another type of holiday or, if there is a low expectation of satisfying needs on the alternative holiday, to stay at home.

This approach to motivation is known as *expectancy theory* (see Witt and Wright, 1992, for more detail). It is a complicated method of analysing motivation, yet it serves to highlight that tourist motivation is, itself, a complex subject. There is a huge variety of push factors that may motivate tourism, and these factors vary between different people. If people's expectations are also taken into account it becomes evident that destination pull factors can play an equally important role in motivation. The implication is, therefore, that to be able to fully understand and predict any one person's motivation for tourism it is necessary to concentrate on that person's preferences, experience, desires and social and economic circumstances.

The situation is further complicated by the fact that tourists may not always be able or wish to reflect upon or express their real motives for travel (Dann, 1981). There is, also, no saying that particular groups of people behave in particular ways, or that particular types of tourism or destinations appeal to particular types of tourist. Essentially, tourist motivation results from a variety of social, economic, demographic and psychological factors peculiar to each individual tourist but, nevertheless, the influence of society and sociological factors, both external and intrinsic to the individual, provide a solid foundation for an understanding of tourist motivation.

INTRODUCTION

The links between authenticity and tourism have been explored by commentators and tourism researchers almost for as long as modern tourism itself has existed. During the nineteenth century attention was initially focused on the way in which emerging forms of mass transport, in particular the railways, diluted the perceived authenticity of the travel experience. At the same time, the early pioneers of package tourism, such as Thomas Cook, also attracted criticism. For example, Charles Lever, writing in *Blackwoods Magazine* in 1865 about Cook's tourists in Italy, described cities as being *deluged with droves of these creatures, for they never separate, and you see them forty in number pouring along a street with their director, now in front, now at the rear, circling them like a sheepdog.* Implicit in this statement is the perceived inauthenticity of the tourists' experience, a theme which Boorstin continues and develops in his essay *From Traveller to Tourist: The Lost Art of Travel* (1964).

In contrast to Boorstin's thesis that tourists are satisfied with inauthentic, pseudo-events, MacCannell (1989) adopts a more positive perspective. He argues that living in modern, alienated societies, tourists are motivated by the need to experience authenticity: *modern man has been condemned to look elsewhere, everywhere, for his authenticity, to see if he can catch a glimpse of it reflected in the simplicity, poverty, chastity or purity of others* (1989:41). Thus, for MacCannell, the entire phenomenon of tourism hinges on a quest for authenticity and reflects the deficiencies of modern life; the tourist is a model for *modern-man-in-general* (1989:1).

The widely quoted Boorstin-MacCannell debate on the meaning and importance of authenticity has largely dominated the sociological treatment of tourism since the late 1960s and, as a result, it has tended to overshadow other equally relevant issues concerned with the connection between authenticity and the tourist experience. For example, the concept of authenticity is frequently used as a marketing tool; holidays are advertised as offering the chance to experience the 'real' Africa, the 'hidden' Asia or, more generally, 'genuine' travel. In many cases, however, the authenticity on offer bears more relation to tourists' expectations (or what tour operators believe tourists want to see) than to what actually exists. This then leads onto the question: what is an authentic tourist experience? Visitors to India on a typical Delhi-Jaipur-Agra (Taj Mahal) tour may well believe that they have experienced the 'real' India but, whilst there is no doubting the authenticity of individual sights, collectively they *represent* India. That is, they are a sign of 'Indian-ness', a physical manifestation of an image far removed from the reality of modern India.

Another problem to be considered is the extent to which any tourist site or experience may be considered authentic once it becomes packaged and sold as part of the overall tourist product. In other words, once a destination, an event or even a cultural artefact becomes caught up in the tourism system it becomes a commodity. Commodities have a value, normally measured by price, and once culture has become commoditised it can lose its meaning and significance for local people and, potentially, its authenticity to tourists (see Greenwood, 1989).

Thus, the relevance of authenticity to tourism and the tourist experience is much broader than might at first be imagined. This chapter examines the relationship between authenticity and tourism and considers the way in which tourists look to heritage and the past in their search for the authentic.

AUTHENTICITY

(i) What is authenticity?
Before looking at the various ways in which authenticity is linked to the tourist experience, it is important to consider what is actually meant by authenticity. It is a word that is frequently used in the literature to describe the tourism experience, tourism attractions and events or the motivation for tourism, yet scant attention is paid to explaining or defining it in relation to tourism. Part of the problem might be that the meaning of authenticity varies according to its use: as Trilling (1974:11) states, *the word 'authenticity' comes so readily to the tongue these days and in so many connections that it may very well resist...efforts of definition.* He goes on to assert, however, that its original usage was in the context of the museum to describe objects which are *what they appear to be or are claimed to be* (1974:93), a usage which continues to be the most widely accepted and understood.

Within the context of tourism, the concept of authenticity has become rather more ambiguous. On one hand, the word 'authentic' is frequently used to describe products, works of art, cuisine, dress, language, festivals, rituals, architecture and so on - in short, everything which comprises a country's culture. Generally, something is considered to be authentic if it is made, produced or enacted by local people according to custom or tradition. Thus, in one sense, authenticity connotes traditional culture and origin, a sense of the genuine, the real or the unique. On the other hand, within tourism, it is also used to describe (and sell!) different types of travel, certain journeys or even entire holidays. Importantly, it is generally used to distinguish between specialist or niche-market tourism products and mass tourism products, the implication being that mass tourism is, somehow, inauthentic. Immediately, then, a difference appears between the two applications of authenticity within tourism. One is based upon the tangible origin of something; a cultural object or event is either real, genuine and authentic, or it is false, or a fake. The second application, however, is based upon a less tangible comparison. For a holiday or a journey to be authentic, it must be perceived to be so in comparison to another experience that is inauthentic. For MacCannell (1989), the inauthentic is modern society, and tourism, therefore, is a search for the authentic. It is easy, then, to see how certain forms of travel and tourism come to be described as authentic because, in a sense, mass, package tourism is an extension of modern society and, hence, inauthentic.

Cohen (1988a) explains how a word that is normally used to describe something that is real or genuine has also become a socially constructed concept (i.e. a description of the condition of modern society). Following Trilling's origination of the word 'authentic' in the museum, curators and ethnographers have tended to view the authenticity of primitive and ethnic art in strict terms; to be authentic, things must have been created by traditional craftsmen using traditional materials. In particular, authentic items must have been made for the use of local people rather than for trade or selling on to strangers; *the absence of commoditisation...*[is]...*a crucial consideration in judgements of authenticity* (Cohen, 1988a). Most importantly, authenticity is a quality that is perceived to be firmly rooted in pre-modern life, a quality *of cultural products produced prior to the penetration of modern Western influences* (Cohen, 1988a). In other words, things can only be authentic if they have been created without the aid of modern materials, tools or machinery; thus, anything, including society, that has been adapted, influenced, altered or, as an anthropologist might describe, contaminated by the modern, Western world has lost its authenticity.

It is here that authenticity develops into a way of describing the state or condition of societies. If the origin of strictly authentic products lies in pre-modern societies then, by implication, modern Western society, with all its characteristics of alienation, materialism, mass production and consumption and so on, is inauthentic. For the tourist, therefore, authenticity is to be found in pre-modern societies or societies that have yet to become Westernised and developed. As discussed later in this chapter, this goes some way to explaining the attraction of the British countryside as a symbol of the pre-industrial, pre-modern era (see Sharpley, 1993) and, more generally, the current fascination with heritage and the past. In a touristic sense, if pre-industrial society is perceived to be authentic then there is much truth in the suggestion that *the past is a foreign country* (Lowenthal, 1990).

(ii) The Boorstin-MacCannell debate

Both Boorstin and MacCannell take the inauthenticity of modern society as the starting point for their arguments. Indeed, both follow the structural line that the behaviour of modern tourists reflects and results from this inauthenticity but their conclusions lie at opposite ends of what may be described as the authenticity-inauthenticity continuum. For Boorstin (1964) modern (American) society is contrived, illusory and unreal. People thrive on pseudo-events and this is reflected in the way that the modern, mass tourist is satisfied with contrived, meaningless events which can be viewed, preferably, from the comfort and surrounding of the familiar world. As Boorstin argues, the tourist...

> *...has come to believe that he can have a lifetime of adventure in two weeks and all the thrills of risking his life without any real risk at all. He expects that the exotic and the familiar can be made to order...expecting all this, he demands that it be supplied to him. Having paid for it, he likes to think he has got his money's worth. He has demanded that the whole world be made a stage for pseudo-events.*

(Boorstin, 1964:80)

The events are supplied by the tourism industry, images of new destinations are contrived by the media and every effort is made to make the tourist feel at home; one of the aims of Conrad Hilton was to create 'a little America' in each of the countries where he opened one of his hotels. As a result, the tourist is increasingly removed from the reality and authenticity of the destination society and *tourism turns into a closed, self-perpetuating system of illusions* (Cohen, 1988b).

MacCannell (1989) adopts the opposite perspective. Rather than simply reflecting or representing the embodiment of the inauthenticity of modern life, the tourist recognises it and becomes a kind of secular pilgrim (MacCannell, 1973) on a quest for authenticity. The very motive for tourism becomes a search for the authentic: *sightseeing is a kind of collective striving for a transcendence of the modern totality, a way of attempting to overcome the discontinuity of modernity* (MacCannell, 1989:13).

The modern tourist looks for meaning in the reality of the life of other people in other places yet, at the same time, accepts the inauthentic condition of modernity. Indeed, as if to perpetuate the differentiation between the modern and the pre-modern, modern society collects and preserves the pre-modern in museums and heritage centres, in arts, music, fashion and decor, in order to provide havens of reality and authenticity in the turmoil of modern life. For the tourist, the challenge lies in the extent to which he or she is allowed to experience the real lives of others. Inevitably, events are staged for tourists but any resulting inauthenticity of experience results not from the demands of tourists for pseudo-events, as Boorstin argues, but rather as *a structural consequence of the development of tourism* (Cohen, 1988b).

(iii) Authenticity and the individual tourist

The arguments of Boorstin and MacCannell represent two extremes and, in reality, it is highly unlikely that tourists who conform to their descriptions exist in any great number, if at all. MacCannell's characterisation of the tourist is more in keeping with a description of an anthropologist and, as McKercher (1993) points out, *it is a mistake to assume that most tourists are anything more than consumers, whose primary goal is the consumption of a tourism experience.* Equally, it is widely accepted that tourists are becoming more discerning and more quality conscious; the tourism industry is having to provide an ever increasing variety of destinations and products to satisfy demand (for example, see Jenkins, 1990, and Lickorish, 1990). Boorstin's tourist, therefore, bears more relation to a caricature of a mass tourist than to anyone who actually exists although, at the same time, it is probable that some tourists come close to his description.

Undoubtedly there are the purists who seek to escape entirely into authentic cultures and societies and others for whom the notion of authenticity does not even come into consideration in their holiday decision-making process. However, the great majority of tourists fall between these two extremes in terms of their search for authenticity. At the same time, the alienation that results from the condition of modern society is not necessarily recognised or experienced to a similar degree by all members of society. For example, many people might be entirely satisfied with their lives, identifying with and accepting the characteristics of modern life, such as a routine job or materialism as a symbol of success. Their centre is firmly rooted in modernity and their sense of alienation is minimal. Other people, however, may reflect on the meaning of their lives and may experience or be more aware of a sense of alienation from modern society. Such differences may result from occupational and educational factors; Cohen (1988a) proposes that intellectuals are, generally, more aware of their alienation than *the rank-and-file middle-classes, and especially the lower middle class, who still strive to attain the material gains which those beyond them already enjoy.*

The important point is that, if there is a link between alienation and the search for authenticity, then different tourists will be more or less disposed to seek authentic experiences elsewhere. Furthermore, the greater an individual's need to experience authenticity, the stricter will be the criteria by which that individual judges something to be authentic (Cohen, 1988a). Thus, the greater a tourist's alienation from society, the greater will be the emphasis on finding and experiencing authenticity and the stricter will be the rules by which authenticity is judged. In other words, a recreational tourist may well perceive a particular attraction or event to be authentic whereas experiential tourists might see through the staged, contrived nature of the same attraction or event, perceiving it to be totally inauthentic. For example, two different tourists staying at a hotel at a beach resort in Spain may witness a show that includes some flamenco music and dancing. One of these tourists may be a non-alienated, recreational tourist with little desire to seek authenticity, the other a person seeking the 'real' Spain. The first, even recognising the staged nature of the show, may accept it as authentic whilst the second would almost certainly write it off as contrived, false and inauthentic.

Authenticity, then, is not a given, measurable quality that can be applied to a particular event or product, nor does it provide a simple scale against which a tourist experience may be judged. Rather, the perceived authenticity (or lack of authenticity) of a cultural product or of an overall tourist experience depends upon relationship between the tourist as an individual and the product with which he or she is concerned. It is not a fixed, static concept, but *negotiable* (Cohen, 1988a). In other words, authenticity *must* be considered from the point of view of individual tourists, their expectations, their experience and their home socio-cultural environment. It is also argued that perceptions of authenticity are dependent on the relationships that tourists have with people in tourist settings (Pearce and Moscardo, 1986). For example, a tourist in an inauthentic environment, such as a Western-style hotel, may still have an authentic experience by interacting with a local person who works in the hotel. Thus, *it is the relationship between the tourist and the host which determines authenticity* (Pearce and Moscardo, 1986).

(iv) Authenticity over time
Just as authenticity is a negotiable process based on the relationship between the individual tourist and the cultural product or event, so too is it possible to suggest that authenticity can develop over time. That is, it is feasible for a product or

event that is originally inauthentic to become assimilated into local culture and to become authentic. No culture or society can be static; new cultural products emerge and, therefore, *emergent authenticity* (Cohen, 1988a) is a valid and realistic process within the context of tourism. Thus, over time, festivals or events originally staged for the benefit of tourists may come to be accepted as a local, authentic custom and crafts or products intended for tourist consumption may also achieve such a status. Tourism may also lead to the revival of old or forgotten rituals or crafts; the passage of time should not be viewed as a sign of diminished authenticity. For example, the traditional craft of greenstone carving in the southern Indian town of Mahabalipuram has been revitalised by the demand for souvenirs; the products, though intended for sale to tourists, are no less authentic than those produced by similar techniques hundreds of years ago:

> *Frequently arts, crafts and local culture have been revitalised as a direct result of tourism. A transformation of traditional forms often accompanies this development but does not necessarily lead to degeneration. To be authentic, arts and crafts must be rooted both in historical tradition and in present-day life; true authenticity cannot be achieved by conservation alone, since that leads to stultification.*

(de Kadt, 1979:16)

Overall, then, authenticity is not simply the antithesis to modern life, something that motivates tourists. Nor is it just a label that may be attached to cultural products, events or tourist experiences as a means of comparing them with the inauthentic, the modern or the spurious. It is something that is unique to each individual tourist, possessing a meaning and importance that can only be assessed alongside an understanding of a tourist's experience, motivation, relationship to his or her home environment and reaction to the tourism environment. In other words, authenticity should be judged through the tourist's own eyes, *what he considers to be the essential marks of authenticity, and which sites, objects, and events on his trip do, in his opinion, possess these marks* (Cohen, 1988b).

STAGED AUTHENTICITY

Of central importance to the consideration of the authenticity of tourist experiences is the notion of *staged authenticity* (MacCannell, 1973 and 1989). MacCannell suggests that although the tourist is motivated by the desire for authentic experience and *may believe that he is moving in that direction* (1973), he is, nevertheless, frustrated in his ambition by the way in which experiences have been set up, or staged. In other words, although he may believe he is witnessing authenticity the tourist is, in fact, experiencing only what local people or the tourism industry are allowing him to see.

MacCannell's concept of staged authenticity is based upon the work of Goffman (1959) who divides the structure of social establishments into what he terms as the *front* and *back regions*. The front region is where the social interaction takes place, where hosts meet guests or where servers attend to customers. The back region is *the place where members of the home team retire between performances to relax and to prepare* (MacCannell, 1989:92). Performers (for example, hosts or waiters) appear in both regions, whereas the audience (guests, diners in a restaurant) are only allowed into the front region. Under this simple dichotomy the performance, the show, takes place in the front region but reality exists in the back region. For example, in a restaurant diners are served and eat their food in the front region, the dining room, but the food is prepared, the plates are washed and so on in the back region, the kitchen. Thus, the front region is removed from reality; the diners do not see their meals being cooked. Conversely, where customers are able to see their food being prepared, the dining out experience might be perceived to be more authentic.

In adapting Goffman's work to tourist settings, MacCannell suggests that the simple front-back dichotomy can be expanded into a continuum which starts at the front and ends at the back and it is from this that the notion of staged authenticity emerges. He proposes that there are six different stages on the continuum which, theoretically, may be identified (see MacCannell, 1989:101):

Stage One: this is Goffman's front region, the setting which tourists attempt to penetrate or get behind.

Stage Two: although still a front region, this stage has been given the superficial appearance of the back region by, for example, having wine racks on display in a restaurant.

Stage Three: this stage is still firmly embedded in the front region but it is totally organised to resemble a back region.

Stage Four: moving into the back region, tourists are permitted to see this stage. For example, tourists may be taken into the workshops to see the production process of local goods.

Stage Five: this is a back region to which tourists are occasionally permitted entry, such as the flight deck on an aeroplane.

Stage Six: this is Goffman's back region, the ultimate goal of the tourist but one which is rarely, if ever, reached.

When these six stages are applied to the setting for tourist experiences it becomes evident that a tourist's quest for authenticity can progress along the continuum, but it is unlikely that the tourist will ever reach the sixth and final stage. Each stage offers the tourist apparently increasing opportunities for authentic experiences yet, from stages two through to five, what the tourist encounters is staged authenticity. The tourist is allowed glimpses of the back region, contrived events and attractions that are passed off as authentic, but the final stage of participating in the lives and culture of the host community is rarely experienced. The tourist in his quest for authenticity is doomed to failure; as more and more countries, regions, societies and cultures are caught up in the tourism net, the opportunity for authentic experience diminishes: *tourists make brave sorties...hoping, perhaps, for an authentic experience, but their paths can be traced in advance... Adventuresome tourists progress from stage to stage, always in the public eye, and greeted everywhere by their obliging hosts* (MacCannell, 1989:106).

One of the main criticisms of MacCannell's model is that it ignores the ability of tourists to understand and interpret the staged authenticity with which they are presented, although it does provide a useful framework for assessing the degree of authenticity inherent in tourist attractions and events. In order to achieve a more realistic model of staged authenticity, the structural approach adopted by MacCannell should be combined with a micro, social action perspective which takes into account the way in which tourists perceive and respond to the situation facing them. Cohen (1979a) combines two types of setting (staged and real) with tourists' impressions of the setting (again, staged and real) utilising a two dimensional approach to identify four different relationships between a tourist and the tourist setting:

(a) The setting is authentic and the tourist recognises it as such.

(b) The setting is staged but the tourist, believing it to be real, fails to recognise its contrived nature.

(c) The setting is real, but the tourist believes it to be staged and is, therefore, suspicious of its authenticity

(d) The setting is staged and the tourist recognises it as such.

Adding the impressions of tourists to the equation removes much of the finality of MacCannell's concept of staged authenticity. Whereas MacCannell's tourist is never likely to be satisfied and will continue to search for authenticity, tourists in Cohen's settings (a) and (d) recognise and accept their situation and will be less frustrated. However, this still represents a rather simplistic approach to the authenticity of tourist experiences and reference should again be made to the arguments presented by Pearce and Moscardo (1986). They identify nine different tourist experiences in which a tourist's relationship with people, with the setting (backstage or frontstage), or a combination of both can add to the authenticity of tourist experiences. For example, meeting frontstage people in a frontstage setting, such as the performers in a tourist show, can be as equally authentic as meeting backstage people in a frontstage setting. In other words, authenticity is not dependent on the position along the back-front region continuum and nor is a tourist's recognition of a situation sufficient to determine the degree of authenticity experienced; a variety of other experiences may contribute to the authenticity of a holiday and, in many cases, the *backstage/*

frontstage distinction is irrelevant or not appropriate (Pearce and Moscardo, 1986).

In short, authenticity may or may not be staged; what tourists experience may be 'real' or it may be planned, a regularly repeated performance. What is important is the *total* tourist experience and what it means to the individual tourist. Different tourists have different motivations, expectations, knowledge and travel experience and the *whole issue of whether or not tourists are satisfied with their holiday experience demands a full consideration of the nature of the tourist environment, the tourists' perceptions of that environment and the tourists' need or preference for authenticity* (Pearce and Moscardo, 1986).

THE SEMIOLOGY OF TOURISM
It is apparent that, within the context of tourism, authenticity is not a fixed, given quality or condition of a cultural product but something which is negotiable. In other words, the degree to which a sight or attraction is perceived to be authentic depends upon the relationship between an individual tourist and that sight or attraction. This relationship, in turn, depends to a great extent upon the attitudes, experience and so on of the tourist but, at the same time, the significance attached to a particular attraction or sight goes a long way to determining its authenticity. Something, such as an article of clothing, a souvenir or a festival, might be seen as authentic simply because it is unusual or different rather than because of its inherent quality or cultural meaning; its authenticity results from its difference or, to put it the other way round, its difference is a *sign* of its authenticity.

Arguably, *as soon as there is a society, every usage is converted into a sign of itself* (Barthes, 1967, quoted in Culler, 1981); that is, everything has a sign as well an original purpose or meaning.

For example, the basic purpose of a Rolls Royce motor car is transport, to carry its occupants from one place to another. To most people, however, a Rolls Royce is more than just a car; it is a sign of wealth, high status and success. Similarly, a Rottweiler is a dog, but it is also a sign of power and, perhaps, of danger; a passport is a legal, internationally recognised proof of nationality but it is also a sign of travel. The study of these signs, of the relationship between the *signifier* (a Rolls Royce) and the *signified* (wealth, status), is known as semiology and it is an approach which can be usefully applied to the consideration of the authenticity of tourist experiences.

Boorstin (1964:106) complains that *the French chanteuse singing English with a French accent seems more charmingly French than one who simply sings in French. The American tourist in Japan looks less for what is Japanese than for what is Japanesey.* However, as Culler argues, most tourists are more concerned with finding and experiencing the image or sign of cultural practices and attractions rather than understanding their basic meaning or function: *all over the world the unsung armies of semiotics, the tourists, are fanning out in search of the signs of Frenchness, typical Italian behaviour, exemplary Oriental scenes, typical American thruways, traditional English pubs* (Culler, 1981). It matters little that pubs are just convenient places for meeting and socialising or that high rise buildings are a logical way of housing a lot of people in a small area of land; for the tourist, the pub is a sign of Englishness, the skyscraper a sign of New York. As Culler (1981) again argues, *gondolas are the natural way to get around in a city full of canals... [but] ... tourists persist in regarding these objects and practices as cultural signs.* What tourists want to see and to accept as authentic is something out of the ordinary, something beyond the threshold of their normal day-to-day existence that they can remember and relate to others when they return home. Thus, authenticity becomes a sign and tourism, rather than a search for authenticity, becomes a search for signs.

The relationship between a tourist and a sight is not, however, a simple, two-way process. The tourist has to know that what is being looked at or experienced is an authentic sign, an attraction, that it is something worth visiting. For example, what is it that singles out the Empire State Building as a sign of New Yorkness, when there are many other skyscrapers (and higher ones, in the case of the World Trade Centre towers) in the city? The answer, according to MacCannell (1989), lies in a three way relationship. *The first contact a sightseer has with a sight is not the sight itself but with some representation thereof* (1989:110). This representation may be in the form of a picture, a souvenir, a model or even just a name on a map and is what MacCannell calls a *marker*. A marker informs the tourist that a sight is worth seeing, that it is an attraction: *the 'real thing' must be marked as real, as sight-worthy; if it is not marked or differentiated, it is not a notable sight* (Culler, 1981). Thus the tourist, in a triadic structure, links the marker with the sight in the process of sightseeing. The Empire State Building appears in all the brochures on New York; it is a symbol, a sign of the city. Therefore, to have an authentic experience of New York the tourist must visit the Empire State Building, along with other recognised symbols of New York, such as Central Park, Times Square and the Statue of Liberty. Preferably, the tourist also buys souvenirs and post cards as a reminder of the experience of New York.

It is the existence of pre-markers (for example, a picture in a brochure or a description in a guide book) and post-markers (souvenirs, photographs, post cards) that confirms a sight or experience as a sign of authenticity. Indeed, *the postcard, along with the photograph, is the most widely disseminated icon of tourist experience* (Edwards, 1993). In other words, for a tourist experience or product to be authentic it needs to be certified as such. The paradox is that many experiences which conform more closely to the traditional meaning of authenticity go by untried or unnoticed if not marked. To continue the example of New York, using the subway is certainly a more authentic means of travelling round the city than joining a guided tour on an air-conditioned coach yet, because of the perceived danger, many tourists are quite happy to forego the experience of travelling on the subway. There is a limit to the New Yorkness they wish to experience, a limit which, as the following section considers, may frequently be dictated by the tourism industry.

THE MARKETING OF AUTHENTICITY

It seems that tourists and indigenous peoples are incommensurately different within the touristic process, and indigenous peoples can only continue to be attractive to tourists so long as they remain undeveloped and, hence, in some way primitive.

(Silver, 1993:310)

Authenticity is not only perceived by tourism researchers and others to be a prime motivator of tourism; it is recognised by the tourism industry as such. Furthermore, it is widely accepted that the tourism industry plays an important role in shaping tourists' motivation and behaviour because, for many people, the travel brochure is the main source of information in planning holidays. Brochures are also influential in determining how tourists perceive a destination: *there seems little reason to doubt that for many people tourist brochures...play a major role in forming their images* (Dilley, 1986), images which result from the information and pictures that tour operators choose to include and, importantly, not to include in their brochures.

Tour operators are motivated by profit and, therefore, market destinations to appeal to the greatest number of people who are likely to be attracted to their product. Thus, in most cases, there is a logical link between the destination and the potential market. Mediterranean countries are marketed to northern European customers primarily as sun, sea and sand destinations whereas to North Americans they are marketed as cultural and historical destinations, the reasoning being that most Americans go to resorts closer to home, such as the Caribbean, for beach holidays (see Buck, 1977, Britton, 1979, and Dilley, 1986, for research into travel brochures). Therefore, beach holiday brochures primarily contain pictures and information about the beach, the hotel, the swimming pool and the nightlife whereas cultural tourism will be marketed by pictures of historical architecture, traditional industries, information about special interest tours and so on.

If this principle is applied to the marketing of authenticity then it is logical to propose that tour operators represent destination countries in a way which potential tourists perceive them to be rather than the how they actually are. These perceptions are not always created by the tourism industry; in an age of mass information and communication, images of many countries in both the developing and the developed world appear regularly in magazines, in films and documentaries and in tourist advertisements. Nevertheless, the tourism industry, through its brochures, may reinforce popularly held images of destinations, in particular of those destinations which offer tourists the opportunity to experience 'true' authenticity in the form of pre-industrial, primitive life styles. In other words, *the tourism industry only markets those images that it anticipates will be verified during travel, for tourists authenticity is not necessarily determined by gaining a genuine appreciation for another culture, but rather by verifying a marketed representation of it* (Silver, 1993).

Inevitably, perhaps, as authenticity is seen to exist in other times and other places (MacCannell, 1989), many destinations marketed on the basis of authenticity are in the developing world. Compared with rapid industrialisation and technological advance (and resultant alienation and inauthenticity) in the Western world, the countries of the developing world are seen as offering authentic, timeless experiences. Brochures describe destinations that have *many unusual and fascinating examples of human cultural activity, past and present;..*[where]*...the pageant of human life is older, more varied, or just different from that at home* (Dilley, 1986). They use clichés such as 'discover the undiscovered' or 'enjoy the unspoilt paradise' to emphasise that, although tourism has arrived, the modern world has yet to penetrate the destination. The images in the brochures tend to be selectively biased towards what a potential visitor expects to see in a country, an image of authenticity based upon pictures, films and historical associations. For example, travel brochures offering tours of India invariably include pictures of the Taj Mahal, the forts of Rajasthan, the houseboats on Dal Lake in Kashmir and of pilgrims bathing in the water of the River Ganges at Varanasi, attempting to recreate, perhaps, the days of the Raj. Furthermore, pictures of local people tend to conform to standard images, such as women wearing colourful saris and adorned with dramatic jewellery. Similarly, Britton (1979) found that *local residents are generally absent from illustrations; when they are shown, they likely appear as stereotyped stage props, such as a smiling Jamaican nimbly balancing a tray of cocktails on his head.*

What the brochures do not usually show are details and pictures of a destination's level of industrialisation, its problems of poverty, over-population and pollution, the signs that it is becoming Westernised. In other words, tourist brochures, not surprisingly, do not include images that are likely to deter visitors. Tourists, even those on a quest for authenticity, are trying to escape, albeit temporarily, from the pressures and problems of the modern world and, therefore, the marketing of a destination and the tourism system within it tends to shield visitors from the realities of the country. In effect, the tourism industry markets and operates a sanitised authenticity; visitors to India may be aware of the poverty, but they do not wish to be reminded of it as they see the tourist sights. However, as the countries of the developing world become more industrialised and more Westernised, the authenticity marketed by the tourism industry is increasingly divorced from the reality of the country; the authenticity marketed and sold becomes a myth, and will become more so as local people and local tourism industries recognise that their appeal and, more importantly, their value to tourists lies in their traditional culture rather than their emerging modernity. In the extreme, authenticity as demanded by tourists may be confined to themed centres, such as the Polynesian Cultural Centre in Hawaii, where *a satisfactory fiction emerges wherein a guest can imagine for a brief time that the idyllic life of Polynesia...described by Robert Louis Stevenson...is a 'reality'* (Stanton, 1989:247).

AUTHENTICITY AND THE COMMODITISATION OF CULTURE

A common thread throughout this chapter is that authenticity, within the context of tourism, is a product, a commodity. It is not a quality or a condition of something but, for many, an essential ingredient of the tourist experience. Tourists are motivated by a search for authenticity, whether as an actual experience or as a sign of something different from their ordinary, everyday existence, and the tourism industry markets authenticity as it would market any other tourism product. As tourism as a whole is a product that is produced, bought and sold then, logically, authenticity and the cultural products that represent it also has a value. It is important to consider, therefore, the extent to which this centrality of authenticity to the tourism experience has led to what Cohen (1988a) describes as the *commoditisation* of culture. In particular, the question must be asked, does the commoditisation of culture dilute, or even destroy, its meaning and authenticity?

One of the most widely held assumptions about the development of tourism is that, generally, it leads to cultural change within the destination society. Mathieson and Wall (1982:159) identify three major forms of culture which attract tourists and are, hence, susceptible to change:

(a) Inanimate forms of culture, such as historical buildings and monuments or traditional arts and crafts.

(b) Forms of culture which are reflected in the normal, day-to-day life and activities of people in destination societies.

(c) Animated forms of culture, involving the participation of people, such as religious events, carnivals, and traditional festivals.

All forms of culture are liable to change over time, with or without the influence of tourism. Worldwide advances in information and communication technology, satellite television and the international spread of symbols of modern Western culture, such as McDonald's, have a far greater influence on cultural change than tourism. Nevertheless, following the onset of tourism the normal life of a host society, its values, lifestyles and customs, may adapt over time through processes known as acculturation and cultural drift. In other words, *when two cultures come into contact of any duration, each becomes somewhat like the other through a process of borrowing* (Nuñez, 1989:266). Generally, tourists are less likely to borrow from their hosts than *vice versa* (although there are exceptions) and tourism is perceived, therefore, to be a powerful agent of change, particularly in those societies with fragile or less dominant cultures. These issues are considered in greater depth in Chapter Seven.

In contrast to a gradual cultural change contributed to by the influence of tourism, certain forms of culture, in particular arts and crafts (i.e. material forms of culture) and festivals or ritual events, can be changed or adapted specifically for tourists. They *come to be performed or produced for touristic consumption* (Cohen, 1988a) or, in other words, they become commoditised. Such a process is inevitable as tourists, constrained by the short duration of their holidays, demand instant culture and authentic souvenirs to take home with them. Furthermore, from the host society's point of view, if the most is to be made of culture as a commercial product, it must be *available and presentable; packaged for consumption into easily digestible and, preferably, photogenic chunks* (Simpson, 1993). Thus, it is a process that is also often perceived as leading to the production of inauthentic, fake art and a loss of meaning to the producers: *local culture...is altered and often destroyed by the treatment of it as a tourist attraction. It is made meaningless to the people who once believed in it* (Greenwood, 1989:173). This, however, need not always be the case.

(i) Arts and crafts
In many destinations both the purpose and the style of many

cultural products have been adapted to appeal to the tourist market. What were once religious or ceremonial artefacts are now mass produced and sold to tourists in a process of cultural commoditisation that can be identified in many countries around the world. Traditional art forms, designs and production techniques tend to disappear as simpler and less sophisticated replacements associated with the techniques of mass production are provided for tourist consumption. One such example are the *raksa* devil dance masks of Sri Lanka (see Simpson, 1993). Originally used in a number of different contexts, such as folk dramas, festivals and rituals of exorcism and healing, the masks represent the images of a variety of deities and demons. They have a fundamental meaning and significance to the performance of such rituals and, at the same time, the production of the masks is also a recognised and socially important activity within the local community. However, the rapid growth of tourism to Sri Lanka during the late 1970s and early 1980s resulted in the masks being recognised as an appealing and commercially attractive representation of Sinhalese culture for the tourist market. As they became mass produced not only did they lose their cultural meaning and authenticity as masks of different sizes, decoration and colours were produced to suit the taste of tourists, but also the status of the manufacturers in Sinhalese society deteriorated.

At best, the reproduction of cultural artefacts for tourism retains the quality and style, if not the meaning or authenticity, of the originals; at worst, they *consist of stylised works which bear only the most tenuous relationship to anything in the traditional culture* (Mathieson and Wall, 1982:168). In short, they typify what has been called 'airport art', manifested by a general deterioration in quality resulting, in particular, from the breaking of the connection between art forms and their original purpose. For example, Buddhist *tankas*, or paintings, which adorn

Buddhist temples in Tibet and Nepal, are now mass produced and widely available for sale to tourists in Kathmandu. They can also be found in specialist shops and markets in the Western world along with a huge variety of other cultural artefacts from areas such as Asia and South America. This export business has further severed the products from their cultural roots, although it can be argued that the internationalisation of culture also leads to a more widespread knowledge and appreciation of such art forms.

Despite the emphasis placed on the perceived negative impacts of the commoditisation of arts and crafts, tourism can also make a positive contribution to the continuation or re-emergence of traditional art forms. For example, Graburn (1976:42) describes how tourists' demands for carvings made by the Canadian Inuit, or Eskimo, has led to a huge increase in production. However, rather than resulting in a dilution of authenticity, the carvings are of a much higher standard than most souvenir crafts and are based upon aspects of the traditional Inuit lifestyle. Through their production of tourist souvenirs the Eskimos are not only able to earn a living but also to preserve their cultural identity. In the case of the Indians of the south-western United States, a variety of art forms have been combined into a new, authentic artistic culture: *massive in-migration and mass tourism have not been disruptive. Rather, the contact with Anglo society offered extended markets that served to heighten artistic productivity and to revive old traditions* (Deitch, 1989:235).

In short, tourism can undoubtedly lead to the mass production of fake cultural objects that bear little resemblance, either in form or in meaning, to their original purpose and are, therefore, inauthentic. Equally, re-emergent or new arts and crafts also result from the demands of tourists for cultural souvenirs. Thus, just as all forms of culture are in a state of constant change and development, these new products are no less authentic to either the producers or the consumers than those from previous cultural periods.

(ii) Festivals, events and rituals

Owing to the constraints that characterise tourism, cultural events which are based upon religious or traditional heritage, such as festivals, re-enactments of historical or mythical events and religious ceremonies, and which are intended as an attraction for tourists, will normally occur outside normal time and space. That is, the reason or tradition underlying the event becomes secondary to the event itself as the timing and content is adapted to suit the needs of tourists. For example, when researching Sinhalese devil dances, Simpson (1993) found that *the necessity for short, concise and essentially visual modes of presentation is at odds with the styles of performance the Berava adopt in their own ritual performances.* In this situation, it is highly likely that the meaning and significance of the event to the performers and local audiences is lost, even though to tourists it may appear authentic.

Examples of commoditised cultural performances occur all around the world, from staged dance performances given by African villagers to 'Hula' girls greeting tourists arriving at Honolulu airport in Hawaii. However, one of the first, and most widely quoted, studies into the tourism-related commoditisation of a cultural event was that by Greenwood (1989). He describes the way in which the *Alarde*, a public ritual in the Basque town of Fuenterrabia, which commemorates the town's victory over the French in 1638, became a major tourist attraction as a result of its taking place during the height of the tourist season. The local authorities decreed in 1969 that, in order to allow large numbers of visitors to witness the *Alarde*, it should be performed twice on the same day. Within two years *what was a vital and exciting ritual had become an obligation to be avoided...* [and] ... *the municipal government was considering payments to people for their participation in the Alarde* (Greenwood, 1989:178). It had become a commercial tourist attraction, devoid of all meaning to the participants. It is interesting to note, however, that, more recently, Greenwood accepts that the *Alarde* is once more a public event, but more significant now as a contemporary political statement than as a recreation of an historical event.

As with arts and crafts, there are also many situations where the commoditisation of cultural performances does not necessarily lead to a loss of meaning and authenticity. On the contrary, the opportunities and the financial rewards presented by the demands of tourists for authentic experiences can lead the preservation and development of traditional, cultural events. Furthermore, as Cohen (1988a) points out, the meaning of such events can change, but remain authentic, for the producers. For example, a festival might lose its religious significance through commercialisation but gain an equally important significance to the participants as a representation of local culture. McKean (1989) describes the case of Bali where ritual performances serve two distinct purposes within Balinese society. On one hand, festivals and rituals are performed for tourist consumption, providing a popular attraction at the same time as representing an important source of income. On the other hand, in a process of *cultural involution*, the commercial tourist version allows the Balinese to retain their traditional cultural skills and practices and to perform to local audiences, thereby preserving authentic cultural events within an increasingly modern social and economic context. Indeed, *younger Balinese find their identity as Balinese to be sharply framed by the mirror that tourism holds up to them, and has led many of them to celebrate their own traditions with continued vitality* (McKean, 1989:132).

In some cases, cultural events and festivals, whilst being major tourist attractions, retain their importance and authenticity within the host society. In other words, although attracting large numbers of tourists and, indirectly, generating tourist spending, their original function and purpose are not adapted or compromised by the demands of tourism but remain firmly rooted in the destination's cultural heritage. For example, the Changing of the Guard at Buckingham Palace in London draws large crowds but its role as a tourist attraction is incidental to its primary function. Similarly, the annual carnival in Rio de Janeiro, historically a celebration of freedom from slavery, is a festival performed by the people for the people. Again, the carnival is a major tourist attraction but it is neither motivated by, nor held for, tourists. It provides an authentic tourist experience but the importance and meaning of the carnival has been retained.

More generally, the commoditisation or commercialism of cultural performances cannot, and should not, lead to accusations of inauthenticity. People all around the world pay to see or experience performed cultural arts and events, from street buskers to major national theatre and dance companies and orchestras. Indeed, many art forms require financial support to survive and it is often tourism that provides that support. For example, it is often stated that many London theatres would go out of business if it were not for tourism. Yet it would be unheard of for a production of a Shakespeare play or a performance of Mozart's music to be described as inauthentic! Therefore, three points deserve emphasis when considering the link between the commoditisation of culture and the authenticity of tourist experiences.

(a) Different tourists, depending on their experience and expectations, have different perceptions of authenticity, but most adopt a broader, less purist stance than would, say, an anthropologist. Thus, many forms of cultural productions, whether performed or material artefacts, are accepted as authentic by tourists even if they have been adapted to the requirements of tourism.

(b) Very often, the tourism induced commoditisation of culture leads to the preservation and recreation of traditional, authentic cultural art forms whilst those which are strongly rooted in local culture retain their integrity and meaning despite tourism. Furthermore, culture is not static but continually evolves and takes different forms. Disneyland is as authentic as a traditional Buddhist festival and perceptions of authenticity or inauthenticity should not be clouded by what may be described as cultural arrogance.

(c) Generally, the decision to commoditise culture lies with the producers, not the consumers. In the extreme, as in the case of the Himalayan kingdom of Bhutan, the number of tourists and where they may go in the country is strictly controlled to protect the authenticity and integrity of religious festivals and ceremonies. As Cohen (1988a) argues, in order to avoid the blanket condemnation of the assumed negative impacts of cultural commoditisation, research should be emic (i.e. from the point of view of the host society) and should assess over time the perceptions of both locals and tourists.

AUTHENTICITY, THE PAST AND NOSTALGIA

If the past is a foreign country, nostalgia has made it the foreign country with the healthiest tourist trade of all.

(Lowenthal, 1990:4)

One of the major themes throughout this chapter is that the notion of authenticity, within the context of tourism, is inextricably linked to the past, to an earlier, pre-modern era. For MacCannell, *reality and authenticity are thought to be elsewhere: in other historical periods and other cultures* (1989:3); that is, in times and places which offer a sense of tradition and authenticity that has been lost in modern society. Similarly, the tourism industry implies, with its promises of 'unspoilt paradise', 'undiscovered peoples and places' and 'authentic culture', that tourists can, somehow, become time travellers; by boarding an aeroplane they can be transported back in time to places which offer the chance to experience life as it used to be. Thus, tourists are motivated by the inauthenticity of modern life, by the alienated, anomic condition of industrialised society, to seek meaning and reality elsewhere. In effect, the past has become a tourist destination.

The past has also become big business, for this concentration on the past is not limited only to tourism; indeed, tourism is symptomatic within the modern world of a much broader and deeper-rooted concern for, and interest in, history and heritage. *Today a great deal of time and energy is dedicated to looking backwards, toward capturing a past which, in many ways, is considered superior to the chaotic present and the dreaded future* (Dann, 1994:55). In many aspects of life, from home decor to clothing fashions, from architecture to advertising, images, designs and styles of the past are used and recreated to signify an era that is, somehow, better than the present. For example, the use of festoon blinds, William Morris style wallpaper, Laura Ashley fabrics, brass lamps and Victorian pine furniture are popular ways of recreating a more traditional, familiar and friendly style of home furnishing in contrast to the perceived stark, characterless quality of many modern homes.

At the same time, saving, conserving and presenting the past is becoming a more widespread concern and activity. Landscape conservation was originally motivated by the desire to protect the natural environment from encroaching urbanisation and industrialisation; nowadays, symbols and relics of that industrialisation are themselves conserved and protected. Moreover, the past that is protected, recreated or simply looked back upon with nostalgia is becoming increasingly close to the present. For example, it is not uncommon for relatively modern, twentieth century buildings, such as Southwark bus station in London, to be added to the ever growing collection of listed buildings in Britain. Indeed, it is in Britain that interest in the past is most prevalent. Almost every town and city boasts a museum or heritage centre and *it seems that a new museum opens every week or so* (Urry, 1990a:104). The National Trust, with over two million members and eleven million visits to its properties each year, is the largest conservation organisation in Europe and the British government spends over £100 million a year on conserving the built environment (Urry, 1990a:106), to say nothing of the financial support provided for landscape conservation.

This ever-increasing interest in the past, feeding what has developed into the heritage industry (Hewison, 1987), is widely believed to be caused by nostalgia, a condition which *now attracts or afflicts most levels of society* (Lowenthal, 1990:11). Nostalgia was once looked upon as a physical illness and even during the Second World War it appeared on the US. Surgeon General's list of standard illnesses suffered by American army personnel. Nowadays it is accepted that nostalgia is not simply an interest in or yearning for the past but, rather, *a positively toned evocation of a lived past in the context of some negative feeling toward the present or impending circumstances* (Davis, 1979:18, quoted in Dann, 1994:65). In other words, nostalgia results from dissatisfaction with the present and concern for the future, a situation that Hewison (1987) links to *Britain in a climate of decline*. Thus, *in the face of apparent decline and disintegration, it is not surprising that the past seems a better place* (Hewison, 1987:43).

Dann (1994) suggests four ways in which nostalgia is linked to tourism and in which the tourism industry attempts to evoke, for the tourist, a sense of authenticity rooted in the past:

(a) Hotels
In an era when hotels are becoming increasingly similar and standardised, when one hotel lobby or room looks much the same as any other irrespective of the city or country in which it is located, a sense of authenticity, distinction and of the luxury of a golden age can be achieved by recreating an image of the past. For example, Indian hotels which utilise buildings which were once, and in some cases still are, the palaces of maharajahs, transport guests back to the days of colonial India. Similarly, the famous Raffles Hotel in Singapore has recently been refurbished to recreate the atmosphere of the early 1900s. Indeed, most cities can boast an hotel noted for its individuality and authentic atmosphere but, undoubtedly, such authenticity is only available to those who can afford it.

(b) Museums
MacCannell writes *the best indication of the final victory of modernity over other sociocultural arrangements is not the disappearance of the non-modern world, but its artificial preservation and reconstruction in modern society* (1989:8). One of the major physical manifestations of the power of nostalgia within the context of tourism is the proliferation of museums and, in particular, heritage centres which attempt to present not only artefacts from the past but also life as it was in

days gone by. Modern methods of interpretation, such as audio-visual displays, re-enactments using actors, 'living museums' (for example, Beamish in County Durham or Williamsburg in Virginia) and the use of 'time cars' to carry visitors back in time through a heritage display (as at the Jorvik Viking Centre in York or The Oxford Story in Oxford), are frequently used to recreate the past. A major problem, however, is that nostalgia acts as a kind of rose-tinted filter, creating a past that safe, secure and devoid of unsavoury facts of past times, such as poverty, illness, dangerous working conditions, child labour and so on. In other words, *myths of the past are created - the past is seen in the way in which we would like to see it, and not the way it was* (Wheeler, 1992). Thus, tourists find a reality based not in the past, but on a modern representation of the past. (See Wright 1985, Hewison, 1987, Lumley, 1988, and Walsh, 1992).

(c) Infamous sites
Whilst the popularity of infamous sites, such as the Auschwitz visitor centre in Poland, the Bloody Tower in London and the Bridge over the River Kwai in Thailand, may be explained by morbid curiosity, the same phenomenon that led to seven mile traffic jams of sightseers on the main road to Lockerbie the day after the explosion of Pan Am Fight 103 (see Rojek, 1993:137 and for a discussion of tourism to 'black spots'), Dann (1994:61) relates it to the ability of nostalgia to discard unpleasant experiences. The reality of the attractions then lies in the evidence they present of past threats to society, to ordered life, to continuity and to identity.

(d) Industrial centres
Much of the growth in the number of heritage centres and museums has been based upon the representation of the industrial past. New Lanark in the Clyde Valley, the Wigan Pier Heritage Centre, and the Rhondda Heritage Park in South Wales

are just three examples of the 464 museums in Britain (Urry, 1990a:104) which display industrial material. Certainly, much of the popularity of such centres is based upon a nostalgia for industrial machinery and processes, such as the steam engine, which are no longer used. However, by drawing attention to the work of others, in other times and under conditions that are unacceptable today, they also represent a yardstick against which the reality and authenticity of modern and post-industrial society may be measured.

Perhaps the best example of the link between tourism and the experience of authenticity as represented by the past is the popularity of the British countryside as a tourist destination (see Sharpley, 1993). If tourism is, indeed, a search for the authentic motivated by the inauthenticity and meaninglessness of modern society then the countryside is the ultimate representation of the pre-industrial life. The countryside originally emerged as an identifiable, distinct tourist destination during the rapid industrialisation and urbanisation of British society during the nineteenth century. Romanticised by the poets and artists of the late eighteenth and early nineteenth centuries, it became the symbol of a life lost to the demands of industry and the capitalists. In the twentieth century, the countryside has come to be seen as the antithesis to modernism; visually and socially it has escaped the regulation and regimentation of modern urban life, representing freedom, nature and reality. Nevertheless, the tourists' rural landscape is idealised by nostalgia. Modern machinery, housing, motorways, electric power cables and, more recently, wind farms, have no place in authentic countryside (Urry, 1990a:98) and the efforts of conservation organisations are firmly directed towards the maintenance of a kind of Wordsworthian image of the countryside within the framework of late twentieth century society. The countryside *has become so imbued with literary and painterly associations that we do not really see the landscape that lies before us. We substitute a countryside of the mind, shaped by our cultural perspectives and reflecting our psychological needs* (Hewison, 1993).

The same criticism may be directed towards the perceived authenticity of tourist attractions and destinations as a whole. By continuing to look to the past for authenticity, reality and meaning, the tourist experience will be increasingly caught in a time warp and the culture that is packaged and presented to tourists will bear less and less resemblance to the reality of the destination. The challenge for the future, therefore, for both tourists and the tourism industry, is to view the culture and authenticity of destinations and host societies in their own right, rather than in comparison to the tourists own culture and society. In other words, authenticity is rooted as much in the present as it is in the past and, as more and more countries develop and modernise, their emerging culture and modernity must be accepted as authentic. To do otherwise, to perceive authenticity as being in other times and places (i.e. the past), would result in tourism becoming based on myth and fantasy, the representations of authenticity in the host societies becoming as meaningless and inauthentic as the societies from which tourists, temporarily, escape.

Chapter Six

The Tourist-Host Relationship

INTRODUCTION

It is virtually impossible to be a tourist in isolation. Unless travelling across uninhabited areas or regions it is inevitable that, sooner or later, tourists come into contact with other people. These may be either fellow tourists or members of local communities in tourism destinations; generally, it will be a combination of both types of contact, the extent or intensity of each being dependent on a variety of factors. For example, mass, institutionalised tourists on a two-week sun, sea and sand holiday are likely to have more inter-personal contact with fellow tourists than with local people, whilst an independent traveller or explorer may actively seek out contact with members of local communities. Indeed, for the explorer, meeting local people and learning about their way of life may be a primary tourism motivator whereas, for the mass tourist, such contact may only incidental to the holiday.

Whatever the type or extent of inter-personal contact that tourists experience, they will, almost certainly, come into contact with local people. Even if not actively seeking to meet locals (or, as is sometimes the case, making a positive effort to avoid contact!), tourists in resort areas stay in hotels, eat in restaurants, drink in bars and buy souvenirs in shops and, therefore, interact with members of the local community. In other words, even within a simple buying-selling context, tourists have a form of relationship with local people, one which is frequently referred to as the *host-guest* relationship (Smith, 1989a). For many tourists this relationship may be fleeting and, indeed, go unrecognised as such; for others, meaningful, two-way and authentic (see Chapter Five) contact with local people may be the basis of the entire tourist experience. In either situation, a variety of social processes are at work which not only determine the nature of the relationship itself but also go a long way towards indicating the potential positive or negative impacts of tourism development on destination communities. Thus, the main practical reason for developing an understanding of the processes involved in encounters between tourists and local people is to be able to plan and manage the development of tourism in a manner which minimises potential negative impacts on host communities.

This chapter examines the varying nature of the relationship between tourists and local people in destination areas. In particular, it considers whether tourism can lead to balanced and equal two-way relationships between tourists and locals, thereby acting, as some would desire, as a vehicle towards greater international harmony and understanding (WTO, 1980), or whether it simply amplifies their social, cultural and economic differences, reinforcing existing attitudes and prejudices. This chapter also serves as a foundation to the discussion of the social and cultural impacts of tourism in Chapter Seven.

CHARACTERISTICS OF TOURIST-HOST ENCOUNTERS

Relationships between tourists and local people are almost infinitely variable (see Pearce, 1994). Tourists are motivated by an enormous variety of factors, they carry with them different attitudes and expectations, they may be more or less experienced as tourists, they are on different types of holiday or trip, and they come from a variety of socio-economic backgrounds. Equally, the economic, social and technological conditions within a tourism destination country or region, the size, type and maturity of its tourism industry, and local cultural and religious factors will all have much bearing on the way in which local communities regard tourists. In short, such is the variety of factors which may influence the relationships that develop between tourists and local communities that it would be logical to conclude that there as many different types of tourist-host encounters as there are tourists and that the analysis of such encounters is a difficult, if not impossible, task.

Despite this variety it is possible to make some general observations about the nature of tourist-host encounters. For example, it would be logical to assume that the greater the economic, cultural and social differences between a tourist and a member of the destination community, the less balanced, or more unequal, will be the relationship between them. The relative wealth of Western visitors to developing countries is a particularly visible basis for an unequal relationship; in many instances, just the cost of the flight to some developing countries may be the equivalent of twice the average annual local income. Less obvious differences, such as conflicting attitudes towards punctuality, may also result in less tolerant contact. Conversely, the relationship between an American tourist and, say, a Canadian host is likely to benefit from a much greater degree of initial commonality in culture, language and outlook. Another general observation is that in most tourist-host encounters the tourist is on holiday whereas the host, more often than not, is employed in the tourist industry and is, therefore, at work. Again, cultural, social and economic distances are likely to amplify potential differences. Thus, links exists between the structure and nature of international tourism development as a whole and the types of tourist-host encounters that result in different destinations around the world. This issue is explored later in this chapter but, as a starting point, it is important to consider a number of characteristics which, to a lesser or greater extent, are applicable to all types of contact between tourists and local people.

One of the earliest attempts to analyse the nature of the contacts between tourists and local people in destination areas identified five particular characteristics common to most situations (see Sutton, 1967). These refer, in particular to international tourism, although certain characteristics may also be applicable tourist-host encounters in the context of domestic tourism. It was argued that, as a rule, contact is transitory, that both parties seek instant satisfaction (for example, the tourist purchasing a souvenir, the shopkeeper making a sale), and that the relationship is asymmetrical or unbalanced (the tourist benefits from greater wealth, the shopkeeper from better knowledge about the value of his goods). Furthermore, it was suggested that the encounter was a new or unusual experience for the tourist and, finally, that a cultural gulf usually existed between the parties involved in the encounter. A similar perspective was adopted by a UNESCO report (1976) which highlights four characteristic features of tourist-host relationships, particularly within the context of mass tourism (see Mathieson and Wall, 1982:136 for more detail):

(a) Most encounters between tourists and members of the local community are transitory. In other words, most tourists stay in a resort for only one or two weeks and although the encounter may be considered unusual, exciting and different from the tourist's point of view, for the host it may be simply 'business as usual'. As a result, the relationship is likely to be shallow, superficial and based upon different expectations. However, where visits are of a longer duration or, as is often the case, tourists return to the same resort year after year, more meaningful relationships may occur.

(b) Most encounters are constrained by temporal and spatial restrictions. Tourism is usually restricted to certain seasons of the year and, within those seasons, tourists are restricted by the length of their visit. Thus, they may try to see as much and do as much as is possible within the time available, a situation which local people may take advantage of by becoming exploitative, charging higher prices and so on. Tourist-host relationships may also be restricted by the location and spread of tourist-related services. Hotels, restaurants, bars, nightclubs and other facilities and attractions in resort areas are frequently concentrated in particular areas, sometimes in tourist zones or 'ghettos' located well away from towns and villages, making it difficult for less interested or motivated tourists to see the 'real' host country. Moreover, tourists are frequently discouraged from venturing out on their own and are sold tours, ensuring that the majority of tourists' spending is within the tourist area and minimising the opportunity for tourist-host encounters based upon anything but commercial interest. In the extreme, such as at self contained Club Med type destinations, tourists have no need to leave the confines of their resort and are unlikely to experience any encounter other than with resort staff.

(c) Tourism is an economic activity. The majority of people who work in the tourism industry do so to earn money and most interaction between tourists and local people is usually a form of economic transaction. As a result, many tourist-host encounters lack spontaneity; shows, tours and even visits to shops are frequently pre-planned to both fit in with tourists' tight schedules and to provide tourists with the maximum opportunity for spending money. Relationships which were once motivated by traditional hospitality may also become commercialised. For example, in the south eastern Turkish village of Harran, famous for its beehive-style houses and religious history, it is not unusual for tourists to be invited in to local people's homes for tea and then for payment to be demanded before departure. Conversely, when the Cyprus Tourism Organisation (CTO) proposed the development of agrotourism in some mountain villages as part of its tourism diversification programme, local villagers were astounded by the suggestion that they should charge visitors for their hospitality.

(d) Tourist-host encounters, on the whole, tend to be unbalanced. That is, local people may feel inferior when faced with ostentatious displays of wealth, and may resent being in a subservient position to people who are on holiday.

A further characteristic applicable to many tourist-host encounters is an apparent lack of knowledge, understanding or sensitivity on the part of tourists to local culture and custom in tourism destination areas. Whilst of greater relevance to the potential impacts of tourism in general, such short-comings, often combined with preconceptions and stereotypical images of the host community and culture, further limit the opportunity for balanced or meaningful tourist-host encounters. Additionally, this characteristic is related to the broader issues of tourist motivation, the nature and structure of international tourism and, in particular, the way in which destinations are marketed to potential tourists. For example, one tour operator's brochure describes The Gambia as *perfect for sun lovers with palm studded beaches, friendly people and year round sunshine. With all its exotic charm, remember this is Africa: life here is slower, standards can vary and public services aren't as reliable as in other resort areas* (Thomsons, 1994). No mention is made of the economic, religious or social structures of the country and first-time visitors to Africa will, almost undoubtedly, carry with them some preconceived images of 'Africa' based upon media images and the connection between The Gambia and Alex Hailey's *Roots* rather than actual knowledge or experience.

This last point raises the question of whether it is the responsibility of the tourism industry to fully inform potential visitors or whether the onus should fall upon tourists themselves to find out as much as possible about their chosen destination (i.e. to be 'good' tourists). Wherever that responsibility lies, it is certain that many tourists arrive at their destination totally unprepared for interaction or social contact with local people and, as a result, tourist-host encounters will be constrained and hampered by their lack of knowledge and understanding.

It is, of course, both easy and somewhat dangerous to generalise the varied and complex social processes and interaction involved in encounters between tourists and local people. Some or all of the above characteristics are likely to be identifiable in most tourist-host encounters and are equally applicable to both international and domestic tourism. For example, there is no reason why contact between a tourist and a local villager in the British countryside will not be as superficial, unbalanced, transitory and influenced by general preconceptions as such contacts in a developing country. Nevertheless, it is important to point out that encounters between tourists and local people occur in a variety of situations and may benefit from positive and informed perceptions and motivations on both sides. de Kadt (1979:50) describes three principal contexts in which tourist-host encounters occur, namely, *where the tourist is purchasing some good or service from the host, where the tourist and host find themselves side by side, for example, on a sandy beach...and where the two parties come face to face with the object of exchanging information or ideas.* Of these, the first two situations are the most common contexts for tourist-host encounters and relate specifically to traditional, mass tourism. Conversely, the third situation, where both the tourist and the local person meet on the basis of equality, mutual respect and shared expectations, relates to the conditions under which tourism could lead, eventually, to greater international understanding. Although such two-way, meaningful and mutually satisfying encounters do occur, there is little doubt that they are relatively rare, largely as a result of mass tourism being of form of modern, mass consumption. In other words, in the majority of encounters, locals are perceived as part of the tourism product and tourists are seen as a potential source of profit; only in de Kadt's third scenario do individuality and personality enter the equation.

HOST PERCEPTIONS OF TOURISTS

It is widely accepted that *tourists are groups or populations with very different characteristics and attitudes, with clearly identifiable preferences, tastes, and perceptions* (Brougham and Butler, 1981); these differences can lead to a variety of tourism impacts in destination areas and to different attitudes towards encounters with local people. It is not surprising, therefore, that a considerable amount of research has been undertaken into the desires, motivation and behaviour of tourists in relation to their impact on destination societies.

Much less research has been undertaken into the opinions and attitudes of local people with regard to tourism and tourists. Indeed, within the context of tourist-host relationships, the host is frequently assumed to be a fixed entity. In other words, whilst tourists are recognised as possessing a variety of characteristics, expectations and behavioural traits, the term host is used as a general description of members of local communities in tourist destination areas. The only distinction made between different categories of hosts is that, more often than not, it will be people who are involved in the local tourism industry who are most likely to come into contact with visitors. This relative lack of research is surprising since *the perceptions and attitudes of residents toward the impacts of tourism are likely to be an important planning and policy consideration for the successful development, marketing, and operation of existing and future tourism programs and projects* (Ap, 1992). In particular, it is essential that local people are favourable towards tourists; if not, the possibility of a *community backlash* (Pearce, 1994:104) may arise, leading to negative attitudes, such as an unwillingness to work within the tourism industry or even demonstrations of outright hostility towards tourists. By implication, the nature of the tourist-host relationship is as dependent on the different characteristics of local people themselves as it is on the varying perceptions, attitudes and so on that tourists bring to the encounter situation.

A number of attempts have been made to analyse the relationship between the different characteristics of host populations and their resulting perceptions of tourism and tourists. For example, Pizam (1978) looked at the attitudes of the residents of Cape Cod, Massachusetts, towards tourists, theorising that their perceptions would be a function of their economic dependency on tourism. He found, perhaps not surprisingly, that a positive correlation existed between residents' work and their attitudes towards tourism: *it was found that the more dependent a person was on tourism, as a means of livelihood, the more positive was his overall attitude towards tourism on Cape Cod.* In another study of resident perceptions, Belisle and Hoy (1980) discovered that local people's perceptions of tourism became less favourable the further their distance from the tourist zone, again indicating that those who are more directly involved in the tourism industry are more likely to have positive feelings towards tourism development. Similarly, Brougham and Butler's (1981) study of resident attitudes on the Sleat Peninsula, Isle of Skye, found that significant differences in perceptions of tourism were identifiable in relation to location of residence, but that other factors, such as age and language, also resulted in varying opinions of the benefits or disbenefits of tourism.

A number of other studies are frequently quoted in the literature (for example, Rothman, 1978, Sheldon and Var, 1984, Perdue, Long and Allen, 1987), the great majority of which tend to be largely descriptive. That is, the studies present the results of various research projects but do not fully explain *why* local people in tourist destination areas have either positive or negative perceptions of tourism. More recently, Ap (1992) proposed that the theory of social exchange, a sociological concept firmly rooted in social action theory, provides a useful framework for the analysis of the tourist-host relationship.

Social exchange theory, which is generally concerned with explaining the exchange of resources (physical or symbolic) between people or groups of people, is similar to Nash's suggestion that *the relationship between tourists and their hosts includes certain understandings that must be agreed and acted upon* (1989:44) or, in other words, is a sort of transaction. When applied to tourism, social exchange implies that both tourists and hosts undergo a process of negotiation or exchange, the ultimate aim of which is to maximise the benefit to each from the encounter. For the tourist, the benefit may be the purchase of a product or service or, more generally, a desired experience and for local people, the benefit may be economic gain.

The exchange process itself follows a sequence of events,

commencing with the identification of *need satisfaction* (Ap, 1992). That is, unless a need or a motivation exists, there is no reason for either party to initiate an exchange; thus, unless a community has a need to develop tourism or sees tourism as a means of economic and social improvement, it is unlikely to be willing to become involved in or to welcome the development of tourism. The one exception may be where a community has a tradition of hospitality with no expectation of payment or reward, although such a tradition is likely to become rapidly commercialised with the advent of regular tourism. Once needs have been recognised, both the tourist and the host enter into an exchange situation that must be rational and that results in satisfactory benefits. In other words, both parties act in a rational manner that will result in the desired benefits, although those benefits will be satisfied rather than maximised. For example, tourism development is normally undertaken for the potential economic and social benefits that it will bring to a community, such as improved standards of living, better transport services and so on. The greater the perceived benefits, the more positive will be local people's attitudes towards tourists. However, certain costs are involved, such as having to put up with crowds or higher costs in the shops during the tourist season; once those costs begin to outweigh benefits, then attitudes towards tourism and tourists will become increasingly negative.

Importantly, the social exchange, or tourist-host encounter, must be reciprocal. *Reciprocity suggests that the resources exchanged should be roughly equivalent* (Ap, 1992) and, therefore, neither party should feel they are being exploited. Once either the host or the tourist recognises a lack of reciprocity, for example, when a tourist feels that he or she is being 'ripped off' by the prices being charged for a souvenir or when hosts believe that they are being taken advantage of, such as when tourists intrude on their privacy by taking photographs, then the exchange becomes unbalanced. In this situation, the host is more likely to adopt a more negative attitude towards encounters than tourists because what is 'business as usual' for local people is a once-off experience for tourists. However, if the conditions of rationality, the satisfying of benefits and reciprocity are fulfilled, then the exchange will be perceived as fair and equitable; if the host and the tourist both feel that they have achieved a fair and satisfactory outcome, then each will have a positive perception of the encounter. For example, Belisle and Hoy (1980) found that the residents of Santa Marta, a resort on the coast of Colombia, South America, had a generally positive attitude towards tourism and tourists. Despite higher seasonal food prices and a greater incidence of robberies, drug smuggling and prostitution, tourism was seen as having led to improved local transport infrastructure and higher employment, benefits which, on balance, outweighed the costs.

Paradoxically, the need satisfaction that initiates the social exchange situation in the context of tourism can also frequently lead to unbalanced tourist-host encounters. Tourism is normally supported and promoted by host communities for the expected benefits of employment opportunities, higher income and social improvement but as tourism in any resort develops, and as the local community becomes relatively more dependent on tourism as a source of income, then a subtle shift occurs in what may be described as the balance of power in tourist-host relationships. Either the social impacts begin to outweigh the benefits to the local community (see Chapter Seven) or local people find themselves in the situation of needing tourists more than tourists need them. In both cases, local people's attitudes and perceptions of tourists will begin to alter and become increasingly negative. In short, tourism development is dynamic and the context for tourist-host encounters can also change, influencing the nature of those encounters. *Encounters between tourists and the local inhabitants must be differentiated according to the stage of tourism development in which they occur* (de Kadt, 1979:50) and it is important, therefore, to consider the tourist-host relationship itself as a dynamic process and one which may change in response to other factors.

THE TOURIST RESORT LIFE CYCLE

Most of the studies into host perceptions of tourism and tourists tend to be undertaken at a particular point in time. That is, research is carried out at certain stage in the development of tourist destinations, at a particular point in what may be described as the life cycle of a resort, although one exception is Pi-Sunyer's (1989) analysis of resident perceptions of tourists in a Catalan resort. Whilst such studies undoubtedly provide a valuable insight into the factors and variables which determine the nature of tourist-host encounters, it is also important to consider how host perceptions change over time, in particular how the nature of the relationship is influenced by the developmental stage of the destination. In a widely quoted study linked to product life cycle theory in marketing, Butler (1980) suggests that tourist destinations evolve through a six or seven stage process:

(i) The exploration stage

The first stage in the development of a tourist destination is characterised by relatively small visitor numbers. It is the stage when a resort or destination is 'discovered' by independent travellers or other explorer-type tourists and, as such, they will be accepted by local residents more as guests than as paying customers. Thus, commercial development of tourism is minimal, contact with local residents is balanced and frequent and little or no marketing or promotion of the resort is occurring.

(ii) The involvement stage

As the number of visitors begins to increase, local people begin to provide facilities and accommodation. The potential for tourism development is recognised and, although still low key, some marketing is undertaken which further increases the number of visitors. As a result, the approach to tourism becomes more commercial although the relationship between tourists and local people remains harmonious.

(iii) The development stage

As tourist destinations progress into the third, development, stage they become transformed from relatively unknown, quiet destinations (what a travel writer would describe as 'undiscovered') into fully fledged resorts. Initially a wide range of locally owned businesses are set up to provide for the needs of tourists, but control of tourism rapidly passes to external organisations such as large hotel groups and international tour operators. The explorer or niche-market visitors have been replaced by mass, institutionalised tourists and the tourist-host relationship suffers as it becomes based on commercial transactions. Indeed, local residents become increasingly marginalised as tourism becomes dominated by external interests.

(iv) The consolidation stage

The consolidation stage is marked by a slow down in the rate of increase of visitors. Rather than new businesses opening up the existing hotels, restaurants and other facilities are more concerned with controlling costs. The destination has lost its exclusivity and 'unique selling points' and it has joined the ranks of many other similar destinations. During the season the resident population is vastly outnumbered by tourists, most of whom stay in an identifiable and distinct tourist zone within the resort. Thus, only local people involved in the tourism industry have any direct contact with tourists, usually on a transitory, business related basis.

(v) The stagnation stage

Eventually the destination reaches a stage where its capacity has been reached or even, at times, exceeded. No new tourists are attracted to the resort which has become dependent on repeat business. The decline in growth has resulted in a lack of investment and so less attention is paid to the upkeep of buildings and infrastructure. Environmental, social and economic problems begin to emerge and the destination, in terms of both visitors and prices, moves downmarket.

(vi) The decline stage

Finally, the destination enters the stage of decline. Visitor numbers begin to fall as newer, more attractive resorts are developed (or, as in the case of British seaside resorts, overseas holidays become increasingly affordable and popular). The larger tourist businesses begin to pull out of the destination and new uses have to found for tourist accommodation and other facilities. Hotels may be converted into retirement flats or nursing homes and tourism activity falls to a low, but perhaps regular, level with minimal contact between visitors and members of the local community.

(vii) The rejuvenation stage

Rather than allowing the destination to completely decline, the signs are recognised and new uses, new markets and new sources of investment are sought. Attractions are updated and efforts are made to re-market the destination with a new, modern image. For example, the resort may begin to market itself as a business and conference centre, the season may be extended with new products, such as summer walking holidays being promoted at winter skiing destinations, or accommodation and facilities are improved and updated to keep in line with developments in other resorts.

A number of attempts have been made to link Butler's model to the 'life cycle' of actual tourist destinations, yet there are conflicting opinions as to its applicability. For example, Ioannides (1992) compares the growth and development of tourism in Cyprus with Butler's exploration, involvement and development stages, concluding that the high level of local involvement combined with increasing dependence on overseas tour operators and a mass, charter market indicates that the development stage has been reached. More recent experience would indicate that Cyprus has, in fact, moved into a period of consolidation. Similarly, the tourism history of British seaside resorts is another example of how destinations can progress through Butler's hypothetical process; some, such as Brighton and Torquay, have undergone rejuvenation, whereas as others are clearly in a state of decline. Conversely, Getz (1992), in a study of tourism development at the Niagara Falls, concludes that Butler's stages of consolidation, stagnation, decline and rejuvenation are not separate and identifiable but a perpetual process. That is, tourism planners and managers respond continually to shifts in demand and other problems which tourism destinations face and, rather than sinking into inevitable decline, destinations enter a stage of maturity: *for old destinations like Niagara Falls, and for most urban tourism areas, 'maturity' will likely be a permanent condition* (Getz, 1992).

The important point to consider is how the developmental process of tourist destinations relates to the tourist-host relationship and, in particular, the perceptions of local people of tourism and tourists. Some links are identifiable through the degree and type of contact that local people have with tourists as

Butler's model develops but, in another widely cited study, Doxey (1975), proposes a four stage process whereby the attitudes of local people change as tourism develops.

At the exploration stage, when there are relatively few visitors and contact between tourists and local people is likely to be frequent and balanced, the attitude of the host population is one of *euphoria*. Visitors are welcome, both as a form of new contact with 'the outside world' and as a new source of income which, in many cases, is an important supplement to household earnings. However, as the level of tourism begins to grow, fewer members of the local population come into contact with tourists. Nor are tourists a rare sight; they begin to be taken for granted and the tourist-host encounter is motivated less by mutual personal interest than by commercial gain on the part of locals. Thus, the attitude of the majority of residents, in particular those who have limited or no contact with tourists, is one of *apathy*. The third stage in Doxey's model is one of *annoyance*. Large numbers of tourists mean that the day-to-day life of residents becomes disrupted; there are queues in shops, traffic jams, local shops turn to the more profitable business of selling souvenirs and, generally, local residents are marginalised in their own town. The perceived benefits of tourism to the host community are beginning to be outweighed by the disruption that tourism is causing, a situation that leads, finally, to *antagonism* towards tourists. Local people have become dependent on tourism; they are no longer in control of the situation, the standard of living in the resort is declining as the quality of tourism facilities and the type of tourist becomes down market. The tourists and their money, once so openly welcomed, are now blamed for the changes that have taken place in the destination. In short, Doxey suggests that the growth and development of tourism can be mirrored by an increasingly negative attitude towards tourists amongst local people.

In a similar vein, Ap and Crompton (1993) identify four different strategies that local residents adopt in response to the level of tourism development. That is, they describe the actions taken by local people that result from their attitudes towards tourists. At the euphoric stage, local people *embrace* tourism; they make positive efforts to meet and develop long term relationships with visitors, many of whom may return on a regular basis. As the number of tourists grows and encounters become more formal, local apathy is marked by *tolerance* towards tourists. Despite some of the problems that tourism brings, the general feeling is that the local economy benefits from the income from tourists and local residents, therefore, tolerate the occasional disruption to their lives caused by tourists. However, as local residents become irritated by the presence of tourist they *adjust* their behaviour: activities, such as shopping, may be rescheduled to avoid crowds or they will go to places which they know will be quieter. Such a strategy is not always possible, in particular when tourism has reached the stage of consolidation, when tourism dominates their lives and local people have become antagonistic towards tourists. In this situation, if they are able to do so, residents may *withdraw*; they either move away temporarily, perhaps during the main season, or they may permanently move away from the area. For example, following the rapid development of Ayia Napa, a mass tourism resort in Cyprus, the entire original village relocated a few kilometres away to avoid the problems and social impacts of tourism.

The implication of these studies is that not only will local people's attitudes and perceptions vary according to the level and type of tourism development, but that they will also adapt their behaviour accordingly. Much depends on the extent to which an individual is involved in the local tourism industry; it is likely that a person who earns a living from tourism will remain at the apathy/tolerance stage until business begins to decline whereas residents who are not directly involved and who, therefore, suffer from the negative impacts without enjoying any apparent benefit, may quickly become antagonistic towards tourists. In either case, the end result is a tourist-host relationship that is unequal and unbalanced, a situation which may be related to the nature of tourism and tourism development itself.

TOURISM AND NEO-COLONIALISM

Much of the literature on the tourist-host relationship adopts what may be described as a micro perspective. That is, it considers the nature of the relationship from the point of view of individuals or localised groups of tourists and locals. However, in order to fully understand the ways in which the tourist-host relationship develops, it is important to consider the broader forces and influences that come into play, in particular the relationship between tourist generating countries or regions and tourist destinations. For example, it would be logical to assume that the local community in a destination that is fully in control of its tourism development would be more favourably disposed towards tourists than, say, local people who feel that, in some way or another, tourism has been imposed upon them or that they have become dependent on tourism and, by implication, tourists. For the latter community, tourism may be considered to be a form of imperialism (see Nash, 1989) or *neo-colonialism* (Mathieson and Wall, 1982:147) and, from a sociological point of view, the tourist-host relationship may be one based upon conflict.

Imperialism, or colonialism, is essentially the expansion of a particular country's economic, political or military interests abroad and, in a sense, international tourism may be viewed as a new, modern form of colonialism. The basis of this argument is that the great majority of tourists originate in the modern, developed countries of the Western world. At the same time, the tourism industry that facilitates the movement of tourists and the development of tourist facilities is itself based largely in the major tourism generating countries. Thus, being the suppliers of large numbers of tourists and, frequently, owning or managing facilities and attractions in destination areas as well as providing the necessary financial investment, the metropolitan centres of Europe and North America are able to exercise some degree of power and control over the development of tourism. This is particularly marked in developing countries but even Mediterranean destinations, such as Spain and Greece, have, in a sense, become colonised by their northern European neighbours. In the case of ex-colonies in the developing world which have gained their political independence from Western powers, this new dependence on the West for both the financial support to develop tourism and tourists themselves is, therefore, seen to be a return to the old days of colonialism, or neo-colonialism.

For example, The Gambia is a small, west African state which gained its independence from Britain in 1965. At that time the country was virtually unknown as a tourist destination; indeed, only three hundred tourist arrivals were recorded for the 1965-66 winter season (Dieke, 1993). Since then, mainly as a result of its popularity as a winter sun destination, there has been a steady growth in the number of tourists travelling to The Gambia and currently about one hundred thousand tourists visit the country each year. Tourism contributes some 10 per cent to the country's Gross Domestic Product (GDP), earning about £16.5 million annually, and The Gambia's Ministry of Information and Tourism hopes to increase tourism's contribution to GDP to 25 per cent. Whilst such figures indicate a reasonably healthy growth in tourism, they hide a number of important facts which demonstrate a less than healthy dependence on overseas finance and organisations. For example, around 60 per cent of visitors to The Gambia come from Britain with about 40 per cent of all visitors using Thomsons, a situation which puts tour operators in a powerful position when negotiating room rates. Also, many of The Gambia's hotels are either owned or managed by overseas organisations and a high percentage of its income from tourism is spent on importing goods to satisfy tourists' needs, whilst the collapse of the national airline in 1993 further increased the country's dependence on international sources of finance. Interestingly, attempts are being made to also develop a summer tourist season in The Gambia. By having to compete with other destinations closer to the main tourism generating countries in northern Europe, holidays in The Gambia are becoming increasingly cheaper and the country is correspondingly gaining less benefit from tourism.

Mathieson and Wall (1982) identify three conditions, some or all of which may be linked to the concept of neo-colonialism and all of which are evident in the example of tourism development in The Gambia, which indicate a country's dependence on an overseas-controlled tourism industry. Firstly, many developing countries have become dependent on tourism as a source of foreign exchange. Thus, although the original policy of developing and promoting tourism may have been to develop and diversify the local economy, thereby enabling a greater degree of self-sufficiency, many countries have been unable to do so. For example, Cyprus turned to tourism to stimulate economic growth and diversification following both independence from Britain in 1960 and the Turkish occupation of northern Cyprus in 1974. Tourism is now the dominant industry on the island, accounting for over 40 per cent of all exports and around 20 per cent of GDP, with the result that the Cypriot economy is largely dependent on tourism and, as with The Gambia, disproportionately dependent on tourism from Britain (see EIU, 1992). Secondly, a large proportion of the earnings from tourism flow directly back to the tourism generating countries, both as profits from investments and as payments for imports to satisfy the needs of tourists. In some countries, such 'leakages' can be as high as 70 per cent of the earnings from tourism. Thirdly, tourism, as a form of neo-colonialism, is evidenced by foreign nationals holding management and other senior positions within the tourism industry, which is also another way in which the profits from tourism leak out of the country.

Often described as the economic costs of tourism development, these characteristics of neo-colonialism are by no means universal. Indeed, many destinations in both the developing and developed world have built up valuable and thriving tourism businesses based on policies which ensure local ownership and the retention of profits. For example, in Thailand foreign ownership of any business is limited to 49 per cent whilst in India no foreign national is permitted to work in the tourism industry. It is, therefore, over-generalistic to claim, as does Nash (1989:39), that it is the influence of tourism generating countries *over touristic and related developments abroad that makes a metropolitan centre imperialistic and tourism a form of imperialism.* Furthermore, many countries have undertaken tourism development programmes voluntarily and willingly and, by retaining their political, if not economic, independence, are able to dictate their own future. Bhutan, which both limits the number of tourists arriving each year and controls their activities so as not to disrupt and commercialise local culture, is an extreme but good example of how the promise of rapid economic growth has been rejected in favour of retaining independence and cultural and political integrity. Nevertheless, in the context of tourist-host relationships, the development of tourism almost inevitably leads to some degree of economic dependence on the part of host communities and, therefore, the concept of tourism as a form of neo-colonialism provides a useful, broad basis for considering the longer-term direction and evolution of interaction between tourists and local communities in all destination areas.

For example, the sense of economic dependence felt by destination communities may serve to undermine the potential for meaningful, balanced tourist-host relationships, especially if an historical, colonial link exists. Thus, local people in India may well perceive that the attitude of British visitors has changed little since the days of the Raj and may therefore, feel resentful towards them whilst in The Gambia, a country once at the centre of the slave trade, local people who work in the poorly paid, foreign dominated tourism industry may feel that little has changed. Similarly, local communities may have generalised attitudes towards visitors which are, again, amplified by their actual or perceived economic dependence upon them. For example, Pi-Sunyer (1989:195) describes how the development of mass tourism in a Catalan resort led to stereotypical descriptions being applied to different nationalities of visitors. In the eyes of local people, Germans, French and Italian visitors lost their individuality and became identified by particular negative attributes, a process resulting from *the pressures and sheer magnitude of mass tourism...and...the sense of loss of control that such an influx implied.*

Nor is economic dependence and the resulting attitude towards tourists limited to international tourism. Local communities in a rural area in England, such as a national park, may be as equally dependent on domestic tourism from towns and cities as is a developing country on international tourists from a modern, Western country. The purchase of large numbers of local houses or apartments by tourists as second, holiday homes, leading to local people being unable to afford to buy their own homes, then becomes little more than a localised form of colonialism. The important point is that the economic dependence which comes hand in hand with virtually all levels of tourism development beyond the exploratory stage implies a lack of absolute control on the part of host communities and, hence, some degree of inequality in the resulting relationship between local people and tourists is inevitable.

TOURIST-HOST RELATIONSHIPS: HARMONY OR CONFLICT?

As pointed out earlier, encounters between tourists and local people in destination areas are frequently described as host-guest relationships, a term which implies a sense of willingness, equality and harmony. In other words, it implies that tourists are invited as welcome (but paying!) guests and that local people are happy and willing hosts. Thus, host-guest relationships within a destination society may be viewed as a form of structural consensus, as long as tourism is seen to be mutually beneficial and that the transactions or social exchanges between visitors and local people is fair, balanced and equitable. However, the analysis of the nature of contacts between tourists and members of local communities leads to a contradictory conclusion. That is, such encounters, when considered within the dynamic context of tourism development and the life cycle of tourist destinations, become identifiable with the gradual erosion of equality and balance in the relationship and the growing domination of the needs of tourism and tourists. In particular, the nature and economic rationale of tourism development indicates that, for the most part, encounters between tourists and local people bear more relation to conflict theory than harmonious inter-action, the exception being contacts in non-tourist areas or where visitors make a conscious effort to meet local, 'backstage' people.

The main point to emerge is that meaningful and balanced encounters between tourists and local people can only occur in situations of mutual dependence and where the local community has retained control over the development of tourism. As residents become more dependent on tourists as a source of income and as control falls into the hands of national or international organisations, the balance of power within the tourist-host relationship falls firmly in favour of the tourist. *Whenever tourism activity is concentrated in time and space, build rapidly, dominates a local economy, disrupts community life, endangers the environment, and ignores community input, the seeds of discontent are sown* (Haywood, 1988). Therefore, if harmony is to be maintained and, by implication, the benefits to both tourists and local people optimised on a continual basis, the solution would appear to lie in maintaining the involvement and control of the community as a whole in the development of tourism, or in what has been called a community approach to tourism development (see Murphy, 1983, 1985 and 1988).

The community approach to tourism development in its original form was, in effect, the precursor of what has become sustainable tourism development. Fundamental to the approach is the recognition that a thriving and healthy tourism industry depends upon an equally healthy and thriving local community. It is the local community that benefits from tourism but, at the same time, it is the local community that bears the costs of tourism and has to pick up the pieces once the tourists have gone. In other words, tourism is a resource industry, and local communities are as much a resource, or part of the tourism product, as are tourist facilities and attractions. Therefore, the basic requirement for the community approach to tourism development is that all members of communities in tourist destination areas, rather than just those directly involved in the tourism industry, should be involved in the management and planning of tourism. The purpose of this approach is to ensure that the objectives of tourism development coincide with the community's wider social and economic goals and that the tourism industry *gives back to the community while extracting a living from it...[and]...that both the industry and its community base can benefit mutually from a long-term partnership* (Murphy, 1983).

The concept of community involvement has been incorporated in a number of tourism planning and development projects, in particular the partnership or Tourism Development Action Programme (TDAP) approach. Primarily intended to develop partnerships between the public and private sectors as a more effective means of planning and financing tourism developments, TDAPs also have the purpose of achieving more widespread support and involvement amongst local communities (see Yale, 1992:23). The extent to which this has been achieved is debatable; involvement tends to be limited to those who have a direct, usually financial interest, whilst decisions may frequently be based upon personal as opposed to community-wide concerns. Nevertheless, it is widely recognised that harmonious tourist-host relationships are dependent, at least in part, on the involvement of local people in tourism planning at a community level. Pearce (1994:117) also includes the education of both local people and communities, community ownership of tourist facilities, the facilitation of local residents' way of life and the undertaking of constant monitoring and research as equally essential ingredients of community based tourism development.

In reality, such involvement is unlikely. Tourism is an economic activity which involves tourists who are willing to spend money in return for certain goods and services, and organisations and businesses which will provide those goods and services at a profit. Under such circumstances, balanced and harmonious tourist-host relationships will only occur when the tourism product is small scale, locally owned and controlled, and not the major source of income and employment for the local community. As soon as the hosts become dependent, either on tourists themselves or on outside organisations, they become, in effect, a commodity. The profits of tour operators and other organisations represent a form of exploitation and the tourists, along with the tourism industry, are the exploiters. The tourist-host relationship becomes based upon conflict and, as considered in Chapter Seven, the local community begins to suffer from the social and cultural impacts of tourism.

The Socio-Cultural Impacts of Tourism

INTRODUCTION

The growth and development of tourism during the latter half of the twentieth century has been remarkable. Between 1960 and 1990 the annual number of international tourist arrivals rose from 69.3 million to 429 million, whilst foreign exchange receipts grew from £4.6 billion to £166 billion. Despite the Gulf conflict in 1991 and its subsequent repercussions throughout the tourism industry, the figures have continued to rise; in 1992, international arrivals amounted to 475.6 million, generating almost £186 billion. If the worldwide earnings from domestic tourism are added to this, the value of tourism is even more staggering. In Britain alone it is calculated that tourism contributes some £25 billion to the economy each year whilst the World Travel and Tourism Council (WTTC) estimates that tourism has become the world's single largest industry, generating more than £1.7 trillion annually (WTTC, 1991).

In short, there is no doubting the economic value of tourism and *many of the world's countries now regard tourism as an important and integral aspect of their development strategies* (Jenkins, 1991:61). In addition to being a significant generator of foreign exchange, tourism can act as a catalyst for economic regeneration and diversification whilst, as a relatively labour intensive industry, it is an important source of employment in both developed and developing countries; around seven per cent of the world's workforce is employed in tourism (WTTC, 1991). It is not surprising, therefore, that many countries have leapt onto the tourism bandwagon, developing and exploiting their natural resources in an attempt to gain their share of the multi-billion pound tourism market.

From a social and cultural perspective, this rapid expansion of tourism is important in two respects. Firstly, within individual destination areas or countries, the development of tourism as a vehicle for economic modernisation and diversification almost invariably leads to changes and developments in the structure of society. Some of these changes may be welcome, such as general, society-wide improvements in income, education, employment opportunities and local infrastructure and services. Other changes may be less welcome; traditional social or family values may be challenged, new economically powerful groups may emerge, or cultural practices may be adapted in order to suit the needs of tourists. In other words, destination societies may both benefit from and suffer the less desirable consequences of tourism as an economic development strategy.

Secondly, *tourism is unique as an export industry in that consumers themselves travel to collect the goods* (Crick, 1989). The tourism product is 'exported' to tourists who travel to the destination, carrying with them the values, beliefs and behavioural modes of their own, home society as a form of cultural baggage. Thus, as the volume of international tourism has increased, so too has the contact between different societies and cultures. To some observers, this interaction between tourists and local communities threatens to dilute or even, potentially, destroy traditional cultures and societies: *tourists seem to be the incarnation of the materialism, philistinism and cultural homogenisation that is sweeping all before it in a converging world* (Macnaught, 1982). To others, it represents an opportunity for sharing, for peace, understanding and greater knowledge amongst different societies and nations.

Whether considering the effects on a destination society brought about by the consequences of tourism development, the influence of ever-increasing numbers of tourists coming into contact with alien cultures, or a combination of both, it is inevitable that tourism, as a fundamentally social activity, will have an impact on those societies and cultures involved in tourism. Indeed, the rapid growth in tourism since the 1960s has been mirrored by increasing concern about the impacts of tourism on host destinations and there exists a large body of literature concerned with both an analysis of the physical, social, political or cultural impacts of tourism development and with potential solutions to the perceived problems (see, for example, Budowski, 1976; de Kadt, 1979; Britton, 1982; Mathieson and Wall, 1982; Holden, 1984; Murphy, 1985; Butler, 1991; ETB, 1991; Smith and Eadington, 1992).

Much of the academic literature, reports in the media and what Mathieson and Wall (1982:134) describe as *colourful stories* adopt a negative stance, highlighting those aspects of tourism which are seen to be destructive or disadvantageous to tourist destinations (see Travis, 1982). Moreover, the analysis and criticism of the social and cultural impacts is frequently based on a number of assumptions which, potentially, distort the overall picture. For example, it is frequently assumed that the social and cultural impact of tourism is a one-way process, that the flood of (usually Western) tourists visiting countries in the developing world almost invariably results in the Westernisation of traditional cultures. This chapter examines both the positive and negative social and cultural impacts of tourism and considers the extent to which the qualitative assessment of socio-cultural impacts can be measured against broader social and cultural change and the tangible, quantitative impacts of tourism development.

TOURISM, SOCIETY AND CULTURE

Murphy (1985:117) describes tourism as a *socio-cultural event for the traveller and the host.* It is a social process which, in the context of both domestic and international tourism, brings together people from different regions and different countries in a form of social interaction (see Chapter Six). The resulting tourist-host relationship may frequently impact upon both the local community and on visitors. Tourism is also, from the point of view of destination areas, a means of improving and modernising the economic and social condition of the host community and, therefore, tourism may be described as an agent of socio-cultural change.

It is difficult to distinguish between changes or impacts that are specifically social and those which are cultural. The condition and structure of a society and its cultural characteristics are interlinked and changes in one almost inevitably lead to changes in the other. Nevertheless, for the purposes of this chapter, the social impacts of tourism may be described as those which have a more immediate effect on both tourists and host communities and their quality of life whereas cultural impacts are those which lead to a longer-term, gradual change in a society's values, beliefs and cultural practices (Murphy, 1985:117). In other words, social impacts are those concerned with issues such as health, moral behaviour, the structure of the family, gender roles, crime and religion whilst cultural impacts may determine behavioural and attitudinal changes, such as dress, food and social relationships, as well as changes in the production of cultural practices and artefacts. Before describing the specific social and cultural impacts of tourism, however, it is important to consider, firstly, the factors which determine the degree of socio-cultural impact and, secondly, the extent to which it is tourism and tourists, as opposed to other factors, that lead to social and cultural change.

(i) Factors influencing socio-cultural change

Although it is possible to make general observations about the potential socio-cultural impacts of tourism, the degree to which these impacts influence or are experienced by host communities and tourists depends on a number of factors. Generally, the greater the gulf between the tourism generating country and the destination in terms of culture and economic development, the more significant are the social and cultural impacts likely to be (WTO, 1981).   Other, more specific factors may also be identified:

(a) Types/numbers of tourists

Both the volume and the type of tourist are significant factors in determining the potential socio-cultural impacts of tourism. As a general rule, explorer-type independent travellers who are relatively few in number and are more willing to seek out, experience and understand local culture are likely to have less impact than large numbers of mass tourists who demand facilities and amenities to which they are accustomed in their home society.   Smith (1989a:12) links tourist types to potential impacts on host societies, following a continuum from low numbers/low impact to high volume charter tourists/high impact, whilst there are also connections between tourist types and behavioural characteristics and the way in which tourists interact with local communities (see Chapter Three).   However, it is important to point out that an independent traveller may have more impact on an isolated community that has not been exposed to tourism than a large number of tourists in an established destination. Conversely, mass tourism in a self-contained club resort may have relatively little impact on the socio-cultural character of the country in which it is located.

(b) Importance of the tourism industry

The primary purpose of tourism development is economic growth and diversification. In those destinations where tourism is part of, or leads to, a mixed economy, the socio-cultural impacts of tourism are likely to be weaker or less widespread than in a country where tourism is the major industry. Where local communities become entirely dependent on tourism, the socio-cultural impacts of tourism are likely to be most keenly felt. Furthermore, diverse economies are more likely to be able to support and supply the local tourism industry, reducing the need for imports and spreading the socially beneficial impacts of employment and income generation.

(c) Size and development of the tourism industry

In a similar vein to the degree of dependence on tourism, both the size of the tourism industry and its stage of development are important factors. A relatively large number of tourists in small communities will have greater impacts on local residents, whereas larger communities are likely to remain relatively unaffected by tourists. It is for this reason that a number of tourist destinations, such as the Seychelles, are adopting the policy of promoting themselves as up-market destinations, hoping to attract a smaller number of higher spending tourists. The purpose of this is to reduce the potential negative impacts of tourism whilst maintaining the economic benefits to the destination. It must also be remembered that the stage of tourism development in a destination will determine the degree of socio-cultural impact; established resorts will experience less continuing change than a newer destination.

(d) The pace of tourism development

Many tourist destinations have experienced the rapid and relatively uncontrolled development of tourism. In such cases, the socio-cultural impacts of tourism are likely to be greater than in countries or destinations which undertake a slow and controlled tourism development programme. In effect, local communities should be allowed to gradually adapt to the needs and benefits of tourism and tourists rather than having to undergo a process of rapid upheaval and change.

All tourism destinations are different and the influence of these factors in determining the degree to which the socio-cultural impacts of tourism are experienced is also variable. Nor are such impacts restricted to developing countries or international tourism in general, although much of the literature concentrates on these areas. For example, the local communities in many rural, coastal and urban tourism destinations in Britain are affected to some degree by domestic tourists. Overall, however, the level of impact in a tourism destination will result from the *interaction between the nature of the change agent and the inherent strength and ability of the host culture to withstand, and absorb, the change generators whilst retaining its own integrity* (Ryan, 1991:148). The implication is, therefore, that the study of the socio-cultural impacts of tourism must be approached with some caution. It is inevitable that some change will occur as a result of tourism but such is the variety of factors influencing socio-cultural change that each case must be considered individually. For example, it would be logical to expect that the changes resulting from the development and growth of tourism in the Greek Cyclades islands would be relatively uniform but a study by Tsartas (1992) indicates otherwise. The islands of Ios and Serifos are similar in size, population and original socio-economic conditions but it was found that, owing to different types of tourism development (mass-charter tourism on Ios, moderate and controlled tourism on Serifos), different socio-cultural impacts were experienced on each island. The speed with which tourism had been developed, the length of time over which development had occurred and a variety of economic and political factors also played a role in determining the perceived socio-cultural impacts on each island.

(ii) Tourism as an agent of socio-cultural change

When visible and identifiable social and cultural changes occur in regions or countries which have adopted a policy of tourism development it is frequently tourism, as opposed to other factors, that is seen to be the cause of such change. Furthermore, the socio-cultural impacts of tourism are generally perceived to be negative, in particular in the context of tourism development in developing countries which are, potentially, more susceptible to Western influences. Yet, whilst there is little doubt that tourism can bring about changes which may both benefit host communities and be viewed as a 'cost', it is important to point out that, in most cases, tourism *contributes* to social and cultural change rather than being the *cause* of such change.

All societies and cultures are changing and, as a global, homogeneous culture emerges (see Chapter Eight), no society is immune from outside influence. For example, there are very few communities which do not have access to a television and, hence, images of other countries and cultures. The activities of multinational corporations, internationalising Western culture (for example, McDonald's in Moscow, Kentucky Fried Chicken in Beijing), are catalysts of social change, whilst many countries are undergoing a process of industrialisation, urbanisation and rapid population growth which, potentially, have a far greater impact than tourism on social and cultural structures and values. As Smith (1989a:9) points out, *culture change, in the form of modernisation, has made impressive inroads into the backward areas and the poverty pockets of the globe, and the process is both ongoing and accelerating.* She goes on to conclude, in her study of Eskimo tourism in Alaska (Smith 1989b:75), that it is the effort of the government to improve housing, education, medical care and infrastructure, rather the growth of tourism, that has been the key element in bringing about modernisation and cultural change.

Frequently, little effort is made to distinguish the effects of tourism from other cultural changes occurring globally and it would seem that, owing to the highly visible nature of tourism and tourists, the development of tourism has become a scapegoat for socio-cultural change (Crick, 1989). It is important, therefore, to recognise the dynamic character of all societies and cultures and to consider the potential socio-cultural impacts of tourism against this background. It is also important to set the parameters within which the impacts of tourism are assessed. In other words, impact studies often display what Wood (1980) describes as a *western ethnocentrism and romanticism,* a bias which, linked with the concept of postmodernism (see Chapter Eight), assumes that it is better to preserve cultures which are traditional or pre-modern rather than allowing them to develop or modernise. Thus, tourism developments which, from the Western point of view, 'threaten' the social and cultural characteristics of many destinations are perceived as negative impacts although it is quite possible that local communities support such changes. Within the study of the socio-cultural impacts of tourism it is necessary, therefore, *to go beyond evaluations based on Western romantic ideals of cultural preservation to analyse the precise components of cultural change* (Wood, 1980) and to assess the extent to which tourism is one of these components.

THE SOCIAL IMPACTS OF TOURISM

Although the social and cultural effects of tourism are linked and distinctions may be difficult to identify (Lea, 1988:62), for convenience they are divided here under separate headings. The social impacts of tourism, those which have a more immediate and visible effect on destination communities and, to an extent, on tourists themselves, may also be sub-divided into impacts resulting from the development of a tourism industry and the impacts of tourist-host interaction.

(i) Social Consequences of Tourism Development

Tourism is normally planned and developed as a source of income and foreign exchange, thereby providing the resources for social and economic improvement within destination communities. The actual economic costs and benefits of tourism development, such as the generation of income and the multiplier effect, are widely discussed in the literature (for example, see Bull, 1991); here we are concerned with the social consequences of these costs and benefits. Generally, *tourism creates new opportunities in the formal and informal sectors of the economy, new criteria of social status, and contributes to changes in such basic social institutions as the family* (Harrison, 1992:22). A number of more specific positive and negative effects are identifiable:

(a) Improvements in the quality of life

In many instances, the development of tourism results, directly and indirectly, in improvements in the quality of life of local communities in destination areas. In less developed areas, basic infrastructural improvements required by tourism, such as roads and transport links, communication and information links, the supply of power, clean water, sewerage disposal systems and so on may all be of benefit to local communities, whilst facilities and amenities provided for tourists in both new and established resorts also represent general social improvements. For example, the income from tourism frequently supports a wider range of shops, restaurants, theatres and other facilities which are of equal benefit to local communities. The development of tourism can also lead to an improvement of the physical environment, supporting the conservation and renovation of traditional buildings or environmental improvement programmes. More generally, tourism should, at least in theory, lead to greater investment in education, health and other social services to benefit the community as a whole although this is not always the case.

Frequently, however, the growth of tourism is not matched by social improvements for local communities. It is generally accepted that jobs in tourism, other than management positions, tend to be low paid, low status and, frequently, seasonal. This is certainly the case in many beach resorts; for example, locals employed as waiters, bar tenders and other similar jobs in hotels in The Gambia earn barely enough to cover their travelling expenses and the work is seasonal. However, it is also interesting to consider the employment situation in a city such as Glasgow where tourism is being promoted as one of the primary ways of transforming the city from a manufacturing to a service based economy. Many of the city's unemployed people used to work in shipbuilding or heavy engineering and it is difficult to consider jobs in tourism as suitable alternative employment (see Damer, 1990). Tourism can also result in inflated land and house prices, extensive second-home ownership (see Coppock, 1977), inflation and loss of services as, for example, local shops convert to more profitable souvenir outlets.

(b) Changes in the role of women
In many traditional societies, the role of women, particularly younger women, has been strictly governed and defined by

social, religious and economic constraints; indeed, the apparent male domination of many societies is plainly evident to tourists visiting many countries in the developing world. Nevertheless, the employment opportunities offered by tourism have gone a long way to reducing women's economic dependency on the family, representing a new freedom which, although putting strains on the traditional family structure and challenging broader social values, has improved the social condition for many women. For example, Reynoso y Valle and de Regt (1979:130) found that the development of tourism opened up a range of job opportunities for women outside the home, challenging the traditional position and machismo of the Mexican male. In other cases, the improved status of women need not necessarily lead to family or social stress. In Cyprus, where the rapid growth of tourism since independence in 1960 has created a large number of new jobs (tourism currently accounts for 20 per cent of all employment in Cyprus), *the improved financial status of females did not create conflicts between parents and children and husbands or wives, nor did it challenge the authority of the parents or husbands* (Andronicou, 1979:249). It has to be added that, under the Cypriot constitution, women enjoy equal rights and many senior positions, including the Director General of Cyprus Tourism Organisation, are currently held by women.

Tourism has also opened up opportunities for women in what may be described as the informal employment sector. In most tourist destinations, particularly in the developing world, the growth of tourism is accompanied by an increase in the number of people who work in unofficial jobs, such as fruit sellers, beach hawkers, garment manufacturers and, perhaps the most emotive subject of all, as prostitutes in the flourishing 'sex tourism' destinations, such as Thailand and the Philippines. This issue is considered in greater detail later in this chapter but there is no doubt that tourism, in both the formal and informal employment sectors, is largely dependent on women. The extent to which this has improved the social status of women varies from society to society; for example, in Bali, *women are central to the culture, and are indispensable to tourism. Without them the industry would collapse* (Osborne, 1993) whereas, in many other countries around the world, the status of women in the industry is still subordinate to that of their male colleagues.

(c) Changes in community structure

The development of tourism can result in a number of changes in the structure and cohesion of local communities in destination areas with, again, developing countries being most susceptible. The lure or attraction of working in the tourism industry, offering not only employment but the opportunity to meet foreign visitors, draws many younger people to tourist development areas. This has resulted in increased rural-urban migration, a phenomenon which, although not directly caused but nevertheless exacerbated by tourism, leaves many rural areas with a disproportionately aged population and a lack of younger people to continue working in traditional agricultural businesses. Within resort areas it tends to be the younger generations who desire the upward social mobility offered by involvement in tourism and studies have shown that tourism tends to accentuate class differences, polarising local populations and creating a new younger, more prosperous group, perhaps with a broader, less traditional approach than the older generations.

(ii) The Social Impacts of Tourist-Host Interaction

It is inevitable that the physical presence of tourists and their behaviour in tourist resorts and destinations will have some form of impact on local communities. Some of these impacts may be immediate, such as inappropriate behaviour, displays of conspicuous consumption or simply the inconvenience and nuisance caused by large numbers of holiday makers who may have little or no intention meeting with or getting to know members of the local population (see Chapter Six). Other effects may be more gradual, such as the local community adopting the behaviour, attitudes or moral codes of visitors through a process of acculturation. Most of the literature on the social impacts of tourism concentrates on the impacts of tourists on host populations but, socially and culturally, tourism is a two-way process. That is, although the physical flows of tourism are largely typified by the annual mass migration from northern Europe to the Mediterranean or, more generally, from the modern, developed nations to lesser developed or developing countries, it does not necessarily imply that the social effects of tourism also flow in one direction.

Relatively little research has been undertaken into how local cultures and people may impact on visitors; indeed, as Holloway (1994:266) points out, there is a need for an examination of tourist-host encounters from the point of view of tourists. In one sense, crimes against tourists, such as pick-pocketing or mugging, fall into the category of impacts on tourists, although this is normally considered a result of tourism development in the destination. Similarly, it is not uncommon for tourists to contract minor, usually stomach, ailments whilst abroad and, as greater numbers of tourists travel to more distant, exotic locations, the incidence of more serious illnesses is on the increase. Interestingly, it has also been reported that a number of 'old' diseases, such as diphtheria, which have virtually eradicated in Western societies, are now spreading as a result of tourism to previously inaccessible areas. Both crime and health problems are common 'reverse impacts' of tourism although, more typically, they are considered to be two of the risks of participating in tourism; nevertheless, it is possible to identify a number of other ways in which local communities impact on visitors in a socio-cultural sense.

It is highly likely that fashions and tastes have become internationalised partly, if not solely, as a result of tourism. The multi-ethnic character of many populations and the influence of the media also play a significant role, but there is little doubt that overseas travel goes some way to reducing what may be described as cultural xenophobia in tourism generating countries. For example, international cuisine, clothing styles and music are now more widely accepted in Britain than some years ago. Local, host communities may also impact on tourists in terms of adapting, for better or for worse, the attitudes and perceptions of visitors towards host societies and cultures. For example, in a study of young, British tourists visiting Greece and Morocco, Pearce (1982:89) found that the tourists saw the Greeks as more religious and less affluent than expected and Moroccans were poorer and more greedy and mercenary than expected. In both cases, the study revealed that tourists returned home with a more positive attitude towards their own country, a finding which implies that an exploration of possible changes in tourists' perceptions of their own society and culture as a result of overseas travel would be a fruitful research topic. It is important to note that the impact of local people on tourists is dependent on the nature of the encounter; in a study of Greek tourists visiting Turkey, Anastasopoulos (1992) concluded that the negative attitude of the Greeks towards their hosts derived largely from the organised, packaged nature of the tour and the role of the tour guides. This study, along with those by Milman, Reichel and Pizam (1990) and Pizam, Milman and Jafari (1991) also found that there is little empirical evidence to support the view that tourism can lead to greater understanding and harmony and that, in certain circumstances, host communities have a negative impact on visitor perceptions.

A further aspect of socio-cultural impacts on tourists is the way in which tourists adapt their behaviour as a result of encounters with local people. It would be logical to propose that the more contact a tourist has with local people, the less institutionalised the setting and the stronger the local culture, the more likely is the tourist to become acclimatised or 'acculturated'. For example, it is accepted that longer-term independent travellers undergo a period of culture shock when first travelling but that they gradually adapt to their new environment, often to the extent that they find it difficult to readjust to their own home culture and society when they return. In some cases, cultural characteristics of the destination society, such as the religion, might be adopted on a permanent basis by the tourist. Again, research is required to explore the two-way nature of the socio-cultural effects of tourism but, generally, it is still local communities which 'suffer' social impacts of tourism to a greater extent. These impacts are manifested in a variety of ways:

(a) The demonstration effect

One of the most visible and common social impacts of tourism, in particular in the context of tourism to less developed or poorer countries, is the introduction of alien values and ways of life into relatively traditional or isolated societies. As a result, local communities begin to adapt and change their own values and modes of behaviour, often in an attempt to emulate those of tourists, in a process known as the demonstration effect.

Up to a point, such a process is inevitable. Whilst on holiday, tourists demonstrate levels of affluence that are usually beyond the reach of local people, affluence which may be apparent simply because tourists can afford to travel in the first place. Frequently, however, they also display their relative wealth by their styles of dress, the camera or video equipment they carry with them or by indulging in conspicuous consumption. Such displays of wealth may often lead to resentment amongst local communities, particularly if they believe that they will be unable to achieve a similar level of affluence themselves. This resentment might be increased by the symbols of tourist development, such as expensive hotels or tourist zones, beaches or clubs which are 'off limits' to local people, and by the behaviour of tourists which do not respect local morals and customs. For example, the development of tourism on the island of Phuket in Thailand has caused considerable local resentment, especially with respect to the 'privatisation' of public beaches, and has led to the formation of the Phuket Environmental Protection Group to fight for the preservation of the remaining undeveloped beaches (Rattachumpoth, 1992). It is also likely, however, that local people, in particular the younger generations, will begin to question and challenge local custom and tradition and will begin to strive after the material and financial affluence so openly displayed by tourists.

At a basic level, this demonstration effect may be manifested by local people adopting Western styles of dress and indulging in types of behaviour that lead to increasing polarisation between the older and younger generations. With the advance and spread of information and communication technology and the influence of mass, international media, such a process is, perhaps, inevitable and is merely accelerated by tourism. However, the regular displays of wealth may entice people to work in the tourism or other service industries or, of greater consequence to host societies, migrating to the tourism generating countries. One way of achieving this is by befriending tourists in the hope of achieving an invitation to visit, offers of financial support or, in the extreme, permanent relationships. For example, in the early days of its tourism development, The Gambia was particularly popular amongst single, middle-aged Scandinavian women. In some cases, relationships between female tourists and local men became more permanent, occasionally resulting in marriage, and a number of couples returned to Scandinavia.

Similarly, in other countries, such as Thailand and the Philippines, it is recognised that younger females often view Western male tourists as potential tickets to a better life and become involved in relationships as a means of migrating abroad.

Thus, the demonstration effect can lead to a number of social impacts in destination communities. On a positive note it may result in economic and social development within the community by encouraging people to work for things they lack but, more commonly, it can amplify the financial and moral gap between generations, it can encourage behaviour that undermines or challenges traditional values whilst advancing the spread of Western, cultural homogenisation, and it may disrupt the social structure of local communities as younger people move to urban centres, tourism development areas or abroad to tourism generating countries. More generally, it can also lead to local communities developing inaccurate, stereo-typical attitudes towards tourists based upon their observations of behaviour which itself is usually untypical, freed as tourists are from the social constraints and rules of everyday life.

(b) Crime

The association between travel and tourism and crime is not a new phenomenon; throughout the centuries travellers had to endure not only slow and uncomfortable travelling conditions but also the regular attention of people anxious to divest them of their belongings. Crime has also been an accepted feature of tourism in some countries for many years, such as in Italy where people on motorbikes snatch handbags from unsuspecting pedestrians. More recently, however, there has been increasing publicity about tourism-linked crime, in particular following the murder of a number of tourists in Florida in 1993 and 1994.

Although there is little evidence to directly link an increase in crime with the development of tourism, there is no doubt that where there are tourists in any significant numbers there will also be people attempting to benefit illegally from the presence of those tourists. One early study found a positive connection between tourism and the level of crime in Florida, noting that the incidence of crime rose during the main tourist season (McPheters and Stronge, 1974), whilst Mathieson and Wall (1982:151), in a review of existing literature, concluded that there is a positive correlation between crime and tourism. It would be logical to suggest that this link exists because, to local members of the criminal fraternity, tourists represent easy pickings. Not only are they in unfamiliar surroundings, but also they will often be carrying large amounts of money or travellers cheques and expensive camera or video equipment. Furthermore, in some countries, British or other passports are a valuable commodity on the black market. Thus, the potential gain for thieves may be high and, as Mathieson and Wall (1982:151) point out, the risk of detection is often low.

In addition to criminal activities which are directed against individual tourists, other illegal activities may also thrive as a result of tourism. For example, in those countries where the official exchange rate overvalues the local currency, it is not unusual for black markets in currency exchange to exist, offering tourists far higher rates than available legally. In China, foreign tourists are required to exchange their cash or travellers cheques for what are known as Foreign Exchange Certificates, a currency which should also be used for all goods and services purchased in China. By maintaining an artificially low exchange rate, the authorities hope to maximise earnings of foreign exchange, but tourists are able to virtually double their money by dealing on the black market and obtaining local currency. Other illegal activities may include gambling, trading in counterfeit goods and so on. For local societies in destination areas, the impacts of tourism related crime are increased expenditure on law enforcement during the tourist season, financial loss as a result of fraud and black market dealings and, potentially, a fall in the number of tourist arrivals should a resort gain an unfavourable reputation for criminal activities, such as theft or mugging.

It should be noted that it is not always tourists who are the victims of crime (Ryan, 1991:159); often, it may be tourists themselves who commit crimes or become involved in illegal activities. This might be simply violent or drunken behaviour, resulting in a fine or a short term in prison, but tourists also engage in more serious crimes, such as drug smuggling, which, as evidenced by the experience of Western travellers in Thailand, can result in long jail sentences.

(c) Language

In most tourist-host encounters, language is the primary means of communication. More generally, however, language is also a significant cultural characteristic of any society and tourism, therefore, can have both immediate and longer term impacts on host communities. This is most likely to occur in larger, more established tourist destinations which attract mass tourists. In this situation local people are, in effect, obliged to learn and use the language of the dominant nationality of visitors in order to be able to deal and communicate with visitors on either a commercial or personal basis. Thus, most local people in Spanish tourist resorts who regularly come into contact with tourists speak English and in the Turkish resort of Alone, German is widely spoken.

It is not only through commercial necessity that foreign languages may be adopted or, in the case of some more isolated areas, that local dialects or languages begin to die out. The demonstration effect may result in local people wanting to learn the language of tourists and, either intentionally or unintentionally, adopting their mannerisms. Similarly, visitors may learn foreign languages or adopt local accents. For example, longer-stay British visitors in the United States frequently develop an American 'twang' in their speech. In more remote areas where the traditional, indigenous language is not widely spoken or only popular amongst the older generations, tourism may represent a threat to the very existence of that language. Thus, Brougham and Butler (1981) found that many local people on the Isle of Skye in Scotland felt that tourism was a major factor in the diminishing use of Gaelic, mainly as a result of increasing second-home ownership and the influx of seasonal workers from the mainland. Conversely, the impact of tourism on language may represent a benefit to local people, resulting in more job opportunities for those who learn a second language or become multi-lingual.

(d) Religion

Traditionally, religion was a major motivating factor of travel and tourism (see Chapter Two) and even nowadays a significant proportion of domestic and international tourism is for religious or spiritual purposes. However, since the advent of modern mass tourism, the relationship between tourism and religion has undergone a fundamental transformation, in as much as the majority of tourist visits to religious shrines, holy cities, temples, cathedrals, churches and other symbols or centres of religion are no longer for purely spiritual purposes. In other words, religion has become a commodity, a tourism product, and religious festivals or buildings have become spectacles to be gazed upon and collected along with other sights and attractions. As a result, in many destinations there has been increasing conflict between local communities, devout visitors and tourists. For example, simply the physical presence of large and often noisy groups of tourists who, frequently, take photographs of religious festivals or people worshipping with little consideration for the participants is a common and widespread problem. Visits to monasteries, religious retreats and centres of learning may also disrupt the lives of the inhabitants; even in Bhutan, where the number of tourists is strictly controlled, the authorities were compelled to prohibit tourists from visiting certain Buddhist monasteries as they were disturbing the monks.

Another situation where conflict may arise is where the traditional importance or meaning of religious rites or practices are not recognised, understood or respected by tourists. For example, in India, tourists frequently attempt to take photographs of the 'burning ghats', places alongside the River Ganges in Varanasi where deceased Hindus are cremated, thereby causing great offence to local people. In the extreme, disrespect for local religious custom may have severe consequences, such as tourists being physically attacked for taking photographs in temples or churches where it is forbidden.

Whilst it is easy to blame tourists for impacting upon local religious custom and practice, they themselves are often exploited by religious institutions, usually as a source of revenue. In some churches or cathedrals, collection boxes are often strategically placed near entrances and it is not uncommon to find book shops, souvenir stalls or even tea shops and restaurants located in religious buildings. In other cases, religious buildings have adopted a clearly definable dual purpose, separating their traditional function as a place of worship from their attraction to tourists and, hence, their earning potential. For example, entrance to a side chapel at St. Paul's Cathedral in London is free for worshippers, whereas entrance charges are levied on tourists visiting other parts of the building, including the crypt and the Whispering Gallery. It may be argued that tourists are being taken advantage of and that the fundamental meaning and purpose of the building is being abused but, nevertheless, tourism represents a significant source of income for essential repair and maintenance work. In this sense, the relationship between tourism and religion is positive in as much as tourism is contributing towards the preservation of a building which is of religious, architectural and national importance (see Bates, 1994, for a consideration of the problems facing Westminster Abbey as both place of worship and a major tourist attraction in London).

(e) Prostitution

One of the most emotive and publicised social impacts of tourism on destination countries, especially in the developing world, is the alleged effect it has on moral behaviour in general, and prostitution in particular. Cities such as Bangkok in Thailand and Manila in the Philippines have gained reputations for being the 'sex capitals' of the world, an image that has undoubtedly been reinforced by media attention and the availability of 'sex tours' that are openly advertised in some tourist generating countries, such as Japan. There is also no doubt that it is this image that draws many male Western tourists to these destinations.

However, prostitution as a tourist 'attraction' is not limited to south east Asian countries. Amsterdam's red light district has long been a tourist sight, London's Soho is famous for its sex shows and, as Ryan (1991:163) points out, the legalised brothels of Nevada are widely advertised in tourist centres such as Las Vegas. Indeed, virtually every major town and city around the world, whether or not a tourist destination, has a red light area. It is difficult, therefore, to assess the extent to which tourism has led directly to an increase in prostitution and, frequently, the role of tourism in this context is overstated. On the one hand, the development of tourism creates the conditions under which prostitution may thrive; tourists have temporarily left the restrictions of their own society and may be willing to indulge in activities which they would not normally consider at home (see Chapter Four). Furthermore, they are assured of anonymity, they may be willing to spend freely and, more generally, sex (the fourth 'S' after Sun, Sea and Sand) has been both an implicit and explicit part of tourism advertising for many years. For example, the Seychelles were once promoted as islands of love (see Turner and Ash, 1975) and at one stage suffered from one of the highest rates of venereal disease in the world.

On the other hand, prostitution as a social impact of tourism must be considered in a broader context. For example, Thailand has a reputation as a 'sex tourism' destination. The clubs and bars of the Patpong area of Bangkok are frequented by tourists and in popular beach resorts, such as Phuket and Koh Samui, it is easy for Western visitors to find a Thai 'girlfriend' who will stay with them for the duration of their stay. However, although the clubs of Bangkok undoubtedly depend on tourism for their business, and prostitution in beach resorts has certainly increased because of tourism, it has been estimated that, overall, there are up to one million Thai women who are involved in prostitution (Harrison, 1992:25). Of these, it has been alleged that only about seven per cent depend on overseas visitors, indicating that tourism has become the scapegoat for a wider social problem. The real cause of prostitution in Thailand possibly lies in the country's role as a rest and recreation centre for American soldiers during the Vietnam War, cultural norms and practices and, as is the case for most women who turn to prostitution, poverty. In countries without social welfare and with a social and cultural tradition which rejects unmarried mothers, prostitution may offer the only hope of survival. In this sense, and putting the wider moral issues to one side, tourism related prostitution may actually be viewed as a benefit to those concerned.

The conclusion must be that, generally, tourism does not actually cause prostitution but contributes to it although there are extreme cases, such as young boys in Sri Lanka being forced into male prostitution, where the link is more direct. Nevertheless, the social impact may be devastating, particularly with the spread of AIDS and other sexually transmitted diseases. It may be hoped that the publicity surrounding sex tourism and prostitution, especially in developing countries, will highlight the wider social problems in those countries and lead to greater controls but, at the same time, sex tourism represents the darker side of tourism induced exploitation of people and their culture.

THE CULTURAL IMPACTS OF TOURISM

Many of the impacts of tourism on host destinations and societies are relatively immediate, affecting family and social structures, gender roles, moral behaviour and so on. However, over time, the culture of host societies may also change and adapt either directly or indirectly as a result of tourism. Much of the literature concentrates on the way in which cultural forms, such as arts and crafts or animate expressions of culture, such as carnivals, festivals, religious events and historical re-enactments change as a result of tourism-related commoditisation (see Chapter Five). For example, traditional art forms and techniques may be trivialised and become mass produced for the tourist market, whilst tourism may be responsible for the transformation of cultural events into commercialised, staged spectacles which are devoid of all cultural meaning to the participants. Equally, tourism can provide both the impetus and the financial support for the preservation or revitalisation of traditional cultural practices. Indeed, one of the principles of sustainable tourism development is that tourism should contribute to the conservation of local culture by, for example, designing and constructing buildings in the vernacular style using traditional materials and methods.

However, artefacts, music, festivals and other practices are only symbols and expressions of culture, or cultural products. That is, the true culture of a society refers to its values and norms, its actual identity. It indicates the meanings people attach to different social institutions, such as education, religion, work and leisure, and, in effect, a society's culture is its way of life. All cultures and societies, unless totally isolated from the outside world, are constantly changing and developing, both as a result of changes within society and from outside influences. Internal economic, social and environmental developments within a society may be reflected in broader, cultural change, whilst international communication and information systems, advances in transport technology and a whole host of other factors have contributed to a sharing and dissemination of national cultures around the world. This has been manifested, in particular, in the spread of Western culture, or what has been referred to as the 'coca-colonisation' of the world.

One such factor which has contributed to cultural change is international tourism, especially tourism to countries which, culturally, are significantly different from the tourism generating country. It is difficult to separate the influence of tourism from other factors which induce cultural change and, as a high profile industry, it is frequently blamed for changes that are almost inevitable with or without the development of tourism. Nevertheless, it is generally accepted that tourism accelerates cultural change through the process of acculturation.

(i) Tourism and Acculturation
The theory of acculturation is that, when two different cultures

come into contact, over time they will become more like each other though a process of borrowing (Nuñez, 1989). That is, each society, to a greater or lesser extent, will adopt the values and attitudes of the other. By implication, if one culture is stronger or more dominant than the other then it is more likely that the borrowing process will be one way. The extent to which this will occur is also dependent on a variety of other factors, such as relative social and economic characteristics, the nature of the meeting, and the numbers of people involved. Thus, tourism, as an economic activity based upon inter-action between different societies and cultures, inevitably results in some form of acculturation.

In many instances, tourism induced acculturation may be slight and impossible to differentiate from broader cultural change. Thus, tourism between Europe and North America has little cultural impact when compared with the influence of television and the steady drift of American culture across the Atlantic. However, in other situations, tourism may be the dominant factor in cultural change, particularly in relatively isolated, developing countries. For example, since the early 1960s, when it became a popular destination for travellers on the Europe to India overland trail, Nepal has become a mainstream tourist destination on the subcontinent (although the area in Kathmandu where the 1960s 'hippies' found lodgings is still known as 'Freak Street'!). From just six thousand arrivals in 1962, about a quarter of a million tourists now visit the country each year (Shackley, 1994), only about 14 per cent of whom go on treks in the mountains. Much of the visible Westernisation of Kathmandu has, therefore, resulted directly from tourism.

The degree of acculturation experienced by a destination society depends on a variety of factors. Different types of tourists have different expectations, demands and motivations and, generally, acculturation is directly linked with the nature of tourist-host encounters (see Chapter Six). When such encounters are minimal or non-existent, such as when local populations are shielded from tourist resorts, then acculturation will also be limited. For example, most of the tourism development at Monastir on the Tunisian coast is in the *Zone Touristique*; there is little contact between tourists and nearby villages with the result that, in comparison with the tourist towns of Monastir and Sousse, there is little evidence of Western culture. Moreover, where tourism is predominantly organised and institutionalised, the level, type and duration of contact between tourists and local people and, hence, the potential for acculturation, is often in the hands of culture brokers. These may be tour operators, tour guides, translators or local representatives of holiday companies, all of whom act as mediators between tourists and local people. As Mathieson and Wall (1982:163) explain, by controlling tourist-host encounters they may also play a positive role in minimising the social and cultural impacts of tourism.

(ii) Tourism and Cultural Dependency

In the extreme, the cultural impact of tourism may result in the situation where the destination society becomes culturally dependent on the tourism generating country (see Erisman, 1983), the difference between this and acculturation being the degree of control exercised by the local community. In other words, the implication of acculturation is that the cultural transformation of a society may be conscious or subconscious but it is, nevertheless, voluntary. Conversely, cultural dependency is an involuntary condition, where the culture of a host society is *so conditioned by and so reflects the expansion of an external culture that there is a dominant/subordinate relationship between the cultural centre...and the cultural periphery* (Erisman, 1983). It results from economic and political dependency, a situation that has emerged in some developing countries which have come to be increasingly reliant on tourism, and represents foreign control over the cultural development of society. In a sense, therefore, cultural dependency signifies the final stage in the process of tourism-related neo-colonialism, the final abdication of the control of a tourism destination's economic, social and cultural future into the hands of a foreign country. Though not widespread, some destinations in the West Indies have, according to Erisman, become culturally dependent on the United States.

MEASURING THE SOCIO-CULTURAL IMPACTS OF TOURISM

As tourism is developed in more and more countries around the world, increasing attention is being paid to the impacts of tourism on the society and culture of host populations. Academics, researchers, pressure groups and the tourism industry itself are becoming increasingly concerned about the negative effects of tourism and new, alternative forms of tourism are being suggested to minimise these impacts. Sustainable tourism development has become the buzz word of the 1990s, tourism development that respects the environment, optimises benefits to tourists and to local communities and which minimises harmful effects on the tourism environment (for example, see Eber, 1992).

It is difficult to argue against the logic of sustainable tourism development although, in practice, it is unlikely to provide any long term solutions to the problems of mass tourism development. Indeed, there is much controversy about the effectiveness and practical worth of sustainable, alternative tourism in a world that appears to be becoming increasingly polarised between the tourism industry on the one hand and pressure groups on the other, although organisations, such as Green Flag International, work as mediators between the industry and environmental lobbies. Nevertheless, tourism development has undoubtedly been responsible for a variety of negative impacts around the world, some of which threaten entire eco-systems. The important point is, whilst it is relatively easy to measure or define physical or environmental impacts, applying concepts such as physical or ecological carrying capacity as the limits to development (see O'Reilly, 1986), the same cannot be said for socio-cultural impacts. In other words, what are the yardsticks by which social and cultural change are measured, and what are the limits beyond which such change should be halted?

In one respect, any form of tourism which impacts upon the life of local communities beyond an agreeable or acceptable limit (from the point of view of the residents) can be said to have exceeded the destination's social carrying capacity. That is, the scale and type of tourism should, in theory, be restricted to that which optimises economic and social benefits to the local community without causing undue problems. When considering social and cultural change, however, impacts are too often judged according to the values of modern Western societies rather than against the actual needs of the communities in destination areas. Too often, a Western cultural arrogance dictates what is right or wrong for other societies and cultures, societies which should be allowed to benefit from tourism, to modernise, to enjoy the standards of health, education, transport and housing that are taken for granted in the developed world. Similarly, with respect to domestic tourism, it is frequently the residents of towns and cities who try to impose their values on the residents of rural areas with little understanding for the needs of rural communities.

Tourism is a contradictory phenomenon (Crick, 1989). It depends upon an attractive environment, yet threatens to destroy it; it trivialises and commoditises cultural production, but can also preserve culture (see Grahn, 1991); it brings economic benefits to communities, yet it undermines traditional family and social structure; it provides opportunities for younger people, yet it polarises generations; it can lead to international understanding, yet it reinforces prejudices and international differences. By its very nature, tourism is a source of conflict and the imposition of the values of tourists, in defining the social and cultural limits for tourism development, does little to reduce that conflict. Tourism does have socio-cultural impacts which may be viewed as either positive or negative but the responsibility for assessing those impacts, for setting the limits of change, lies not with tourists or the tourism industry, but with host communities themselves.

Chapter Eight

Tourism in Postmodern Society

INTRODUCTION

Tourism, in particular mass tourism, is frequently described as a phenomenon of modern society. It is modern society, through the development of fast, efficient and economical forms of mass transportation, increasingly high levels of disposable income and the provision of socially-sanctioned free time (e.g. bank holidays and holidays-with-pay) that has provided the means and the opportunity for people to participate in tourism. Similarly, as discussed in Chapter Four, modern society is a major factor in tourist motivation. Whether to simply escape from the pressures and stress of modern life or to seek authentic, satisfying and meaningful experiences elsewhere, people increasingly believe that the only way to survive in modern society is to regularly remove themselves from it, albeit on a temporary basis. Thus, in short, tourism is both caused and sustained by modern society.

Yet, whilst there is much truth in this proposition, the relationship between the development of tourism and modern society is not so simple or clear cut as it may at first appear. The link between technological advance, increases in wealth and free time and the growth, in terms of both spread and volume, of tourism is universally accepted, but there is no indication as to why it is tourism, as opposed to other forms of leisure activity, that has become so widespread. Nor is tourism a single, well defined activity; tourism encompasses an enormous variety of holidays, modes of transport, destinations and activities, each of which increase or decrease in popularity over time. For example, in 1986, beach hotel holidays accounted for 72 per cent of all early (i.e. by December of the preceding year) holiday bookings out of the UK and beach self-catering holidays accounted for 17 per cent. By 1993, the proportion had changed to 38 per cent and 36 per cent respectively (McCarthy, 1994). This shift in demand may be put down to changes in fashion, but are changes in fashion related, in turn, to changes in the nature of modern society itself? In other words, the developments and trends that have, and continue to, occur in tourism cannot be simply explained as resulting from the modernisation of society.

It is important, therefore, to consider what is meant by the term 'modern society'. In particular, a distinction must be drawn between modern society in a temporal or periodic sense (i.e. modern as opposed to old, pre-modern or traditional) and modern society in the cultural sense. When analysing and explaining the development of tourism as a modern phenomenon it is, generally, the former approach that is adopted. That is, the birth of tourism as we know it today occurred when society was undergoing a process of industrialisation. Rapid technological advances throughout the modern era, commencing with the development of the railways during the nineteenth century, followed by the introduction of the motor car and, latterly, developments in aircraft technology, have resulted in the opportunity to travel being more widely available. At the same time, the mass tourism industry has been able to spread its net ever wider around the world; more and more countries now lie within what has been called the *pleasure periphery* (Turner and Ash, 1975) of modern, industrialised societies.

However, in order to fully understand the link between society and the development of tourism, in particular trends and changes in tourism practices rather tourism as an overall human activity, it is necessary to consider the nature or condition of modern societies. That is, modern, industrial societies are characterised by a combination of economic, political, social and cultural processes that together create a form of social life that sociologists call 'modernism'. These processes are constantly evolving and adapting according to the needs and demands of society so that, whereas modern in the temporal sense is a fixed state, modernity as a social condition is dynamic. Indeed, it has been suggested that as modern societies become post-industrial, with their economies becoming increasingly dependent on the service sector, modernity is being replaced by the condition of postmodernity (see Harvey, 1990). This chapter introduces the concept of postmodernism and examines the relationship between tourism and contemporary culture, in particular the way in which certain characteristics of postmodern society impact on tourism. It concludes with a consideration of the future of tourism from a sociological perspective.

FROM MODERNISM TO POSTMODERNISM

It is difficult to grasp the notion that society or, more specifically, the social and cultural character of life in modern society, is undergoing an identifiable process of transformation from one condition to another. Indeed, there is much debate amongst sociologists themselves as to whether modern society has moved beyond modernity and is now identified by a set of characteristics that may be amalgamated and described as the condition of postmodernity. As Urry (1990a:83) states, *in some ways it is difficult to address the topic of postmodernism at all. It seems as though the signifier postmodern is free-floating, having few connections with anything real, no minimal shared meaning of any sort.* What is certain is that many of the economic, political, social and cultural forms that characterise modernism have changed or are in a process of change. The extent to which these changes are inter-related and signify an identifiable and all-embracing development in the nature of contemporary society is arguable but, nevertheless, postmodernism is a term that can be usefully applied to the organisational and cultural condition of modern society in the late twentieth century.

The purpose here is not to analyse the arguments for and against postmodernism (for example, see Harvey, 1990; Lash, 1990; Jameson, 1984; Lyotard, 1984; and, more generally, Hall, Held and McGrew, 1992). Nevertheless, it is important to outline what is meant by postmodernism and to highlight common themes among its various definitions before considering the links between postmodern society and tourism. A problem is immediately evident in as much as there is little agreement as to what postmodernism actually is. For example, it can be used in a specific sense to describe new styles of art or architecture, it may be considered as an emergent sociological theory and a new basis for analysing and understanding the social world, or it may be viewed as the social and cultural response to economic development, the *cultural logic of late capitalism* (Jameson, 1984). Generally, however, postmodernism is seen to represent the end of the structured, organised and rational state of society; it signifies the replacement of *the dominance of an overarching belief in 'scientific' rationality and a unitary theory of progress* (Jary and Jary, 1991:487) with an emphasis on choice, a plurality of ideas and viewpoints, image and the ephemeral. In other words, postmodernism represents a departure from modernism; a logical starting point is, therefore, to briefly consider modernism, or the modern condition, from which postmodernism has evolved.

(i) Modernism

The emergence of modern societies in a temporal, periodic sense can be traced back to the Europe of the sixteenth and seventeenth centuries with successive agricultural, scientific and industrial revolutions. It was during this period that, rather than being dependent on and controlled by nature, societies were increasingly able to dominate their natural world to their own advantage. Thus, the advent of the modern era was dependent on technological advance and scientific knowledge and, therefore, those increasingly few societies today which have yet to embrace or to come under the influence of modern technology are described as pre-modern, traditional or authentic (see Chapter Five).

It was much later, however, that modernism, *that distinct and unique form of social life which characterises modern societies* (Hall, Held and McLennan, 1992:2), became an identifiable social condition.   Its origins lie in what is known as the Enlightenment Project, a period of intellectual thought dating back to the eighteenth century but the major tenets of which are reflected modernist thought and culture. During an age when *the scientific domination of nature promised freedom from scarcity, want and the arbitrariness of natural calamity* (Harvey, 1990:12), the Enlightenment thinkers envisaged a similar situation whereby society, through the accumulation and application of rational, scientifically-based knowledge, could be released from the constraints of irrational forms of thought, such as religion, superstition, myth, prejudice and ideology. Distancing themselves from history and tradition, they foresaw the triumph of reason and objective, rational knowledge and, through scientific progress and social scientific knowledge, they sought *mental liberation and social betterment amongst humanity generally* (McLennan, 1992:330). In particular, the Enlightenment thinkers believed that all natural and social phenomena could be scientifically explained and, therefore, that there was only one solution to any problem, a position that was soon to be challenged. Nevertheless, their support for scientific, technological and economic progress in pursuit of an improved human condition continued through to the height of modernism.

The real foundations of modernity were laid during the industrialisation and urbanisation of society during the nineteenth century, based upon the social and political institutions that evolved in the wake of rapid change. Five main processes, in particular, emerged to give modernism its identifying character:

(a) The development of political, secular systems and the concept of the nation-state, supported and sustained by large-scale bureaucratic systems which increasingly sought to organise, regulate and control social life.

(b) The growth and expansion of the capitalist economy based upon private ownership, leading to mass production and consumption and, internationally, the distinction between the industrialised, developed countries of the West and the rest of the world.

(c) The evolution of national and international society into a system determined by class, gender, race, occupation and wealth.

(d) The cultural transformation of societies from religious to secular and the emergence of popular forms of art, entertainment and music.

(e) The demise of individuality and development of the mass market with the public perceived as a homogeneous group with similar tastes and attitudes.

The major characteristic of modernism which emerged from the nineteenth century onwards, however, was that virtually every aspect of society and social life became differentiated. Guided by the over-riding objective of human and technical progress, modernism eschewed history and tradition; the past, the present and the future became separated, the present providing the opportunity to work towards an assured, better future. Time itself became a resource and, whereas during the pre-modern, agricultural era leisure and work intermingled within social life, a distinction came to be made between work time and leisure time. As tourism developed as an identifiable, widespread leisure activity it became a differentiated, separate sphere of social life with its own distinct time. It was also differentiated by location; work and home life was in the towns, tourism took place at the seaside. Urbanisation led to the differentiation between the countryside and towns and cities and their associated social systems, so much so that modernism largely came to be associated with the structure and order of urban society. For example, the inner-city tower-block architecture of the post-war period is often considered to be the most visible physical representation of modernism. Employment and work practices in capitalist industry resulted in differentiation between classes and occupation, the family became differentiated by gender roles; even nature and society became differentiated. Internationally, distinctions emerged between nation-states, between East and West, between North and South. In short, *modernism involves 'structural differentiation', the separate development of a number of institutional and normative spheres, of the economy, the family, the state, science, morality, and an aesthetic realm* (Urry, 1990a:84).

This differentiation, according to Urry, is both horizontal (i.e. distinctions between different institutions, roles, activities, etc.) and vertical (i.e. differentiations within different spheres of

226

social life). In other words, not only is there a distinction between, say, tourism and other forms of leisure activity but also, in modernist culture, a distinction between travel and (mass) tourism. Similarly, distinctions exist classical and popular music and within other art forms and between mass and elite production and consumption. In recent years, however, this horizontal and vertical differentiation has become less distinct; society has embarked on a process of *de-differentiation* (see Lash, 1990:11), the fundamental trait of postmodernism.

(ii) Postmodernism

Although much of the literature on postmodernism is concerned specifically with changes in cultural styles in literature, films, architecture and art, during the latter half of the twentieth century a number of changes in society, its institutions and its direction indicate that a much more fundamental and widespread social movement is underway. In other words, the postmodern style of, for example, architecture which incorporates classical or traditional styles (such as that preferred by Prince Charles) is symptomatic of a much deeper rooted shift in both the structure of society as a whole and its values and culture. Whether this shift has been towards a new, distinctive social and cultural experience is open to debate, yet there is little doubt that many of the ideas, objectives and cultural representations of modernism have been rejected and replaced by a new set identifying characteristics. Thus, postmodernism is, in effect, *a very loose term used to describe the new aesthetic, cultural and intellectual forms and practices which are emerging in the 1980s and 1990s* (Thompson, 1992:226).

Postmodernism can be considered from a variety of viewpoints. For example, in terms of the development of society, the modernist project of progress and change which rejected history and tradition has been replaced by a new concern for conserving, representing or recreating the past. Whether as a particular style of interior decoration, a style of building or as a tourism product in the form of heritage attractions, the past is being merged into the postmodern present. In other words, the past and the present have become de-differentiated as society appears to be gaining a preference for stability rather than change. Similarly, the distinction between society and nature has become de-differentiated as it has become increasingly recognised, under the aegis of the environmental movement, that, in order to survive, society must co-exist with rather than dominate nature.

Other structural differentiations, both horizontal and vertical, have also been reversed or removed. For example, class distinctions and boundaries are becoming less clear cut and bear more relation to family background and tradition as opposed to wealth or occupation. The emergence of multinational corporations and the interdependence of economies and organisations across international borders has diminished the distinct status of the nation-state whilst the increasingly cosmopolitan character of many societies has led to a de-differentiation of race, religion and culture. Thus, it is claimed that in Sydney it is possible to eat out at a culturally different restaurant every night for a year! Paradoxically, the globalisation of society has also served to heighten the awareness of how various societies and peoples are culturally different, in some cases leading to a resurgence of nationalism and fundamentalism. *Postmodernism is...*[also]...*anti-hierarchical* (Urry, 1990a:85); distinctions between high and low culture are disappearing as classical music becomes popular (for example, the music played by the violinist Nigel Kennedy and, in 1994, the Gregorian chants performed by the monks of the Benedictine monastery of Santo Domingo de Silos in Spain have both appeared in the Top 20 album charts), as art and commerce merge and, through techniques such as audience participation, contemplation of art becomes entertainment.

Further evidence of de-differentiation is to be found in the way in which reality is represented. That is, a major distinction between the cultures of modernism and postmodernism is that *modernism conceives of representation as being problematic whereas postmodernism problemises reality* (Lash, 1990:13). Modernism was concerned with reality and fact based upon logical and scientific explanation; representations of reality, through the arts, advertising and the news media, reflected the importance placed on reality. Under postmodernism, however, it is claimed that there is a diminishing distinction between reality and representations of reality. Indeed, such has been the growth in the production of images, representations and simulations, exacerbated by the explosion in electronic imaging, such as television, video, films and home computers, that image is merging into reality. In some instances, such as computer games, representations and simulations, replace reality. Social life in general and social identity in particular have become dependent on image; for example, styles and fashions represented in the media are translated into reality by an increasingly image conscious consumer society. The result is that postmodern society is dominated by image, by pastiche and by reproductions that lack depth and substance. It has become a *world of sign and spectacle...in which there is no real originality...Everything is a copy, or a text upon a text, where what is fake seems more real than real* (Urry, 1990a:85).

There are number of identifying characteristics, therefore, which indicate that, socially and culturally, modern society is evolving from a condition of modernism into a new state that may be described as postmodernism. Not all modern societies are becoming, or have become, postmodern and some may be more or less postmodern than others. For example, America may be described as more postmodern than the majority, if not all, European countries. Furthermore, different areas or regions within societies may possess cultural attributes which, to a greater or lesser extent, resemble those proposed by postmodernists, whilst not all aspects of culture within society need to be postmodern. Nevertheless, modern societies are increasingly adopting the characteristics of postmodernism, these being:

(a) a plurality of viewpoints and ideas, replacing the modernist concept of a uniform, mass society, and a corresponding rejection of all-embracing sociological theories. *The idea that all groups have a right to speak for themselves, in their own voice, and have that voice accepted as authentic and legitimate is essential to the pluralistic stance of postmodernism* (Harvey, 1990:48).

(b) the fusion (de-differentiation) of distinct areas of social and cultural activity and structure and the unification of popular, mass consumer (i.e. 'low') culture with 'high' culture.

(c) lifestyles which are increasingly dominated by spectacle, image, visual media and what has been called the 'three minute culture', resulting in ephemerality and a concentration on surface appearance rather than cultural depth.

(d) the merging of the past into the present and a preference for stability, implying a condition of discontinuity and a lack of historical progression (even though, paradoxically, postmodernism is considered to be the next stage in society's development after pre-modern and modern). *Post-modernism abandons all sense of historical continuity and memory, while simultaneously developing an incredible* *ability to plunder history and absorb whatever it finds there as some aspect of the present* (Harvey, 1990:54).

(e) the breaking down of traditional social structures and the emergence of new groupings and movements, such as conservation groups, political groups, New Age travellers, women's associations, special interest groups and so on which cross over ethnic, class, occupational and religious boundaries.

There are many other elements and characteristics of contemporary society that theorists claim to be indicative of a move into postmodernism. At the same time, there are others who completely reject the notion of postmodernism, either as a cultural paradigm or as a new social and cultural epoch, writing it off simply as a term used to describe developments in society and culture that depart from the sense of order, rationality, cohesion and uniformity that typified modernism. Whichever viewpoint is adopted, a number of fundamental changes are occurring in society which may have a corresponding effect on tourism.

POSTMODERNITY AND TOURISM

Tourism, according to Urry (1990a:87), is *prefiguratively postmodern because of its particular combination of the visual, the aesthetic, and the popular.* In other words, certain characteristics of postmodernism have always been identifiable in tourism, in particular the emphasis on spectacle and entertainment. For example, the English seaside resorts of the late nineteenth and early twentieth centuries, through to the heyday of holiday camps in the 1950s (see Ward and Hardy, 1986), vied for business by offering the best entertainment, the longest pier, the brightest lights or the most exciting funfair. Blackpool, with its tower, ballrooms, piers, promenade, zoo, illuminations, gardens and Pleasure Beach was, perhaps, the most postmodern resort of all, offering a world of image, illusion and fantasy in contrast to the reality of social life in the northern industrial towns and cities. Importantly, the social life of the tourists in the seaside resorts, thriving on spectacle and mass entertainment, made little or no distinction between art, culture and society; the holiday experience was characterised by the de-differentiation that has come to identify postmodernism.

Yet, even though tourism has displayed some of the characteristics of postmodernism, that postmodernism has, until recent times, been limited to the social sphere of tourism. In other words, whilst on holiday the social condition of tourists was essentially postmodern but tourism remained a distinct social activity, separate and differentiated from normal, modern, day-to-day social life. Specific periods of time were set aside for tourism, such as bank holidays and the annual week or fortnight's holiday, and tourism took place in distinct places, such as the seaside or the countryside. Thus, tourism, both temporally and spatially, provided a contrast to normal life; indeed, it was, and still is, that contrast which is the major attraction of tourism. To a large extent, however, the contrast or differentiation between tourism as a separate and identifiable sphere of social activity has diminished; it has become de-differentiated from, or merged with, other cultural and social activities to the extent that it may be suggested that most people are tourists most of the time. This can be better explained by considering how tourism place and tourism time have become de-differentiated and how developments in contemporary tourism are linked to postmodern culture.

(i) Tourism Place
Traditionally, people have travelled away from their place of residence and work in order to participate in tourism, a process

still typical of much contemporary tourism. This relocation is not purely in the simple sense of moving from one place to another, from the city to the seaside or from one country to another; it also involves a change of social and cultural environment from, for example, the urban environment (signifying work, constraint, normality) to the holiday environment (signifying fun, escape, relaxation and so on). Throughout the modern era the popularity of the traditional seaside resorts may have waned in favour of an ever increasing choice of different and more distant overseas destinations, but the basic formula has remained the same. More recently, however, new tourism destinations and attractions have emerged which indicate that the tourism place (i.e. where people participate in tourism) has become increasingly de-differentiated from the normal, day-to-day social place and, implicitly, the need for a change of environment has diminished.

A primary example of this 'postmodernisation' of tourist place is the development of urban tourism. If the residents of Bradford in the early 1900s had been able somehow to see into the future, they would have no doubt been amazed to discover that, in the 1990s, about six million people each year choose to visit their city as tourists! Virtually every major town and city in the UK now promotes itself as a tourist destination, frequently basing their tourism product on heritage which is a major manifestation of postmodern tourism. The important point is, however, that there no longer needs to be a contrast between tourism place and normal work/residence place; people can be tourists in their own town as the social activity of tourism itself becomes entwined with other social and cultural activities. Factories and other workplaces, both historical and modern, have become tourist attractions, whilst the development of new complexes which permit a variety of social activities literally under one roof has further spread the location and diversity of tourist place into the urban area. Shopping malls, in particular, have served to de-differentiate between activities such as shopping, eating, going to the cinema and other forms of entertainment; Urry (1990a:147) cites the West Edmonton Mall in Canada which, in 1987, attracted over nine million people making it the third most popular tourist attraction in North America after Disneyland and Disney World.

The best British example of the shopping centre as a tourist attraction is the Metrocentre in Gateshead. Along with some three miles of shopping malls, a multi-screen cinema, restaurants and an indoor fairground, it includes a number of themed areas, such as the Mediterranean village where restaurants and cafés are designed in Greek and Italian styles. Thus, an attempt has been made to represent overseas cultures and styles in an artificially created tourist place; image and fantasy have replaced reality, a situation that has been taken to its extreme by the development of inland resorts, such as the Center Parcs complexes. Here, simulation has been superimposed on reality in the ultimate manifestation of the de-differentiated, postmodern tourist place, an artificially created 'tropical' environment built in the normal, traditionally non-tourism place.

(ii) Tourism Time

As tourism has increasingly merged with other social and cultural activities, so too has the time spent being a tourist become less distinct from other time, such as work time and shopping time. Indeed, shopping, eating out, going to the theatre and participating in sports or hobbies have, in many instances, become tourist activities. For example, a weekend city-break may include the traditional activities of sightseeing and staying in a hotel, but shopping and visiting the theatre or cinema are also likely. Furthermore, the time made available for tourism has also increased, as has the definition of what tourism time is. Thus, tourism is no longer restricted to the annual holiday; weekend breaks, additional short holidays, day and even half-day trips are now considered to be tourism time.

Nor does an individual have to leave home to be a tourist. As discussed in Chapter Three, the tourism experience does not start and end with the physical departure from and return to the home environment. Anticipation and daydreaming in the planning process and remembering or reminiscing after the holiday are equally part of the tourism experience but, in the context of postmodern culture, such is the bombardment of images of other cultures, peoples and places presented by the media, whether incidentally or in specialist television programmes and newspaper and magazine articles, that armchair tourism has become a reality. The future development of electronic imaging technology, particularly in the field of virtual reality, will ensure that people can become tourists whenever they desire and without ever having to leave there own homes. Additionally, the plurality and multi-ethnicity of many modern societies, evidenced by the cultural diversity of restaurants, shops and entertainment in many towns and cities, means that, consciously or subconsciously, people are tourists for much of the time.

(iii) Time compression and tourism

One of the main characteristics of postmodernism is the merging of different time periods. Postmodernists look to the past as a sign of stability, and symbols of the past are reconstructed or represented in the present. Styles of architecture, interior design and clothing fashions are the most common examples where the past is visually represented in the present, but tourism is also a sphere of social activity where the past, and the future, become compressed into the present. Moreover, postmodernism's fondness for pastiche and image is particularly evident within the context of tourism.

There are two areas where the past, or representations of the past, influence tourism. Firstly, the enormous growth in the heritage industry (see Chapter Five) and the ways in which the past is represented are indicative the attraction of nostalgia as a tourist attraction. *Postmodernism and the heritage industry are linked, in that they both conspire to create a shallow screen that intervenes between our present lives, and our history* (Hewison, 1987:135). The past is brought into the present and is put on display through a variety of modern interpretative techniques, such as videos, the re-creation of noises and smells and live re-enactments, which represent the past, not as it was but as we wish to see it. History thus becomes a commodity, a tourist attraction based upon visual spectacle that is devoid of any true analysis of the past, a representation that bears little, if any, resemblance to reality. *The postmodern past is one where anything is possible, where fantasy is potentially as real as history because history as heritage dulls our ability to appreciate the development of people and places through time* (Walsh, 1992:113). In short, tourism based upon heritage is fundamentally postmodern.

The second way in which a relationship exists between the postmodern compression of the past into the present and tourism is linked to the issue of tourist experiences and the search for authenticity. If true authenticity is seen to lie in other times and places (i.e. in destinations or countries that have yet to adopt the characteristics of modern, Western societies), then tourism that is motivated by the desire to experience cultures that are essentially pre-modern is an attempt to merge the past into the present. Tourists who travel to developing countries superimpose different, past cultures onto their own, modern experience; in effect, they compress the past into their own present. It is, however, an unreal past. Just as heritage presents a rose-tinted version of history, so too do tourists in many destinations experience a sanitised experience of local, historical culture. They experience visual representations, a romanticised version that is confirmed by the images reproduced in the media, that in many cases bears little resemblance to the reality of life in the countries being visited. It is famous sights, colourful festivals, exotic food and the promise of adventure that sells tourism, not images of poverty, starvation, illness and other problems that beset many developing countries. This has important implications for the future development of tourism, particularly with respect to the way in which many destinations are permitted to represent themselves (to become modern), in a world that, some would argue, is transforming into a global village.

TOURISM AND THE GLOBAL VILLAGE

It is frequently stated that the world is getting smaller, that the world is becoming a global village and that, internationally, society is undergoing a process of globalisation. *'Globalisation' has become a widely used term within media, business, financial and intellectual circles, reflecting a fairly widespread perception that modern communications technology has shrunk the globe* (McGrew, 1992:65). Information technology that allows us to see history in the making and to communicate with people on the other side of the world at the touch of a button, transport technology that has brought distant countries ever closer in terms of travel time and opened up the whole world to international tourism, twenty-four hour dealings on the world's financial markets and a whole host of other factors have led to the impression that, in a physical sense, the world is, indeed, becoming smaller.

However, globalisation is concerned with rather more than the increasing speed and ease of international travel and communication. It is about a world where there is greater inter-dependence between nation-states; where the activities and influence of political, economic, industrial, religious and environmental organisations transcend national boundaries; where the events in one country can have serious and immediate effects on another country far away; where there has been a significant migration of people; above all, where there is increasing recognition that 'spaceship earth' is one world shared by a huge diversity of peoples with the potential to develop into the first global civilisation (see Perlmutter, 1991).

There is little doubt that globalisation is an identifiable process. For example, the demands made upon the United Nations as a peace keeping force, the expansion of multinational corporations, the attention paid to international problems, such as drug production and smuggling, pollution and international aid, the inter-dependency of the world's financial markets (as shown by the October 1987 crash), the world-wide impact of the Gulf conflict on international tourism, and the internationalisation of communities based upon religious, ethnic and cultural factors all point to the dissolving of national boundaries. Tourism itself has undoubtedly contributed to, and is affected by, the process of globalisation; increasing knowledge and understanding of different nationalities and cultures has broadened peoples horizons whilst the internationalisation of many countries populations has undoubtedly led to a significant increase in tourism.

As to the cause of globalisation, there is less agreement; it is variously attributed to technological advance, the development of a world economy, political factors, or a combination of all three (see McGrew, 1992). Equally, there is disagreement as to the longer term consequences of globalisation, although it is generally accepted that it will not be a smooth, harmonious process. In particular, the greater uniformity, integration and homogeneity of society that some envisage in the global village of the future is likely to be countered by efforts to retain national or local control and identity. For example, the move towards European union has served to highlight national differences, pluralistic societies emphasise cultural and religious differences and, as discussed in Chapter Seven, tourism can both increase and decrease the gulf between different nation-states. Nevertheless, a number of links can be identified between globalisation and tourism.

(a) One of the major characteristics (and causes) of globalisation has been the rapid advance in information technology. Tourists now have access to information and images of virtually every destination in the world which may be combined with visual images on the television (for example, 'reality' images, such as news programmes, specialist travel programmes and nature programmes, or representational images, such as the Australia of *Neighbours* or the California of *Baywatch*) and in other media. As a result, tourists demand greater choice and variety and are able to make better informed decisions. At the same time, the tourist industry is more rapidly susceptible to localised problems reported on the world stage. For example, the activities of terrorist groups or threats of muggings and other crimes can lead to rapid cancellations of holiday bookings.

(b) The continuing globalisation of the international economy has a number of characteristics, in particular the greater inter-dependency of nation-states and the ability of one country's financial policies to have an impact on the economies of other nation-states. Indeed, such is the extent of international financial dependency that some people question whether the concept of the nation-state as a separate, identifiable form of society is still applicable in the 1990s. Of equal importance has been the collapse of the centrally planned economies and the emergence of the free market in the former Eastern Bloc countries, which has signalled the advent of a truly worldwide capitalist economy and the gradual post-industrialisation of the advanced, Western economies. The latter has been matched by the industrialisation of a number of developing countries, in particular in the Far East, which means that, in a sense, the capitalist system which was once limited to individual nation-states has emerged as a worldwide economic phenomenon. This is part of what has been described as the age of *disorganised capitalism* (Lash and Urry, 1987). The implication for tourism is that international tourism will continue to increase but with much of the growth accounted for by tourism from newly industrialised nations and also from those countries whose economies have been released from central control. For example, the Cyprus Tourism Organisation signed an agreement with its Russian counterpart in March 1994 as the first step towards the development of charter package tourism to the island.

(c) It is generally accepted that globalisation is leading towards greater cultural homogeneity amongst nation states. For example, it is not unusual to see younger local people in many developing countries adopting the Western dress code of jeans, T-shirts and baseball caps whilst the spread and popularity of symbols of American culture, such as McDonald's, is testament to the increasing uniformity of the world. This homogeneity is exacerbated to an extent by tourism although the activities of multinational corporations and worldwide communication have done more to spread Western culture around the globe. Cultural homogenisation may be linked to tourism in contrasting ways. On the one hand, it may lead to an increase in tourism as countries which have become Westernised appear 'safer' to potential tourists whilst, on the other hand, increasing cultural homogeneity may reduce the attraction of some destinations. In the latter case, it will be necessary for resorts and destinations to improve the quality of their tourism product in order to compete against other similar destinations. Such a situation already exists around the Mediterranean coastal resorts where, for example, in the late 1980s, Turkey capitalised on the poor image of the Spanish resorts. Efforts by the Spanish to improve the quality of their destinations and Turkey's growing reputation for a lack of quality have now succeeded in returning Spain to its position as the most popular European tourist destination.

(d) The international tourism industry is becoming increasingly dominated by large, multinational corporations (MNCs). Both vertical and horizontal integration (see Holloway, 1994:62-66) within the industry has resulted in the creation of large organisations with operations in many countries and which own or control, through management agreements and franchises, many, if not all, elements of a tourism 'package'. Thus, it is not unusual to book a holiday, travel to the destination, stay in accommodation and go on organised tours with different companies that are all owned by one parent company. Deregulation of the airlines and a number of other factors will continue to lead to the domination of the industry by a few major 'players', with the result that tourists, smaller businesses and even some entire tourist destinations will be increasingly at the mercy of the large MNCs. For example, Thomsons controls some 40 per cent of all tourism into The Gambia, a situation that seriously weakens the country's ability to determine the future of its own tourism industry.

TOURISM, POST-FORDISM AND POST-INDUSTRIALISM

Modern society and the more general characteristics of modernism are inextricably linked to the industrialisation of society. The nineteenth century modernist project of progress and economic growth, based upon the control and domination of nature and the resulting transformation of natural, raw materials into tangible and saleable commodities, was firmly rooted in the development of industrial processes and systems. These processes, in turn, led to the rapid urbanisation of Western societies and the corresponding evolution of social structures and institutions which came to represent the differentiated condition of modern society. During the first half of the twentieth century modern industrial methods of mass production dominated Western economies but, more recently, there has been a recognisable shift towards new forms of production and consumption which reflect certain characteristics of postmodern society. This shift is marked by a growth in service, rather than manufacturing industries and a reorganisation of economic processes based upon flexible production but, in particular, the new, post-industrial age has signalled the end of the organised, rigid socio-economic structures of modernism and the advent of what has been termed post-Fordism.

Following the pioneering work of Henry Ford in developing mass production techniques for the manufacture of motor cars, the term Fordism has been used to describe both the system of mass production and the resultant mass consumption of the modern industrial era. Fordism was based on four main principles which became applicable to the production of most mass-produced goods (see Murray, 1989). Firstly, all products were standardised, which meant that, in turn, each part and task involved in production could also be standardised. Following from this, certain, standardised tasks could be undertaken by machines. Thirdly, those tasks which could not be relegated to machines were performed by workers who concentrated on one particular task. Finally, the assembly line system introduced greater efficiency by bringing the task to the worker rather than *vice versa*. The main characteristic of mass production was high set-up costs but low unit costs and, overall, its success depended on, amongst other things, economies of scale, long runs of standardised products, a willing workforce and, most importantly, a mass market that would accept mass produced, standardised products.

A similar, but more simple, process is identifiable in the development of mass tourism and, in particular, the package holiday. The product, the holiday, is 'manufactured' by tour operators using the standard components of transport, accommodation and attractions. Each component part is further standardised by, for example, providing one-class, charter air travel and a minimum choice of basic meals in hotels. Unit costs (i.e. the cost of the holiday) are minimised by high levels of 'production' and are ensured by techniques such as the block booking of hotel rooms and fitting a greater number of seats into aeroplanes used for charter flights than would normally be found on scheduled flights. Equally, as with all forms of mass production, the continued success of the mass, package holiday is dependent on the acceptance of the product by the consumer. In other words, tour operators are only able to sell cheap, mass produced package holidays to a large number of tourists if the tourists themselves are willing to accept the lack of choice, the impersonal service, basic standards of food and accommodation, and cramped transport. (Indeed, a common criticism of package holiday tourism is that the tourist is frequently treated more like a unit of production than as a customer!). Once an element of choice or a demand for non-standard products enters the system then the basis of mass production is undermined; the principles of Fordism no longer apply.

Since the late 1960s Fordist methods of mass production in general have been challenged by both workers and consumers alike and some have suggested that modern societies have entered the era of post-Fordism, an age where the consumer has begun to dictate, rather than accept, what is produced. Production methods have become more flexible as manufacturers, aided by advanced production technology and improved information systems, have had to become responsive to more rapid changes in consumer demand. Consumers themselves have become more quality conscious and demand a greater variety of products and styles, whilst products have a shorter 'life' as fashions change according to the image portrayed in the media. Many changes in demand are related to surface appearance; the basic product remains the same but the demand for colour, style or accessories changes. For example, the success of the clothes manufacturer Benetton is largely based on the company's ability to react quickly to changes in fashion colours, producing the same basic garments but in each year's new colours. Additionally, manufacturers have had to become more aware of different specialised and niche markets; the mass market approach has been replaced by market segmentation and the need for a variety of market research techniques.

Within the context of tourism, the transformation from a Fordist to a post-Fordist system of production and consumption is, interestingly, less marked than in other areas. It is frequently forecast that tourists are becoming more quality conscious and are demanding more specialised, tailor-made forms of holiday and travel experience (for example, see Lickorish, 1990) and, certainly, there is an ever-increasing variety of tourism products on offer. Newer, more distant destinations are being added to the range of package holidays offered by tour operators and different types of holidays, from adventure trips in the more exotic or remote regions of the world to winter-sun holidays for the older generations, are being supplied by specialist operators. At the same time, new products and attractions have been developed to satisfy the demands of an increasingly tourism and leisure oriented public whilst many popular overseas destinations, such as Spain and Cyprus, have recognised the importance of improving standards and quality to maintain market share. Nevertheless, recent experience, at least in Britain, demonstrates that the original Fordist-type basis of the package holiday remains as popular as ever. Early in 1994 a discounting campaign mounted by major tour operators and travel agents resulted in a level of bookings which was some 40 per cent up on the same period in 1993, the implication being that price is still the dominant factor is mass market holiday purchasing. Similarly, it was reported in April 1994 that Britannia, Thomsons' charter airline, was to increase the number of seats on its long-haul Boeing 767 flights, sacrificing passenger comfort for cheaper holidays (Atkins, 1994). Thus, mass tour operators in Britain appear to be resisting the trend towards a consumer-oriented industry, although this is, perhaps, evidence of the effects of post-industrialisation.

Rather than looking at changes in the manufacturing and consumption process in particular, the concept of post-industrialisation is concerned with the transformation of modern economies in general, the main proposition being that modern, industrial societies are becoming increasingly dominated by service economies. Within service economies, both the kinds of work that people do and traditional social structures based upon occupation have fundamentally altered. Manual jobs have been replaced by machines and some would argue that the expansion of the service sector has led to jobs which involve creativity, social interaction and the delivery of a service rather than the production of an inanimate object, jobs which are, therefore, more satisfying and worthwhile. Others would argue that, although the nature of work has changed, resulting in a less clear distinction between the traditional working class and an expanding middle class, new social distinctions are appearing. In a postmodern society that is increasingly dominated by information technology and communication, power resides with those who have access to and use of information; in conflict theory, the capitalists (i.e. the owners of the production process) have been replaced by the bureaucrats, but the relative position of the workers remains unaltered. Whichever viewpoint is adopted, the evidence suggests that, in the case of tourism, there is a move towards the provision of specialist, niche market products and an expansion in both the range and quality of holidays on offer yet, despite the generally accepted post-Fordist attitudes towards production and consumption, mass market package tourism remains firmly embedded in the industrial era.

TOURISM AND THE ENVIRONMENT

One of the principle areas in which postmodernism differs from modernism is within the context of the environment or, more precisely, *concern* for the environment. Continuing the basic tenet of the Enlightenment project, modernism sought human and economic progress through the domination and exploitation of nature and modern, Western societies appear, by and large, to have achieved that aim. Most Western societies are able to live beyond the constraints of nature; natural resources are exploited to provide fuel, shelter and food, there are cures for most common illnesses, and people are generally able to travel where and when they want without having to wait for favourable weather conditions. In short, most people, at least in the developed world, are able to live in societies that have overcome their subordination to most of nature's constraints, although natural disasters, such as earthquakes, hurricanes and floods, do not respect national or developmental boundaries.

In recent years, in particular since the early 1980s, modern society has become increasingly concerned with the conservation, rather than the exploitation, of the environment. Governments, societies and individuals alike have become more aware that, in the long run, the survival of the human race depends not on the domination of nature and the environment but the harmonious, sustainable co-existence with our natural surroundings. Issues such as the destruction of the rain forests, the greenhouse effect and global warming resulting from the burning of fossil fuels, acid rain, and the depletion of the ozone layer have all become of international concern. Similarly, specific cases of resource depletion, such as excessive and indiscriminate whaling, have been publicised by the activities of conservation organisations, whilst green political parties have challenged the policy of economic growth which is the driving force behind capitalist economies. The history, political and social development of environmentalism and the green movement is beyond the scope of this chapter (for example, see Porritt, 1984, Adams, 1990, Yearley, 1991) yet concern for the environment is not only evidence of the reflexive nature of postmodern culture (the interest in preserving the past being another example) but also one of the greatest challenges facing the future of the international tourism industry.

Concern about the negative impacts of tourism has been expressed for almost as long as tourism itself has existed as an identifiable, modern leisure activity. For example, in 1848 Thomas Cook wrote in his handbook for visitors to Belvoir Castle that *to the shame of some rude folk from Lincolnshire, there have been just causes of complaint at Belvoir Castle: some large parties have behaved indecorously...conduct of this sort is abominable, and cannot be too strongly reprobated* (Quoted in Ousby, 1990). In Britain the national park movement, culminating in the National Parks and Access to the Countryside Act 1949, was the first attempt to reconcile the demands of tourists with the need to protect the environment, but it was not until the late 1960s and early 1970s that concern about the effects of tourism became more widespread. A number of authors (see Mishan, 1969, Young, 1973, Turner and Ash, 1975, Rosenow and Pulsipher, 1979) expressed alarm at the rapid spread of mass, package tourism, predicting that the economic benefits of tourism could soon be outweighed by the costs associated with tourism's negative impacts: *the time has now come...to take the Goddess of Tourism off her pedestal and to place her in the garden with other statues* (Young, 1973:168).

Since the 1980s new, alternative forms of tourism have been suggested to counter the impacts of mass tourism; variously termed as responsible tourism, green tourism, appropriate tourism, good tourism or eco-tourism, they all share the viewpoint that tourism should be sustainable. At the same time, an enormous volume of literature produced by academics, researchers and tourism organisations has been published, all suggesting that tourism should be developed in harmony with the environment, maintaining a balance between the needs of local communities, visitors, the tourism industry and the physical, social and cultural environment. Various organisations, such as Tourism Concern, Green Flag International, the Centre for the Advancement of Responsive Travel (see Millman, 1989) and the Ecumenical Coalition On Third World Tourism, strive to increase awareness of the impacts of tourism and to promote forms of tourism (other than mass tourism) that respect the local environment and the needs of local communities. Others stress that the responsibility for sustainable tourism lies with tourists themselves, seeing the way forward as the development of 'good' tourism (Wood and House, 1991).

The impacts of tourism on the environment, the mechanisms and principles of alternative, sustainable tourism development and the arguments surrounding the viability of alternative forms of tourism to mass tourism are widely discussed and described in the literature. The purpose here, however, is to consider the extent to which the growth in tourism environmentalism is linked to the reflexive nature of postmodern culture.

Concern for the environment as a general and widespread social transformation is undoubtedly a major characteristic of postmodernism, representing the de-differentiation of society and its natural environment. It is also evidence of a significant departure from the Enlightenment/modernist project of progress through the control and exploitation of natural resources. The relationship between environmental concern, tourism development and postmodernism is not, however, quite so clear cut. Three points, in particular, cast doubt on the underlying motivation for the promotion of environmentally friendly, sustainable tourism.

(a) Much of the research into tourism is concerned with ways in which it may be more sustainable. In other words, it suggests methods of optimising the economic benefits of tourism to host countries whilst, at the same time, minimising the impacts of tourism on the environment. Rarely, however, is the question about the sustainability of tourism, in particular international tourism, as an overall social and economic activity ever raised. *There is no example of tourist use that is completely without impact. If the primary goal is one of protection and preservation of the environment in an untouched form then, in all truth,*

there cannot be tourism development at all (Cater, 1993).
Unlike other forms of economic activity that impact upon
and deplete the world's natural resources, the continuing
existence of tourism is generally accepted, no doubt because
it is an activity that is enjoyed by a large number of people.
It is also frequently motivated by the desire to escape from
modern society, which includes escaping from the concerns,
such as environmentalism, of modern life. Thus, it may be
argued that much of the environmental concern surrounding
tourism is motivated not by the need to protect the
environment *per se*, but to sustain it as the resource upon
which tourism depends. In short, the ultimate purpose is to
sustain tourism itself (see Jenner and Smith, 1992).

(b) Tourism is a global activity and, increasingly, new tourism
generating countries are emerging. Nevertheless, the great
majority of tourists originate in the developed, industrialised
countries which, to a greater or lesser extent, are becoming
postmodern and, not surprisingly, most of the multinational
corporations involved in tourism are also based in the main
tourism generating countries. Conversely, many tourism
receiving nations have yet to achieve modern status in an
economic and technological sense and are, in effect,
culturally pre-modern. Furthermore, many developing
countries cannot afford to be environmentally aware; caring
for the environment is a luxury to be indulged in once basic
needs have been catered for. In other words, they require
far greater amounts of foreign exchange than can be
realistically earned from the small-scale, sustainable
approach advocated by the (Western) promoters of
sustainable tourism. Therefore, unlike those countries which
have established and profitable tourism industries and
diverse economies and can afford conservation programmes,
developing nations depend on larger scale tourism

development as a vital source of income. Much of the concern for the impact of tourism is, therefore, an attempt to impose postmodern social values on nations which are unwilling, or in no position, to accept those values.

(c) It is important not to confuse genuine environmental concern with the postmodernist de-differentiation of the past and present. To a great extent, the concept of sustainable tourism proposes the conservation or protection of both the physical and the socio-cultural environment of destination areas. Whilst the protection of the natural environment from excessive or inappropriate tourism development and use falls entirely within the parameters of environmentalism, the desire to preserve social and cultural traditions and practices is linked to the issues of authenticity (see Chapter Five) and time compression. In other words, the preservation of the socio-cultural environment in tourist destinations, as proposed by the tourism industry, is the preservation of *signs* of past cultures (in comparison to postmodern culture). Such 'environmentalism', therefore, is based upon the need to maintain the appeal of the environment to potential tourists and is, again, an effort to impose postmodern cultural values upon other societies.

Overall, then, the issues of postmodern environmental concern about the impacts of tourism should be considered from a global perspective. Whilst many tourism generating countries reflect the broader, international concern for the environment as a whole it must be remembered that many countries, particularly in the developing world, are either unwilling or unable, for financial reasons, to embrace the concept of environmentalism and sustainable development. For them, the development of tourism is seen as a valuable tool to aid economic growth and diversification; only when a certain level of economic, technological and social development has been achieved can such countries begin to consider environmental issues. At the same time, distinctions need to be drawn between the conservation of scarce natural resources, including those upon which tourism depends, and the preservation of societies and cultures which, to tourists from modern societies, symbolise different, past ages. The challenge for the tourism industry is to question its own motives in promoting sustainable or alternative forms of tourism; the challenge for postmodern, environmentally sensitive societies is to allow other societies to develop and modernise.

TOURISM AND SOCIETY: TOWARDS THE FUTURE

Predicting the future of any sphere of social or economic activity is fraught with difficulties. At best, a reasonable picture can be built up from the analysis of past trends, historical evidence, relevant current information and educated guesswork; at worst, it can amount to little more than crystal-ball gazing. Attempting to forecast future trends in tourism is no exception. Statistics which detail the historical growth in tourism arrivals, tourism flows and other information can be combined with relevant factors, such as demographic trends and changes in the supply of tourism, to provide a reasonably accurate idea of the shorter term future. However, accurate predictions require accurate information and it is generally accepted that, on a worldwide basis, tourism statistics tend to be of variable quality. Furthermore, tourism is a notoriously fickle business; it can be affected by exchange rate fluctuations, economic recessions in tourism generating countries, adverse political conditions in destination regions, wars, changes in taste or fashion, and a whole host of other factors. Nevertheless, since the 1960s, international tourism has grown at a steady, if not spectacular, rate and, in the longer term, has proved to be relatively immune to short term political and economic upheavals. Thus, since 1980, the number of international tourism arrivals has grown at between four and five per cent annually, a rate of growth which is likely to continue well into the next century.

The World Tourism Organisation (WTO, 1992) has identified two sets of variables which will influence the way in which tourism develops into the future. These are market forces, or factors which include changes in the demand for and supply of tourism products and services, and exogenous variables, factors which although not directly connected with tourism can, nevertheless, have an impact on it. The latter group includes political, economic, legislative, technological and social trends. From a sociological perspective there are factors identifiable in both sets of variables which will combine to influence the future direction and growth of tourism in both a domestic and an international context.

The demand for tourism in the major generating countries will be influenced by a variety of factors. Demographic and social trends, such as ageing populations, increasing numbers of single or childless households, couples having children later in life, people who have retired early and, generally, populations which enjoy greater levels of both free time and disposable income, will result in both the absolute numbers of tourists increasing and an increase in the number of holidays taken by individuals. Importantly, however, the present middle-aged and younger generations are those which have grown up with tourism. They are used to tourism, they do not see it as a luxury but an essential feature of modern, social life, and many are experienced tourists. This may result in a two-tier demand structure for tourism, namely, those who are content with the traditional, institutionalised type of package holiday, and those who demand a greater variety of destination and type of holiday. The latter may also become identified as the new type of environmentally aware tourists, 'good' tourists who demand sustainable tourism products although, as discussed earlier in this chapter, this is more likely to result from the cultural (postmodern) values in tourism generating countries than from a genuine concern for the environment.

New tourism generating countries will also appear on the world tourism map, both as a result of the industrialisation of some developing countries and the spread of democracy. The countries of eastern Europe and the former Soviet Union are regarded as valuable potential source of tourists although political unrest and economic instability will limit growth in the early years. However, the emergent economic powers in the Far East, such as Korea and Taiwan, will join Japan as major tourism generators. These new tourism generators will also become tourist destinations in their own right; indeed, the East Asia and Pacific region accounted for the largest growth in international arrivals between 1980 and 1990, achieving growth of about 10 per cent per annum compared with less than four per cent annual growth in Europe. Nevertheless, the European region will continue to be the world's largest generator and receiver of tourism, accounting for over 60 per cent of all international arrivals. The growth in tourism will be facilitated by increasing efficiency within the tourism industry, in particular within the context of air transport where technological advances in both aircraft and information/management systems will ensure that, subject to energy costs, prices will remain at a low level.

There is undoubted optimism that tourism, as an *economic* activity, will maintain and strengthen its reputed position as the world's largest industry. That optimism must be tempered, however, by the recognition that tourism, perhaps more importantly, is a *social* activity. Some societies generate tourism, others receive and depend on tourism; the international travel and tourism industry depends on the continuing desire of individuals to travel. Thus, developments and changes in the structures and values of societies may influence future developments in tourism both positively and negatively. For example, globalisation is a double-edged sword; firstly, it may lead to greater homogenisation, integration and universalisation amongst the world's nations which, as discussed earlier, may result in either an increase or a decrease in tourism. Secondly, it may lead to a resurgence in nationalism and, perhaps, an eventual reaction against the inherently imperialistic nature of international tourism. In a similar vein, much of the tourism to destinations outside the developed, western world depends upon and is motivated by the 'otherness', the distinct social and cultural characteristics, of those destinations. Maintaining those characteristics in order to remain attractive to tourists, those destinations may, in the extreme, become little more than 'living museums' satisfying the thirst of tourists for 'authentic' experiences. In short, international tourism may, in the longer term, achieve the opposite of its primary purpose of economic, technological and social modernisation in destination countries.

Societal change in tourism generating countries may also influence the future development of tourism. For example, less than one hundred years ago it was unfashionable to have a suntan. If fashions were to change once again, or concern about the cancer risks of sunbathing were to increase, the impact on the traditional sun, sea and sand summer package business could be catastrophic. Changes in work practices and more flexible approaches to education, such as a change in the traditional three term and long summer holiday system of schooling, would be of benefit to tourists, the industry and destinations alike as the constraints of seasonality are removed. In a more general sense, the quality of life in modern, Western countries may improve to the extent that, as Krippendorf (1987) hopes, people will no longer feel the need to escape. Equally, the development of technology, such as virtual reality, or the spread and acceptance of attractions such as the Center Parcs concept, may prove to be a more enjoyable and relaxing experience than the 'actual reality' of tourism which is becoming increasingly characterised by crowds, delays, pollution, traffic jams, mass production, and so on. Whatever the future holds for tourism, it is essential that knowledge about the interdependence between tourism and the societies that motivate, generate and receive tourists is increased and used to guide its future development to the benefit of all.

References

Adams, William, 1990, *Green Development: Environment and Sustainability in the Third World*, Routledge, London

Adler, Judith, 1989, Origins of Sightseeing, *Annals of Tourism Research*, 16(1), 7-29

Anastasopoulos, Petros, 1992, Tourism and Attitude Change: Greek Tourists Visiting Turkey, *Annals of Tourism Research*, 19(4), 629-642

Andronicou, Antonios, 1979, Tourism in Cyprus, in *Tourism: Passport to Development?*, E. de Kadt (ed), Oxford University Press, New York

Ap, John, 1992, Residents' Perceptions on Tourism Impacts, *Annals of Tourism Research*, 19(4), 665-690

Ap, John and Crompton, John, 1993, Residents' strategies for Responding to Tourism Impacts, *Journal of Travel Research*, 32(1), 47-50

Atkins, David, 1994, Britannia Waives the Legroom, *Daily Telegraph*, April 16th

Barthes, Roland, 1967, *Elements of Sociology*, Hill and Wang, New York

Bates, Paul, 1994, Pilgrims or Tourists?, *In Focus*, Tourism Concern, 11, 14-15

Belisle, Francois and Hoy, Don, 1980, The Perceived Impact of Tourism by Residents: A Case Study in Santa Marta, Colombia, *Annals of Tourism Research*, 7(1), 83-101

Bilton, Tony; Bonnett, Kevin; Jones, Philip; Stanworth, Michelle; Sheard, Ken and Webster, Andrew, 1987, *Introductory Sociology*, 2nd Edition, Macmillan, Basingstoke

Boorstin, Daniel, 1964, *The Image: A Guide to Pseudo-Events in America*, Harper & Row, New York

Brendon, Piers, 1991, *Thomas Cook: 150 Years of Popular Tourism*, Secker & Warburg, London

Britton, Robert, 1979, The Image of the Third World in Tourism Marketing, *Annals of Tourism Research*, 6, 318-329

Britton, Steve, 1982, The Political Economy of Tourism in the Third World, *Annals of Tourism Research*, 9, 331-358

Brougham, J. and Butler, R., 1981, A Segmentation Analysis of Resident Attitudes to the Social Impact of Tourism, *Annals of Tourism Research*, 8(4), 569-590

Buck, R., 1977, The Ubiquitous Tourist Brochure: Explorations of its Intended and Uneintended Use, *Annals of Tourism Research*, 4(4), 195-207

Budowski, Gerado, 1976, Tourism and Conservation: Conflict, Co-existence or Symbiosis?, *Environmental Conservation*, 3(1), 27-31

Bull, Adrian, 1991, *The Economics of Travel and Tourism*, Pitman, London

Butler, Richard, 1980, The Concept of a Tourism Area Cycle of Evolution, *Canadian Geographer*, 24, 5-12

Butler, Richard, 1991, Tourism, Environment, and Sustainable Development, *Environmental Conservation*, 18(3), 201-209

Butler, Richard, 1992, Alternative Tourism: The Thin End of the Wedge, in *Tourism Alternatives*, Smith, V. and Eadington, W., (eds), University of Pennsylvania Press, Philadelphia

Buzard, James, 1993, *The Beaten Track*, Oxford University Press

Casson, Lionel, 1974, *Travels in the Ancient World*, George Allen and Unwin, London

Cater, Erlet, 1993, Ecotourism in the Third World: Problems for Sustainable Tourism Development, *Tourism Management*, April, 85-90

Clarke, John and Critcher, Chas., 1985, *The Devil Makes Work: Leisure in Capitalist Britain*, Macmillan, Basingstoke

Cohen, Eric, 1972, Towards a Sociology of International Tourism, *Social Research*, 39(1), 64-82

Cohen, Eric, 1974, Who is a Tourist? A Conceptual Clarification, *Sociological Review*, 22(4), 527-555

Cohen, Eric, 1979a, Rethinking the Sociology of Tourism, *Annals of Tourism Research*, 6(1), 18-35

Cohen, Eric, 1979b, A Phenomenology of Tourist Experiences, *Sociology*, 13, 179-201

Cohen, Eric, 1984, The Sociology of Tourism: Approaches, Issues and Findings, *Annual Review of Sociology*, 10, 373-392

Cohen, Eric, 1988a, Authenticity and Commoditisation in Tourism, *Annals of Tourism Research*, 15(3), 371-386

Cohen, Eric, 1988b, Traditions in the Qualitative Sociology of Tourism, *Annals of Tourism Research*, 15(1), 29-46

Cohen, S. and Taylor, L., 1976, *Escape Attempts: The Theory and Practice of Resistance in Everyday Life*, Penguin, Harmondsworth

Cooper, Chris (ed), 1991, *Progress in Tourism, Recreation and Hospitality Management Vol III*, Bellhaven Press, London

Cooper, Chris; Fletcher, John; Gilbert, David and Wanhill, Stephen, 1993, *Tourism: Principles & Practice*, Pitman, London

Coppock, J., 1977, *Second Homes: Curse or Blessing*, Pergamon Press, Oxford

Crick, Malcom, 1989,, Representations of International Tourism in the Social Sciences, *Annual Review of Anthropology*, 18, 307-344

Crompton, John, 1979, Motivations for Pleasure Vacation, *Annals of Tourism Research*, 6, 408-424

Culler, Jonathon, 1981, Semiotics of Tourism, *American Journal of Semiotics*, 1(1-2), 127-140

Dalen, E., 1989, Research into Values and Consumer Trends in Norway, *Tourism Management*, 10(3), 183-186

Damer, Sean, 1990, *Glasgow: Going for a Song,* Lawrence and Wishart, London

Dann, Graham and Cohen, Eric, 1991, Sociology and Tourism, *Annals of Tourism Research,* 18(1), 155-169

Dann, Graham, 1977, Anomie, Ego-Enhancement and Tourism, *Annals of Tourism Research,* 4(4), 184-194

Dann, Graham, 1981, Tourist Motivation: An Appraisal, *Annals of Tourism Research,* 8(2), 187-219

Dann, Graham, 1989, The Tourist as Child: Some Reflections, *Cahiers de Tourisme,* Série C, 135, CHET, Aix-en-Provence

Dann, Graham, 1994, Tourism: The Nostalgia Industry of the Future, in *Global Tourism: The Next Decade,* Theobald, W (ed), Butterworth Heinemann

Davis, F., 1979, *Yearning for Yesterday: A Sociology of Nostalgia,* Free Press, New York

de Kadt, Emanuel, 1979, *Tourism: Passport to Development?* Oxford University Press, New York

Deitch, Lewis, 1989, The Impact of Tourism on the Arts and Crafts of the Indians of the Southwestern United States, in *Hosts and Guests: The Anthropology of Tourism (2nd edition),* Smith, V., (ed), UPP, Philadelphia

Dieke, Peter, 1993, Tourism and Development Policy in The Gambia, *Annals of Tourism Research,* 20, 423-449

Dilley, Robert, 1986, Tourist Brochures and Tourist Images, *Canadian Geographer,* 30(1), 59-65

Doxey, G., 1975, A Causatiuon Theory of Visitor-Resident Irritants, Methodology, and Research Inferences, *The Impact of Tourism,* Sixth Annual Conference Proceedings of the Travel Research Association, San Diego, 195-198

Dunning, J. and McQueen, M., 1982, Multinational Corporations in the Hotel Industry, *Annals of Tourism Research,* 9(1), 69-90

Eber, Shirley (ed), 1992, *Beyond the Green Horizon: Principles for Sustainable Tourism,* WWF/Tourism Concern, Godalming

Edwards, A., 1987, *Choosing Holiday Destinations: The Impact of Exchange Rates and Inflation*, Special Report No.1109, Economic Intelligence Unit, London

Edwards, Elizabeth, 1993, The Tourist Icon in Tourism, *In Focus*, Tourism Concern, 6, 4-5

EIU, 1992, Cyprus, *International Tourism Reports No.2*, Economic Intelligence Unit, London

Emery, F., 1981, Alternative Futures in Tourism, *International Journal of Tourism Management*, March, 241-255

Erisman, H. Michael, 1983, Tourism and Cultural Dependency in the West Indies, *Annals of Tourism Research*, 10, 337-361

ETB, 1991, *Tourism and the Environment: Maintaining the Balance*, English Tourist Board, London

ETB, 1993, Holiday Tourism by the British, *Insights*, F-6, English Tourist Board, London

Feifer, Maxine, 1985, *Going Places*, Macmillan, London

Forster, J., 1964, The Sociological Consequences of Tourism, *International Journal of Comparative Sociology*, 5(2), 217-227

Gerakis, A., 1965, The Effects of Exchange Rate Devaluation & Revaluation on Receipts from Tourism, *IMF Papers*, 12(1)

Getz, Donald, 1992, Tourism Planning and Destination Life Cycle, *Annals of Tourism Research*, 19(4), 752-780

Gilbert, David, 1991, An Examination of the Consumer Behaviour Process Related to Tourism, in *Progress in Tourism, Recreation and Hospitality Management Vol III*, Cooper, C. (ed), Bellhaven Press, London

Goffman, Irving, 1959, *The Presentation of Self in Everyday Life*, Penguin, Harmondsworth

Goodall, B., 1991, Understanding Holiday Choice, in *Progress in Tourism, Recreation and Hospitality Management Vol III*, Cooper, C. (ed), Bellhaven Press, London

Gottlieb, A., 1982, Americans' Vacations, *Annals of Tourism Research*, 9, 165-187

Graburn, Nelson, 1976, *Ethnic and Tourist Arts: Cultural Expressions from the Fourth World*, University of California Press, Berkeley

Graburn, Nelson, 1983, The Anthropology of Tourism, *Annals of Tourism Research*, 10(1), 9-33

Graburn, Nelson, 1989, Tourism: The Sacred Journey, in *Hosts and Guests: The Anthropology of Tourism (2nd edition)*, Smith, V. (ed), UPP, Philadelphia

Grahn, Patrik, 1991, Using Tourism to Protect Existing Culture: A Project in Swedish Lapland, *Leisure Studies*, 10, 33-47

Gray, H., 1970, *International Travel-International Trade*, DC Heath, Lexington

Greenwood, Davydd, 1989, Culture by the Pound: An Anthropological Perspective on Tourism as Cultural Commoditisation, in *Hosts and Guests: The Anthropology of Tourism (2nd edition)*, Smith, V. (ed), UPP, Philadelphia

Hall, Stuart, Held, David and McLennan, Gregor, 1992, Introduction to *Modernity and its Futures*, Hall, S., Held, D. and McGrew, T., (eds), Polity Press, Cambridge

Hall, Stuart; Held, David and McGrew, Tony, (eds) 1992, *Modernity and its Futures*, Polity Press, Cambridge

Harrison, David, 1992, Tourism to less Developed Countries: The Social Consequences, in *Tourism and the Less Developed Countries*, Harrison, D., (ed), Bellhaven Press, London

Harvey, David, 1990, *The Condition of Postmodernity*, Blackwell, Oxford

Haywood, K. Michael, 1988, Responsible and Responsive Tourism Planning in the Community, *Tourism Management*, 9, 105-118

Hewison, Robert, 1987, *The Heritage Industry: Britain in a Climate of Decline*, Methuen, London

Hewison, Robert, 1993, Field of Dreams, *The Sunday Times*, January 3rd

Holden, Peter, (ed) 1984, *Alternative Tourism with a Focus on*

Asia, ECTWT, Bangkok, Thailand

Holloway, J. Christopher, 1994, *The Business of Tourism (4th Edition)*, Pitman, London

Ioannides, Dimitri, 1992, Tourism development Agents: The Cypriot Resort Cycle, *Annals of Tourism Research*, 19(4), 711-731

Iso-Ahola, Seppo, 1982, Toward a Social Psychological Theory of Tourism Motivation: A Rejoinder, *Annals of Tourism Research*, 9(2), 256-262

Jameson, Fredric, 1984, Postmodernism, or the Cultural Logic of Late Capitalism, *New Left Review*, 146, 53-92

Jary, David and Jary, Julia, 1991, *Collins Dictionary of Sociology*, Harper Collins

Jebb, Miles, 1986, *Walkers*, Constable, London

Jenkins, Carson, 1990, Tourism: Is Future Demand Changing? in *The Horwath Book of Tourism*, Quest, M (ed), Macmillan, London

Jenkins, Carson, 1991, Tourism Development Strategies, in *Developing Tourism Destinations*, Likorish, L (ed), Longman, Harlow

Jenner, Paul and Smith, Christine, 1992, *The Tourism Industry and the Environment*, Special Report No.2453, Economic Intelligence Unit, London

Johnson, Peter and Thomas, Barry, 1992, *Choice and Demand in Tourism*, Mansell Publishing, London

Krippendorf, Jost, 1986, Tourism in the System of Industrial Society, *Annals of Tourism Research*, 13(4), 517-532

Krippendorf, Jost, 1987, *The Holiday Makers*, Heinemann, Oxford

Lash, Scott, 1990, *Sociology of Postmodernism*, Routledge, London

Lash, Scott and Urry, John, 1987, *The End of Organised Capitalism*, Polity, Cambridge

Lea, John, 1988, *Tourism and Development in the Third World*, Routledge, London

Lett, James, 1983, Ludic and Liminoid Aspects of Charter Yacht Tourism in the Caribbean, *Annals of Tourism Research*, 10(1), 35-56

Lett, James, 1989, Epilogue to Touristic Studies in Anthropological Perspective, in *Hosts and Guests: The Anthropology of Tourism (2nd edition)*, Smith, V., (ed), UPP, Philadelphia

Lickorish, Leonard, 1990, Tourism Facing Change, in *The Horwath Book of Tourism*, Quest, M (ed), Macmillan, London

Lowenthal, David, 1990, *The Past is a Foreign Country*, Cambridge University Press

Lowyck, Els; Van Langenhove, Luk and Bollaert, Livin, 1992, Typologies of Tourist Roles, in *Coice and Demand in Tourism*, Johnson, P. and Thomas, B., (eds) Mansell Publishing, London

Lumley, R., (ed) 1988, *The Museum Time-Machine*, Routledge, London

Lyotard, Jean-Francois, 1984, *The Postmodern Condition: A Report on Knowledge*, Manchester University Press, Manchester

MacCannell, Dean, 1973, Staged Authenticity: Arrangements of Social Space in Tourist Settings, *American Journal of Sociology*, 79, 589-603

MacCannell, Dean, 1976, *The Tourist: A New Theory of the Leisure Class*, Shocken Books, New York

MacCannell, Dean, 1989, *The Tourist: A New Theory of the Leisure Class (2nd Edition)*, Shocken Books, New York

Macnaught, Timothy, 1982, Mass Tourism and the Dilemmas of Modernisation in Pacific Island Communities, *Annals of Tourism Research*, 9, 359-381

Mannell, Roger and Iso-Ahola, Seppo, 1987, Psychological

Nature of Leisure and Tourism Experience, *Annals of Tourism Research*, 14, 314-331

Mansfeld, Yoel, 1992, From Motivation to Actual Travel, *Annals of Tourism Research*, 19, 399-419

Maslow, A., 1943, A Theory of Human Motivation, *Psychological* Review, 50,370-396

Mathieson, Alister and Wall, Geoffrey, 1982, *Tourism: Economic, Physical and Social Impacts*, Longman, Harlow

McCarthy, Terry, 1994, Booking Trends, *Travel Weekly Plus*, 2, March, p.35

McGrew, Anthony, 1992, A Global Society?, in *Modernity and its Futures*, Hall, S., Held, D. and McGrew,T.,(eds), Polity Press, Cambridge

McIntosh, Robert and Goeldner, Charles, 1990, *Tourism: Principles, Practices and Philosophies*, Wiley, New York

McKean, Philip, 1989, Towards a Theoretical Analysis of Tourism: Economic Dualism and Cultural Involution in Bali, in *Hosts and Guests: The Anthropology of Tourism (2nd edition)*, Smith, V., (ed), UPP, Philadelphia

McKercher, Bob, 1993, Some Fundamental Truths About Tourism, *Journal of Sustainable Tourism*, 1(1), 6-16

McLennan, Gregor, 1992, The Enlightenment Project Revisited, in *Modernity and its Futures*, Hall, S., Held, D. and McGrew,T., (eds), Polity Press, Cambridge

McPheters, L. and Stronge, W., 1974, Crime as an Environmental Externality of Tourism, *Land Economics*, 50, 359-381

Middleton, Victor, 1988, *Marketing in Travel and Tourism*, Heinemann, Oxford

Mill, Robert and Morrison, Alistair, 1985, *The Tourism System*, Prentice Hall International, New Jersey

Millman, Roger, 1989, Pleasure Seeking vs the 'Greening' of World Tourism, *Tourism Management*, December, 275-278

Milman, Andy, and Reichal, Arie and Pizam, Abraham, 1990,

The Impact of Tourism on Ethnic Attitudes: The Israeli-Egyptian Case, *Journal of Travel Research*, 29, 45-49

Mishan, E., 1969, *The Costs of Economic Growth*, Penguin, Harmondsworth

Moutinho, Luiz, 1987, Consumer Behaviour in Tourism, *European Journal of Marketing*, 21(10), 5-44

Murphy, Peter, 1983, Tourism as a Community Industry, *Tourism Management*, 4(3), 180-193

Murphy, Peter, 1985, *Tourism: A Community Approach*, Routledge, London

Murphy, Peter, 1988, Community Driven Tourism Planning, *Tourism Management*, 9, June, 96-104

Murray, Robin, 1989, Fordism and Post-Fordism, in *New Times*, Hall, S. and Jacques, M., (eds), Lawrence & Wishart, London

Nash, Dennison, 1981, Tourism as an Anthropological Subject, *Current Anthropology*, 22(5), 461-481

Nash, Dennison, 1989, Tourism as a Form of Imperialism, in *Hosts and Guests: The Anthropology of Tourism (2nd edition)*, Smith, V., (ed), UPP, Philadelphia

Nash, Dennison and Smith, Valene, 1991, Anthropology and Tourism, *Annals of Tourism Research*, 18(1), 12-25

Nuñez, Theron, 1963, Tourism, Tradition and Acculturation: Weekendismo in a Mexican Village, *Ethnology*, 2(3), 347-352

Nuñez, Theron, 1989, Touristic Studies in Anthropological Perspective, in *Hosts and Guests: The Anthropology of Tourism (2nd edition)*, Smith, V., (ed), UPP, Philadelphia

O'Reilly, A, 1986, Tourism Carrying Capacity: Concept and Issues, *Tourism Management*, 7(4), 254-258

Osborne, Christine, 1993, Making the Most out of Tourism, *In Focus*, Tourism Concern, 10, 10-11

Ousby, Ian, 1990, *The Englishman's England: Taste, Travel and the Rise of Tourism*, Cambridge University Press, Cambridge

Owen, Robert, 1991, *A New View of Society and Other Writings*,

Penguin, Harmondsworth

Parker, Stanley, 1983, *Leisure and Work*, Allen and Unwin

Parrinello, Giuli, 1993, Motivation and Anticipation in Post-Industrial Tourism, *Annals of Tourism Research*, 20, 233-249

Passariello, Phyllis, 1983, Never on Sunday? Mexican Tourists at the Beach, *Annals of Tourism Research*, 10(1), 109-122

Pearce, Douglas and Butler, Richard (eds), 1992, *Tourism Research: Critiques and Challenges*, Routledge, London

Pearce, Philip, 1982, *The Social Psychology of Tourist Behaviour*, Pergamon Press, Oxford

Pearce, Philip, 1988, *The Ulysses Factor*, Springer-Verlag, New York

Pearce, Philip, 1992, Fundamentals of Tourist Motivation, in *Tourism Research: Critiques and Challenges*, Pearce, D. and Butler, R., (eds), Routledge, London

Pearce, Philip, 1994, Tourist-Resident Impacts: Examples, Explanations and Emerging Solutions, in *Global Tourism: The Next Decade*, Theobald, W (ed), Butterworth Heinemann

Pearce, P and Caltabianao, M., 1983, Inferring Travel Motivation from Travellers Experiences, *Journal of Travel Research*, 22, 16-20

Pearce, Philip and Moscardo, Gianno, 1986, The Concept of Authenticity in Tourist Settings, *Australian and New Zealand Journal of Sociology*, 22(1), 121-132

Perdue, Richard; Long, Patrick and Allen, Lawrence, 1987, Rural Resident Tourism Perceptions and Attitudes, *Annals of Tourism Research*, 14, 420-429

Perlmutter, Howard, 1991, On the Rocky Road to the First Global Civilisation, *Human Relations*, 44(9), 897-1010

Pfaffenberger, Bryan, 1983, Serious Pilgrims and Frivolous Tourists, *Annals of Tourism Research*, 10(1), 57-74

Pimlott, J., 1947, *The Englishman's Holiday*, Faber & Faber, London

Pi-Sunyer, Oriel, 1989, Changing Perceptions of Tourism and Tourists in a Catalan Resort Town, in *Hosts and Guests: The Anthropology of Tourism* (2nd edition), Smith, V., (ed, UPP, Philadelphie

Pizam, Abraham, 1978, Tourism's Impacts: The Social Cost to the Destination Community as Perceived by its Residents, *Journal of Travel Research*, 16, 8-12

Pizam, Abraham; Milman, Ady and Jafari, Jafar, 1991, Influence of Tourism on Attitudes: US Students visiting USSR, *Tourism Management*, 12, 47-54

Plog, Stanley, 1977, Why Destination Areas Rise and Fall in Popularity, in *Domestic and International Tourism*, Kelly, E., (ed), Institute of Certified Travel Agents, Wellesley, Mass.

Poon, Auliana, 1993, *Tourism, Technology and Competitive Strategies*, CAB International, Wallingford

Porritt, Jonathon, 1984, *Seeing Green*, Blackwell, Oxford

Rattachumpoth, Rakkit, 1992, Phuket: holiday paradise where locals are banned, *Contours*, 5(8), 13-15

Reynoso y Valle, Augustin and de Regt, Jacomina, 1979, Growing Pains: Planned Development in Ixtapa-Zihuatanejo, in *Tourism: Passport to Development?*, de Kadt, E.(ed), Oxford University Press

Riley, Pamela, 1988, Road Culture of International Long-Term Budget Travellers, *Annals of Tourism Research*, 15, 313-328

Rojek, Chris, 1993, *Ways of Escape*, Macmillan, Basingstoke

Rosenow, J. and Pulsipher, G., 1979, *Tourism: The Good, The Bad and The Ugly*, Three Centuries Press, Lincoln

Rothman, R., 1978, Residents and Transients: Community Reaction to Seasonal Visitors, *Journal of Travel Research*, 16, 8-13

Ryan, Chris, 1991, *Recreational Tourism: A Social Science Perspective*, Routledge, London

Selwyn, Tom, 1992, Tourism, Society and Development, *Community Development Journal*, 27(4), 353-360

Shackley, Myra, 1994, the land of Lo, Nepal/Tibet: The First Eight Months of Tourism, *Tourism Management*, 15(1), 17-26

Sharpley, Richard, 1993, *Tourism and Leisure in the Countryside*, ELM Publications, Huntingdon

Sheldon, P. and Var, T., 1984, Resident Attitudes Towards Tourism in North Wales, *Tourism Management*, 5 40-48

Sigaux, Gilbert, 1966, *History of Tourism*, Leisure Arts Ltd, London

Silver, Ira, 1993, Marketing Authenticity in Third World Countries, *Annals of Tourism Research*, 20, 302-318

Simpson, Bob, 1993, Tourism and Tradition: From Healing to Heritage, *Annals of Tourism Research*, 20, 164-181

Smith, Valene, (ed) 1989, *Hosts and Guests: the Anthropology of Tourism (2nd Edition)*, University of Pennsylvania Press, Philadelphia

Smith, Valene, 1989, Eskimo Tourism: Micro-Models and Marginal Men, in *Hosts and Guests: the Anthropology of Tourism (2nd Edition)*, Smith, V.(ed), UPP, Philadelphia

Smith, Valene and Eadington, William, (eds) 1992, *Tourism Alternatives: Potentials and Problems in the Development of Tourism*, University of Pennsylvania Press, Philadelphia

Stanton, Max, 1989, The Polynesian Cultural Centre: A Multi-Ethnic Model of Seven pacific Cultures, in *Hosts and Guests: the Anthropology of Tourism (2nd Edition)*, Smith, V.(ed), UPP, Philadelphia

Sutton, W., 1967, Travel and Understanding: Notes on the Social Structure of Touring, *International Journal of Comparative Sociology*, 8, 217-233

Swingewood, Alan, 1991, *A Short History of Sociological Thought*, Macmillan, Basingstoke

Thomsons, 1994, 1994/5 Winter Sun Brochure, Thomsons Tour Operations, London

Thompson, Kenneth, 1992, Social Pluralism and Post-Modernity, in *Modernity and its Futures,* Hall, S., Held, D. and McGrew, T., (eds), Polity Press, Cambridge

Thurot, Jean Maurice and Thurot, Gaétane, 1983, The Ideology of Class and Tourism: Confronting the Discourse of Advertising, *Annals of Tourism Research,* 10, 173-189

Towner, John, 1985, The Grand Tour: A Key Phase in the History of Tourism, *Annals of Tourism Research,* 12,297-333

Travis, Anthony, 1982, Physical Impacts: Trends Affecting Tourism. Managing the Environmental and Cultural Impacts of Tourism and Leisure Development, *Tourism Management,* December, 256-262

Trilling, Lionel, 1974, *Sincerity and Authenticity,* Oxford Paperbacks, Oxford University Press, London

Tsartas, Paris, 1992, Socioeconomic Impacts of Tourism on Two Greek Isles, *Annals of Tourism Research,* 19, 516-53

Turner, L. and Ash, J., 1975, *The Golden Hordes: International Tourism and the Pleasure Periphery,* Constable, London

Turner, Victor, 1973, The Centre out There: the Pilgrim's Goal, *History of Religions,* 10, 191-230

Turner, Victor and Turner, Edith, 1978, *Image and Pilgrimage in Christian Culture,* Columbia University Press, New York

UNESCO, 1976, The Effects of Tourism on Socio-Cultural Values, *Annals of Tourism Research,* 4(1), 74-105

Urry, John, 1988, Cultural Change and Contemporary Holiday-Making, *Theory, Culture and Society,* 5, 35-55

Urry, John, (!990a, *The Tourist Gaze,* Sage Publications, London

Urry, John, 1990b, The Consumption of Tourism, *Sociology,* 24(1), 23-35

Urry, John, 1992, The Tourist Gaze and the Environment, *Theory, Culture and Society,* 9, 1-26

Wahab, Salah, 1975, *Tourism Management,* Tourism International Press, London

Walsh, Kevin, 1992, *The representation of the Past: Museums and Heritage in the Post-Modern World*, Routledge, London

Walter, J., 1982, Social Limits to Tourism, *Leisure Studies*, 1, 295-304

Walton, John, 1983, *The English Seaside Resort: A Social History, 1750-1914*, Leicester University Press, Leicester

Walvin, James, 1978, *Beside the Seaside*, Allen Lane, London

Ward, Colin and Hardy, Dennis, 1986, *Goodnight Campers! The History of the British Holiday Camp*, Mansell Publishing, London

Wheeler, Marion, 1992, Applying Ethics to the Tourism Industry, *Business Ethics*, 1(4), 227-235

Wheeller, Brian, 1991, Tourism's Troubled Times, *Tourism Management*, 12(3) 91-96

Wheeller, Brian, 1992a, Eco or Ego Tourism: New Wave Tourism, *Insights*, ETB, Ma

Wheeller, Brian, 1992b, Alternative Tourism: A Deceptive Ploy, in *Progress in Tourism, Recreation and Hospitality Management Vol IV*, Cooper, C.(ed), Bellhaven Press, London

Witt, Christine and Wright, Peter, 1992, Tourist motivation: Life after Maslow, in *Choice and Demand in Tourism*, Johnson, Peter and Thomas, Barry (eds), Mansell Publishing, London

Witt, S., Brooke, M. and Buckley, P., 1991, *The Management of International Tourism*, Unwin Hyman, London

Wood, Katie and House, Syd, 1991, *The Good Tourist: A Worldwide Guide for the Green Traveller*, Mandarin, London

Wood, Robert, 1980, International Tourism and Cultural Change in South East Asia, *Economic Development and Cultural Change*, 28, 561-581

World Tourism Organisation, 1980, *Manila Declaration on World Tourism*, WTO, Madrid

World Tourism Organisation, 1981, *The Social and Cultural Dimension of Tourism*, WTO, Madrid

World Tourism Organisation, 1992, *Tourism Trends to the Year 2000 and Beyond,* WTO Madrid

Wright, Patrick, 1985, *On Living in an Old Country,* Verso, London

WTTC, 1991, *Travel and Tourism in the World Economy,* World Travel and Tourism Council, Brussels

Yale, Pat, 1992, *Tourism in the UK,* ELM Publications, Huntingdon

Yearley, Steven, 1991, *The Green Case: A Sociology of Environmental Issues, Arguments and Politics,* Routledge, London

Young, Sir George, 1973, *Tourism: Blessing or Blight?* Penguin, Harmondsworth

Zuzanek, J. and Mannell, R., 1983, Work Leisure Relationships from a Sociological and Social Psychological Perspective, *Leisure Studies,* 2

Index

INDEX

From Tourist Attractions to Tourism Heritage - Pat Yale

From museums to stately homes, castles, palaces and gardens, religious buildings, archaeological sites and ancient monuments, including industrial and transport heritage. A standard reference work for tutors as well as a good, advanced level class text. Level PG Diploma, degree, etc. Book, pbk, 256pp, 1 85450 016 3

Tourism in the U.K. - Pat Yale

The business and management of tourism. With commentary on UK tourist attractions. Adopted by many colleges and schools as as set text for those new to the business of tourism. Level BTEC Nat., A level +. Book - maps/charts/diagrams, 320 pp, 1 85450 017 1 Tutor's Manual - exercises/notes/OHPs, 1 85450 094 5

Tourism Law, 2nd edition - Jim Corke

Updated and revised edition of the first text specially written on the law relating to tourism and travel. New material on EC regulations. Level HND +. Book, pbk, 480pp, 1 85450 028 7 Tutor's Manual, 1 85450 140 2

Tourism, Tourists and Society - Richard Sharpley

An in-depth study of the relationship between tourism and the societies that both generate and host tourism & tourists. Includes: the effects of social change on the pattern of tourism consumption; motivation for tourism; impact of tourism on host societies; and commoditisation & authenticity. Book, pbk, 224pp, 1 85450 159 3 Tutor's Manual - exercises/notes/OHPs, 1 85450 233 6

Travel and Tourism, 2nd edition - Patrick Lavery

Introduction to the main sectors of the tourism industry, defining & outlining the development in the UK, Europe, USA, & including transport deregulation. Level HND +. An adopted and recommended text in many colleges. Book, pbk, 224pp, 1 85450 120 8 Tutor's Manual - exercises/notes/OHPs, 1 85450 024 4

Water Based Recreation: managing resources for leisure -Fiona McCormack
Comprehensive treatment of water based resources for leisure. Aspects of management, marketing, environmental issues, conservation, conflicting uses, access and future trends. The first full coverage of this growing area of leisure management. Book, pbk, 320pp, 1 85450 154 2 Tutor's Manual, exercises, notes, OHPs etc, 1 85450 154 2

HUMAN RESOURCES MANAGEMENT

Employee Relations - Ken Whitehead
Describes the system by which employers & Trade Unions seek to resolve their differences. Level HND+.
23   Book, pbk, 224pp, 0 946139 76 8 ....£8.95
23TP   Tutor's Manual - exercises/notes/OHPs, 0 946139 81 4 ..... £59.00

Human Resources *Standing Start* Pack - Celia Golding - **updated edition**
Updated to July, 1994, classroom-tested sessions for mixed ability groups. NO textbooks needed. Follows GNVQ syllabus order. The tutor can present complex topics in a clear and interesting way and handle several groups at one time (to about 25). Individuals learn at their own pace in the group. Level - GNVQ Advanced.
Packs of workshop notes, examples on OHPs, 30 posters & exercises
Full set - Parts A, B & C, ISBN 1 85450 238 7 .... £79.00

Human Resources Management - McIlwee & Roberts
A set book at many colleges for IPM Stage 1. A manual for both professional personnel managers and for students. Level PG Diploma+.
59   Book, pbk, 484pp, 1 85450 022 8 ....£12.95

People in Organisations - Pat Armstrong
Introduction to the management of people at work. Organisations, communication, information systems, interpersonal skills, appraisal, job/workplace design, health, welfare & safety, satisfaction/performance, working groups.
Level BTEC National, also A level.
16   Book, pbk, 160pp, 0 946139 80 6 ....£5.95
16TP   Tutor's Manual - exercises/notes, 0 946139 85 7 .... £39.00

People in Organisations, 4th edition - Armstrong & Dawson
Best-selling text for managers and students on courses like DMS, HND and BA Business Studies years 1-2, and for GNVQ Level 3.
07   Book, pbk 368pp., 0 946139 55 5 ....£7.95
07TP   Tutor's Manual - exercises/notes, 0 946139 60 1 .... £29.00